# The Ark of the Covenant
## IN ITS EGYPTIAN CONTEXT

# The Ark of the Covenant IN ITS EGYPTIAN CONTEXT

*An Illustrated Journey*

DAVID A. FALK

HENDRICKSON ACADEMIC

*an imprint of Hendrickson Publishing Group*

**The Ark of the Covenant in Its Egyptian Context: An Illustrated Journey**



Published by Hendrickson Academic
an imprint of Hendrickson Publishing Group
Hendrickson Publishers, LLC
P. O. Box 3473
Peabody, Massachusetts 01961-3473
www.hendricksonpublishinggroup.com

ISBN 978-1-68307-267-6



*Printed in the United States of America*

*First Printing — December 2020*

Library of Congress Control Number: 2020944578

Cover Photo: Image of four priests carrying a *kar* shrine on poles at Abydos Temple of Ramesses II. Photo courtesy of the author.

To my wife Kiara
whose love, faith, and editorial skills
have always supported me

And to Bill and Cindy Kozel
whose loving generosity has kept
this research alive over the years.

# Contents

# Abbreviations

## General Abbreviations

| | |
|---|---|
| ill. | illustration |
| *O.* | Ostracon, a text written on a pottery shard |
| *P.* | Papyrus |
| pl. | plate |
| pt. | part |
| rt | recto, or the righthand side or front of a page |
| vs | verso, or the lefthand side or back of a page |

## Journals, Series, and Reference Works

| | |
|---|---|
| *ASAE* | *Annales du Service des antiquités de l'Égypte* |
| *BASOR* | *Bulletin of the American Schools of Oriental Research* |
| *BIFAO* | *Bulletin de l'Institut français d'archéologie orientale* |
| *CAD* | *The Assyrian Dictionary of the Oriental Institute of the University of Chicago*. 21 vols. Chicago: The Oriental Institute of the University of Chicago, 1956–2010 |
| *CD* | *A Coptic Dictionary compiled with the help of many scholars.* Walter Ewing Crum. Oxford: Clarenden, 1939 |
| *CG* | *Catalogue Générale des Antiquities Égyptiennes du Musée de Caire* |
| *COS* | *The Context of Scripture: Canonical Compositions from the Biblical World.* Edited by William W. Hallo and K. Lawson Younger. 3 vols. Leiden: Brill, 1997–2002 |
| CT | Coffin Text |
| EA | El-Amarna, an Amarna letter |
| *ECT* | *The Egyptian Coffin Texts.* Edited by Adriaan De Buck and Alan H. Gardiner. 7 vols. Chicago: University of Chicago Press, 1935–1961 |
| Gardiner Sign | Hieroglyph signs that appear in Alan H. Gardiner, *Egyptian Grammar*, 3rd ed. rev. (Oxford: Griffith Institute, 1957), 442–543. |
| GM | Göttinger Miszellen |

| | |
|---|---|
| *HALOT* | *The Hebrew and Aramaic Lexicon of the Old Testament.* Ludwig Koehler, Walter Baumgartner, and Johann J. Stamm. Translated and edited under the supervision of Mervyn E. J. Richardson. 4 vols. Leiden: Brill, 1994–1999 |
| *Hier. Ostr.* | *Hieratic Ostraca.* Jaroslav Černý and Alan H. Gardiner. 2 vols. Oxford: Griffith Institute, 1957 |
| JARCE | Journal of the American Research Center in Egypt |
| JBL | Journal of Biblical Literature |
| JEA | Journal of Egyptian Archaeology |
| JETS | Journal of the Evangelical Theological Society |
| JNES | Journal of Near Eastern Studies |
| JSSEA | Journal of the Society for the Study of Egyptian Antiquities |
| *KRI* | *Ramesside Inscriptions: Historical and Biographical.* Kenneth A. Kitchen. 8 vols. Malden, MA: Blackwell, 1975–1990 |
| *LD* | C. R. Lepsius. *Denkmäler aus Aegypten und Aethiopien.* 5 vols. Leipzig: Hinrichs, 1897 |
| *LEM* | *Late-Egyptian Miscellanies.* Alan H. Gardiner. Brussels: Fondation Egyptologique Reine Elisabeth, 1937 |
| *LESt* | *Late-Egyptian Stories.* Alan H. Gardiner. Brussels: Fondation Egyptologique Reine Elisabeth, 1932 |
| PM | *Topographical Bibliography of Ancient Egyptian Hieroglyphic Texts, Reliefs, and Paintings.* Bertha Porter and Rosalind L. B. Moss. 2nd ed. 7 pts. Oxford: Clarendon, 1960–1995 |
| PT | Pyramid Text |
| *RAD* | *Ramesside Administrative Documents.* Alan H. Gardiner. Oxford: Griffith Institute, 1948 |
| *REg* | *Revue d'Égyptologie* |
| *RecTrav* | *Recueil de traveaux relatifs à la philologie et à l'archéologie égyptiennes et assyriennes* |
| Sethe | *Die altaegyptischen Pyramidentexte.* Kurt Sethe. 2 vols. Leipzig: Hinrichs, 1908 |
| TT | Theban Tomb |
| *Urk.* | *Urkunden des ägyptischen Altertums.* Edited by Kurt Sethe, Heinrich Schäfer, Siegfried Schott, and Herman Grapow. 7 vols. Leipzig: Hinrichs, 1904–1958 |
| *WÄS* | *Wörterbuch der aegyptischen Sprache.* Adolf Erman and Hermann Grapow. 5 vols. Leipzig: Hinrichs; Berlin: Akademie, 1926–1931. Repr., 1971 |
| *ZÄS* | *Zeitschrift für ägyptische Sprache und Altertumskunde* |

# Figures and Illustrations

# Glossary

| | |
|---|---|
| Barque | A shrine shaped like a small boat. The French-derived form of the word is used instead of the modern English form to prevent confusion with other meanings of the word *bark*. |
| Bier | A bed or chest used for a dead body prior to burial. |
| Determinative | In the Egyptian written language, a letter with no phonetic component that gives visual clues to indicate the meaning of a word. |
| Frieze | A decorative horizontal border with a repetitive pattern along the upper section of a wall, column, or object that is used as an architectural or design element. |
| Great Throne | The central, most holy, section of a temple. It was typically made of special materials and housed a sacred barque. |
| Hypostyle | A columned hall that was completely covered by a ceiling. |
| Inner Shrine | The rear portion of a temple that contains the *naos*. |
| Liminal | The transition between profane space and sacred space. |
| Liminal Inertia | The impedance between moving objects or persons between sacred and profane spaces. |
| Nomarch | A regional, often hereditary, overlord who governed one of the provinces (nomes) of Egypt. |
| Palanquin | A litter or chair used to transport a person. |
| Peristyle | A columned court that had columns along the edges with a ceiling partially covering the court and open in the center. |
| Shrine | A cabinet or chest used to hold or contain something divine. |
| Shrine Cabinet | A shrine that has doors on its vertical sides. |
| Vizier | The highest ranking official in Egypt after the king. Egypt was effectively governed by the vizier, much like a prime minister. Depending upon the period, Egypt was governed by either a single vizier or (New Kingdom) by a pair who managed Upper and Lower Egypt. |
| Votive Image | A statue of a person or god that is dedicated, sequestered, or buried out of sight. |
| Uraeus | The sacred cobra goddess 𓆗. |

# CHAPTER 1

# Discovering the Ark for the First Time

Snakes spitting fire, entrapped demons, and gods wandering the land. This is the true story behind the account of the ark of the covenant. This story is unlike any that you have heard before. Like a lone tree hidden in a forest, the ark has a message that is easy to overlook. The ark's story is about God dwelling with his people. It is a message written in a visual language that everyone knew 3,330 years ago but is lost to us today—a message still important to you and me because it relates the identity of God through ordinary objects used in extraordinary ways.

The story I have discovered about the ark is the story of its context. It is a story with sweeping implications. The context of the ark can tell us about the origins of the Pentateuch. The context can narrow down the date of the exodus. The context shows us a structuring of ritual space that makes sense of the tabernacle. The context even affects how we understand the symbolism of the ark. And in turn this affects the relationship between God and humanity, which impacts every one of us.

Over the last 150 years, ancient Near Eastern scholars have shown that the Pentateuch emerged from a bounty of beliefs and cultures stretching back thousands of years. The ancient writers derived new religious expressions using ideas and symbols already existing in their culture. It is a bit like building a castle one ancient stone at a time. Even though Moses had physically led the Israelites out of Egypt, the people still had an Egyptian mindset and religious understanding. Early Israelite ritual built upon that understanding to construct a unique expression of religion.

Yet, few authors engage the wealth of Egyptian material culture in relation to the ark. To dig deep into the meaning behind the ark, we will delve into the mysteries of Egyptian ritual and its furniture. This will open a door to tell the story of an important biblical object and to take a journey through the unique world of the Bronze Age, the ark's historical context.

## What Is the Ark?

Let's pretend we are archaeologists discovering the ark for the first time. The first thing we would do—after popping the champagne corks and yelling *eureka!*—is try to describe the object. Put most simply, the ark of the covenant was the reliquary that held the tablets of the ten commandments. The term *reliquary* comes from the word *relic* and was a container that held sacred artifacts. Reliquaries were commonly used in the medieval period to hold the bones of the Christian saints.

God spoke to Moses upon Mount Sinai, and God inscribed two tablets with his finger. Moses brought the tablets down from the mountain and placed them in the ark. The ark was one of four pieces of furniture created for the Israelite tabernacle. The other tabernacle furniture included an incense altar, a bronze altar of burnt offering, and an offering table.

While the ark would not be signed like a European oil painting, the biblical texts say that the ark was made by a craftsman named Bezalel son of Uri son of Hur (Exod 37:1). Ancient people normally devoted little effort to describing inanimate objects. But the ark is described not once but twice, and the writers said more about the ark than about any other object in the ancient world. We have details of its design and specifications in Exod 25 and its actual construction in Exod 37.

Figure 1. Reconstruction of the ark of the covenant (illustration by author).

Bezalel was said to have crafted the ark's chest from acacia wood. Today few trees exist in the Sinai, but during the Early Bronze Age, the Sinai was a savanna. Acacia, along with almond trees, were common in the Sinai during the Late Bronze Age. Timbers from Middle Kingdom boats recovered from the Red Sea caves indicate that the acacia trees from the Middle Bronze Age were tall enough to be used as ship planks.[1]

With a rudimentary saw mill and bronze tools, Bezalel could make an unadorned wooden box measuring two and a half cubits long by one and a half wide by one and a half high, approximately 45 by 27 by 27 inches, with a cubit being about 18 inches (Exod 25:10). He overlaid the ark inside and out with gold foil. A gold molding was fitted around the piece that held the lid in place (Exod 25:11). Two poles of acacia wood were made and overlaid with gold (Exod 25:13). Four pole rings were attached to the feet of the chest unit (Exod 25:12). These poles were inserted into rings with the purpose of carrying the ark (Exod 25:14).

Bezalel created a lid measuring two and a half cubits long by one and a half cubits wide (45 by 27 inches), which could be placed on the box (Exod 25:17). English translations call the lid the "mercy seat." The translation "mercy seat" comes from Wycliffe's and Luther's translations of the Septuagint.[2] The translation from the Greek is more of a theological construct than a strict translation, blending the ideas of propitiation and a throne.

Finally, Bezalel made two cherubim (winged angelic beings) of hammered gold and attached them to each end of the lid (Exod 25:18). The wings of each cherub were spread upward, covering the lid. He placed the two cherubim so they faced each other (Exod 25:20).

## Covenant and Conspiracy

The first stop on our journey will look at the language used about the ark, which will give us a big-picture view of what the ark is all about. The English word *ark* comes originally from the Latin *arca*, "chest" and enters into the language as the Old English *ærc*. However, this translation represents two different Hebrew words in the Pentateuch.

The first word is *tēbāh*, "chest or casket,"[3] and is commonly used of Noah's ark. This was the boat used to save humans and land animals from the world-destroying flood. Without getting too far ahead of myself, the ark of the covenant shares qualities with Noah's ark, that is, it is a chest that transforms profane things into something sacred. Noah's ark can be thought of as a sacred chest, and I will discuss this more later. Until then, I will leave it to you to ponder.

The other Hebrew word, the one that is used with the ark of the covenant, is *ʾărôn*, "coffin, money-chest."[4] This word comes from a Semitic root related to the Babylonian word *arānu*, "chest, coffer, cashbox, coffin,"[5] where it was used mostly in nonreligious contexts. For the Egyptians, a coffin was a proxy body that the spirit of a dead person could inhabit to participate in the world after death. Thus, the ark as a kind of coffin is not so much a burial casket as a facility given to a god to influence the world. Perhaps this is not necessary for an all-powerful god, but it is a notion consistent with Bronze Age views of divinity. Going forward, we will refer to the ark as a *reliquary* until we get into the sticky wicket of trying to figure out the ark's function. What can I say? It's complicated.

The ark did not always go by the name "ark of the covenant of the Lord." When Bezalel built the ark in Exod 37, its name was originally the *ark of the testimony* (Exod 25:22). The Hebrew word *ʿēdût,* "testimony," is a Semitic word that shares a history with the Akkadian *adû*, "a formal (written) agreement," and the Ugaritic *'dt*, "assembly." After the word entered into West Semitic languages, the Egyptian language picked it up as *ádet*, "conspiracy." By the time of Ramesses III (ca. 1191–1160 BC), the word was associated with criminal conspiracy.[6]

This raises the question of what kind of testimony or conspiracy is being suggested by the ark. God had already conspired with Moses to free his people from Pharaoh, but I think there is more to it. I think that the testimony is a "conspiracy" of terms in brokering an agreement. A buyer and a seller will "conspire" to create a contract and, once they agree to the terms, they now have a contract or *covenant*. At its simplest, a covenant (Hebrew: *bĕrît*) is an agreement or treaty made between two opposing sides.

In the ancient Near East, suzerains (occupying overlords) made covenant agreements with their vassals. After a king conquered a city, he told the vassals that if they behaved and sent him lots of loot, he would protect their city. If they disobeyed, he would rain terror down upon them. These treaties had a specific structure that became less complex over time.[7]

We find that the reason for the existence of the ark revolves around the word *covenant*. The holiness of Yahweh (the suzerain) facilitated, by way of a treaty or concession, the ark. He provided a means where he could dwell in close proximity to his people (his vassals). He did this so that they could have relationship with him. The ark was a visible symbol of the agreement with his people. Having this agreement, God could set aside hostilities and the Israelites could be his people (Gen 17:8; Jer 24:7; Heb 8:10).

In the Scriptures, the books of Exodus, Leviticus and the first half of Numbers called this reliquary the *ark of the testimony*. Numbers 7:89 is the last use of *ark of the testimony* in the Pentateuch. The first use of *ark of the covenant of the Lord* is in Num 10:33. The *ark of the covenant* is then consistently used through the rest of Numbers and Deuteronomy.

The event marking the name change was when the glory of the Lord hovered over the tabernacle (Num 9:18). A name change occurs in other places in the Bible often when one has a life-changing encounter with God. For example, Abram's name changed to Abraham (Gen 17:5). The patriarchs also renamed towns when a theophany appeared. For example, Jacob renamed Luz to Bethel (Gen 28:19). But the ark is the only name change that happens to an inanimate object. After Num 7:89, the writers of Scripture use *ark of the testimony* one last time in Josh 4:16. The name change shows a change of state—from parties in pre-agreement opposition to God to parties under the covenant.

## Bezalel's Story (The Imaginative Retelling)

To help the reader understand the historical setting of the ark, a story about the ark's creator might help. The story of Bezalel begins at Avaris, a city on the Pelusiac branch of the Nile in Lower Egypt. Bezalel lived in Avaris when it was long past its glory days.

Back in the days of the Hyksos (ca. 1666–1520 BC), many entered Egypt when the delta still provided water, fish, and fowl. Avaris was a city of Libyan and Asiatic immigrants that settled in the Nile Delta.[8] These groups entered Egypt when the Neolithic Wet Phase dried up, and food in the neighboring savanna became scarce.

Joseph had arrived in Egypt as a slave, but he soon gained the reputation as an interpreter of dreams. The Egyptians believed in the power of dreams to tell the future.[9] The Hyksos king appointed Joseph to be vizier over the land of Egypt (Gen 41:41). Jacob and his seventy sons settled near Avaris during the Second Intermediate Period (ca. 1650–1530 BC) and they arrived to an already established city (Gen 46:27).[10] Joseph's plan to buy all the land of Egypt made the Hyksos wealthy beyond their dreams. And the wealth of Egypt flowed through the city and was exported across the Mediterranean: wine, salted fish, grain, leeks, chairs, beds, gold, and bronze.

However, the harsh taxation of the Hyksos created resentment, and the rulers of the Theban province drove out the Hyksos. When the Hyksos rulers heard that the Theban king Ahmose was coming, they packed as much wealth as they could carry and hightailed it out of Egypt, leaving the remaining population of Asiatics to the mercy of the not-so-benevolent new regime, a regime that cared nothing about Joseph, his deeds, or his people (Exod 1:8). To the Egyptians, Avaris was nothing but a city of parasitic foreigners that could never be trusted.

By the time Bezalel was born, the Egyptians had controlled Avaris for almost three hundred years and long forgot any memory of Joseph. When Bezalel was as young as six, his father Uri loaded a donkey with goods. He picked up Bezalel, placed him upon the donkey, and led it out of the city. Uri brought the donkey to a neighborhood outside the old city walls built by the Hyksos when they had ruled Egypt.

Bezalel and his father arrived at a compound with several low buildings. The courtyard was littered with clay kilns, broken pottery, and heaps of smoldering ash. The acrid smell of smoke and wood pitch burned Bezalel's nose. He wanted to go home.

A pair of Medjay guards armed with spears stopped Uri and the donkey at the gate. The Medjay were a tribe that originally lived in Upper Egypt between Thebes and Cush. They served as mercenaries for King Ahmose (ca. 1538–1513 BC). After Ahmose conquered Avaris (ca. 1520 BC), the Medjay relocated throughout Egypt, serving local communities as armed guards, police officers, and community leaders.

An Egyptian man, deeply tanned and naked except for a loincloth, emerged from a workshop. He was the master of the workshop. He shuffled out to meet Uri at the gate, and the two men quickly finalized terms. Uri lifted Bezalel off the donkey and set him down. Then he gave the master all the goods from the donkey: grain, dried fish, wine, clothing, sandals, and decorative boxes. Uri placed the hand of Bezalel into the hand of the master. Bezalel watched as Uri left with donkey in tow, leaving him at his new home. Uri had bought Bezalel an apprenticeship with a master craftsman who would teach Bezalel everything he knew about the arts of Egypt.[11] That would be the last time Bezalel saw his father until he had grown into a man.

Figure 2. Statue of King Thutmosis III (photo by author).

Figure 3. Relief of the Hittite god of weather, Tarkhunna (Berlin Pergamonmuseum VAG 01024) (photo by author).

Early in the occupation of Avaris, the Egyptians built palaces and renovated temples to show their supremacy. King Thutmosis III (ca. 1477–1423 BC) built a palace at Avaris to keep an eye on the Asiatics but seldom used the palace himself, leaving the city to manage its affairs under a policy of benevolent neglect. But when King Tutankhamun (ca. 1334–1324 BC) died without an heir, his widow, Queen Ankhnesuamun, wrote a letter to the Hittite King Suppiluliuma I (ca. 1348–1326 BC) for a son to marry to become king over Egypt. Suppiluliuma I was naturally suspicious but sent one of his sons. General Horemheb and the vizier Ay conspired to seize power and assassinated the Hittite prince en route. The successful plot created a state of war between Egypt and the Hittites. Despite the palace and temples the Egyptians had built at Avaris to discourage revolt, the Egyptians were afraid that the Asiatics would side with their enemies (Exod 1:10).

With instability in the royal succession and the country in a state of war, attention turned to Avaris with its booming Asiatic population. Egyptians considered the Hittites to be Asiatics and believed the Asiatics at Avaris could side with their enemies at any time. The Egyptians soon pressed the population of Avaris (including the mixed multitude and sons of Jacob that were soon-to-be Israelites) into servitude making mud bricks. Each day the taskmasters expected them to produce an unrelenting quota of bricks. Construction crews then used these bricks to make storage depots for the temples of Egypt.[12] When King Seti I (ca. 1303–1288 BC) broke the ground at Qantir for his new royal residence, Bezalel was still a boy. The interminable war that had begun sixteen years earlier continued to seesaw in the Levant in a series of indecisive military actions. And with each military stalemate, the Egyptians grew ever more suspicious of the foreigners in their midst.

By the time Bezalel turned ten, Seti I had died and Ramesses II (ca. 1288–1222 BC) ascended the throne. Living conditions went from bad to worse as Ramesses II expanded the residence to become the capital of Egypt. The king renamed his island city Piramesses, "the house of Ramesses." And his eye was ever watchful over the affairs of Avaris. After all, Piramesses was a mere two kilometers from Avaris. Ramesses II set the people of Avaris to hard labor. When Ramesses II cut off the supply of straw for brickmaking, any straw the Israelites had was quickly consumed by their livestock, leaving nothing left for making bricks (Exod 5:7). This forced the people to search all over Egypt for straw (Exod 5:12).

From the courtyard of the workshop, Bezalel tended the truyeres, the nozzles or pipes through which air was blown into a furnace, for smelting bronze. As he worked, he saw the Levantine women take out their flocks of five or six goats or sheep. Even though Avaris was a city, verdant pastureland was just outside the limits. The Israelites lived with their livestock in the bottom floor of their homes. The men headed out soon after the women. They traveled to the banks of the Pelusiac branch of the Nile where they worked the clay pits. The men mixed straw with the clay and formed the mixture into molds to make mud brick. In the evenings the women returned, their sheep burdened with bundles of straw for the next day's bricks.

Figure 4. Modern Qantir, the site of the city of Piramesses (photo by author).

Day after day, Bezalel watched the backbreaking toil in the hot sun and oppressing humidity of the delta climate. But God had a different destiny for Bezalel. Making bricks would not be his lot.

As the years passed, Bezalel learned to make boxes, chests, chairs, and beds for domestic use. He created funerary furniture such as biers and coffins. His teacher taught him to make tents and woven cloth. He could cut gemstones, smelt copper, and cast gold. And he became skilled with the forge and paintbrush. He even learned the written language of Egypt. To become a skilled craftsman, Bezalel became deeply familiar with the meaning of every ritual required to satisfy the gods of the Egyptians (Exod 31:2–3).

When he became a young man, Bezalel would spend the warm summer nights talking with his master as they drank beer to beat the heat. They would talk about the stars and share stories about the gods. Stories about how Ptah and Re created the world.

One night his teacher asked. "We make jewelry and funerary objects for people, kings, and gods. Do we not?"

"We do, master," Bezalel replied.

"Is not our jasper known throughout Egypt?"[13] His teacher took a sip of beer. And he took a deep breath. "Is our work not desired? I have heard that it is has even come to the attention of the Great House."[14]

Bezalel shifted a bit as the discussion progressed.

"Looks like we will have to expand the compound. It's going to mean more workers and more work. I cannot oversee every task myself." His teacher looked up at the star-filled sky. "What kind of work interests you?"

"I'm not sure I'm ready," said Bezalel. "But I want work that serves a true god."

"Perhaps, but a good craftsman can choose his assignments," answered the teacher. "Which god do you wish to serve?"

"Which one is the greatest?"

"My people, the Egyptians, say there are hundreds of gods. They say Amun-Re is king of the gods. And even Ramesses himself is a living god." His teacher smirked. He was well aware of the cultural and religious differences between the native Egyptians and the Asiatic residents at Avaris. The teacher was aware that making furniture was not inseparable from religious service, so he tested his young apprentice to gauge Bezalel's awareness of what may be expected in the future. "Your people, the Asiatics, don't they worship Baal, Reshef, and Astarte? Whose gods would you serve?"[15]

Bezalel's skills and wisdom grew with time, and the local community sought out his crafts (Exod 31:2–3). Even when the taskmasters supplanted other Israelites from their occupations to make bricks, they passed him over. Egypt never overlooked the value of a man with specialized, highly desired skills. The requirements for the afterlife were onerous, and few skilled craftsmen were able to meet those needs.

For ten days each (Egyptian) week, Bezalel worked in the service of the master craftsman.[16] From a distance he watched his relatives forced to make mud bricks. Armed guards prevented the craftsmen from leaving the compound. The king trusted the craftsmen with expensive tools, costly metals, and precious stones. The Medjay scrutinized all transactions to prevent theft. Bezalel was powerless, watching the people come and go. Patiently he plied his craft.

The master recognized the work of Bezalel with greater responsibility and more expensive tasks, the pinnacle of which was the creation of a barque for a god or a palanquin for the king's relative. The king provided Bezalel, as a skilled craftsman, with an allowance of beef, dried fish, bread, and wine. He ate much better than either the Egyptian peasants or the Israelites living in Avaris. Representatives of the king occasionally visited the compound requesting ritual items. Bezalel watched as the temples at Piramesses with their towering pylons and flags rose up from the island capital. The people from Avaris came by asking the master for coffins, chairs, or chests. And the master always accepted their requests for work even though he knew they could not pay him except by a worthless promissory note.[17]

Then one day, Moses arrived at Avaris and with him, plagues. He brought the name of a god no one had ever heard of, Yahweh. Suddenly, the guards were no longer there. Nobody knew if they lived or died. They were just gone. Food deliveries ceased and Bezalel's fellow craftsmen started to leave. Bezalel was no longer a prisoner in his gilded cage. With no idea what else to do, Bezalel returned to his father's home in the heart of the city. There he learned about the ways of his fathers Abraham, Isaac, and Jacob.

At the home of his father, Bezalel celebrated the first Passover. And when a great cry was heard in Egypt, Moses led Bezalel and his people out of the land of Egypt through the Wadi Tumilat (Exod 12:30). Even though the Israelites were mostly Asiatics, the group was a mixed multitude that included pastoralists and a small number of non-Asiatics (Exod 12:38).

While they lived in Avaris, the sons of Israel lived in houses and bartered for leeks, cucumbers, melons, onions, and grains either grown locally or brought in by boat. The people traded their produce for salted fish and beer. When the Israelites were promised a land flowing with milk and honey, what they were *actually* promised was goat milk and wild honey, which were hallmarks of a pastoral lifestyle (Exod 3:8). Even in those days, big cities attracted a greater variety of goods than what a pastoral lifestyle could offer. For city dwellers like the Israelites, living in tents and tending flocks was an alien lifestyle.

Bezalel was probably in his early thirties when the Israelites abandoned Avaris. But even so, he had about twenty years of experience in his trade. Not only was he an expert craftsman, but he was also the son of Uri and grandson of Hur. After Moses and Aaron, Hur was the most respected man among the Israelites. Bezalel probably witnessed Hur and Aaron holding up the arms of Moses when the Amalekites attacked Rephadim (Exod 17:12). And two months after the Israelites left their homes at Avaris, Bezalel son of Uri and Oholiab son of Ahisamach were charged with the task to build the tabernacle and all its furniture (Exod 19:1). With the offerings of gold and silver, wool and wood, and leather and bronze before him, Bezalel knew what to do and set his mind to the task.

## The Exodus Date

The story of Bezalel above was written using what is called the *late date, late exodus view*, or *Ramesses-Merneptah theory*. This view maintains that the exodus took place during either the reign of Ramesses II (ca. 1288–1222 BC) or Merneptah (ca. 1222–1212 BC). This is the majority position among Egyptologists today who still believe that there was an exodus as described in the Hebrew Scriptures.

The late exodus view is not a recent view as is sometimes suggested.[18] The view leverages the chronological work first introduced in late antiquity by Rabbi Hillel Hanassi (AD 344), deriving an exodus date (1312 BC) from Jewish tradition.[19] With the advent of modern Egyptology, C. R. Lepsius (AD 1853) thought that the exodus pharaoh was Merneptah and that the exodus occurred in ca. 1314 BC, which he determined based upon the Hebrew date correlated with Manetho.[20] Lepsius's approximation turned out to be close to what we have since learned.

Over time, Egyptian chronology was refined. With the discovery (AD 1896) of the *Merneptah Victory Stela* (a.k.a. the "*Israel Stela*"), Egyptologists now recognize that the Israelites arrived in Canaan no later than the fifth regnal year of Merneptah. The stela celebrates the victory of King Merneptah over a coalition of Libyan invaders. In its poetical section, the stela lists the foreign nations that were overcome by Merneptah. Among these are included the Hittites, Canaan, Ashkelon, Gezer, Yenoam, the Hurrians, and Israel. Poetic sections mentioning Egyptian dominance over foreign powers are common in royal memorial inscriptions. Merneptah's stela is dated to his fifth regnal year (ca. 1218 BC), so we know that Israel had to have been founded as a foreign nation to Egypt by this year.

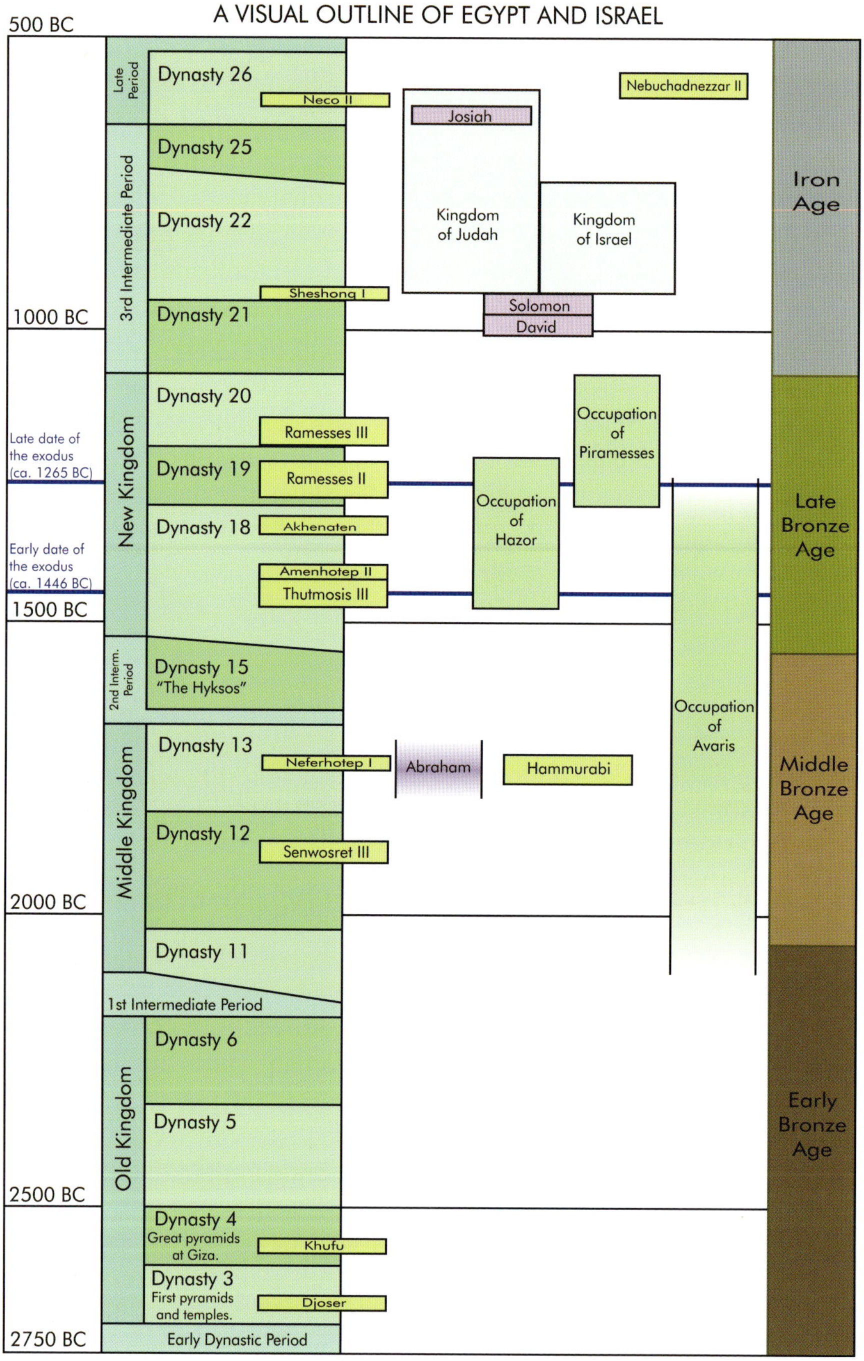


Figure 5. Timeline showing the relation between the exodus and ancient Egypt (illustration by author).

Figure 6. The *Merneptah Victory Stela* with "Israel" marked in red (photo by author).

Furthermore, the cities of Ramesses (Piramesses) and Pithom ("House of Atum") mentioned in Exod 1:11 are place names that did not occur any earlier than Ramesses II.[21] This narrows down the range to sometime during the 66-year reign of Ramesses II during the mid-thirteenth century BC.

Without delving into issues of chronology, discussing the date of the exodus is almost impossible. Chronology and the exodus have been tied together since the nineteenth century. Fortunately, the reigns of Egyptian kings can be linked to other kingdoms in the ancient Near East, and we now have advanced technologies that can establish the validity of various chronologies. These data points allow us to test different theories and put us on much firmer ground than in past eras.

While I will not discuss most of the alternative views, I will discuss the *early exodus view*, a theory that states the exodus took place in the mid-fifteenth century BC based upon the "480th year" found in 1 Kgs 6:1. Most ancient Near Eastern specialists no longer consider this view viable, even though it still has some admirers among Old Testament scholars.

On the surface, the early exodus view claims to support tradition and a simple, literal reading of the Bible. It is sometimes misidentified as the "traditional date," even though the view is only a little over a hundred years old. Laying out the history of this debate can help us to see where this view came from and how it got its traction.

In 1654, Bishop James Ussher published what would come to be an influential chronology among Christian circles.[22] Ussher relied upon the medieval belief that 4,000 years had passed between the creation of Adam and the birth of Christ. He adjusted the date for Dionysius Exiguus' error in dating Christ's birth,[23] which led him to arrive at a 4004 BC date of creation.[24]

Ussher calculated his chronology by taking the only fixed date he thought he could rely upon, the creation epoch, and counted forward through the generations of Genesis. Ussher calculated his exodus date (1491 BC) from the moment of creation and only then added 480 years to get the date for the Solomon's temple. He did not date the exodus according to Solomon's temple dedication as is commonly assumed. Instead, Ussher used lunar dating as his primary supporting evidence. However, the speculative nature of these observations began nearly a century of debate that resolved little.

The modern notion of an early date exodus (ca. 1450 BC) was first suggested in AD 1906 and is based upon the foundation of the Solomonic temple.[25] This "new hypothesis" held that the exodus occurred in the first years of Amenhotep II.[26] The date is calculated starting with the conventionally accepted year Solomon built his temple (ca. 967 BC) and then 480 Julian years are added. Defenders of the view elevate one verse (1 Kgs 6:1) as more important than every other verse for dating the exodus.[27]Although the exodus dates in Ussher's chronology and the early date view are reached by different methodologies, they are only fifty years apart (1491 vs. 1446 BC). The revised *Scofield Reference Bible* (AD 1917), which was popular in American dispensational and fundamentalist circles during the early twentieth century, included a version of Ussher's chronology and inadvertently popularized the early date hypothesis. The influence of the Scofield Bible continues to this day in certain circles, and the early date view along with it.

I will now lay out the challenges to the early date view that have made it impossible for me to adhere to it. The first challenge to this view is the mention of "Ramesses" in the biblical text (Gen 47:11; Exod 1:11; 12:37; Num 33:3, 5). Even today, the city of Ramesses remains a problem because it dates to no earlier than the thirteenth century BC (while the early date view holds to an exodus date in the 1440s). Some early defenders of the view claimed that Ramesses was changed in the text by *redactors*, a fancy name for "editors" who changed the Bible's content. Not satisfied with that suggestion, some have attempted to place the name Ramesses in the fifteenth century BC, which I have found unconvincing.[28] Even if the name Ramesses was mentioned in the fifteenth century (for which there is currently no evidence), the problem of thirteenth-century locations as the setting for a fifteenth-century event remains. The actual city of Ramesses didn't exist before the thirteenth century.

The early date view began to face other challenges as our knowledge of Egypt grew. During the excavation of Amarna, the capital city of King Akhenaten (ca. 1351–1335 BC), several diplomatic letters from well-known ancient Near Eastern kings were discovered. The Amarna letters, published in 1907 and 1915, affected scholars' understanding of Egyptian chronology and made the early date view much harder to hold onto.

The Amarna letters linked the reign of King Burna-Buriash II of Babylon (ca. 1360–1333 BC) with the reigns of Amenhotep III (ca. 1389–1351 BC), Akhenaten, and Tutankhamun (ca. 1334–1324 BC). They also linked Kadashman-Enlil I of Babylon (ca. 1375–1360 BC) with Amenhotep III, and Ashur-Uballit I of Assyria (ca. 1358–1323 BC) with Akhenaten.[29] This lowers the dates for Amenhotep II, believed by many supporters of the early date to be the pharaoh of the exodus, by about twenty-five years, putting his dates at ca. 1423–1399 BC. Yet, the early view depends upon the exodus taking place no later than the mid-1440s.

Furthermore, the Amarna letters opened a window into Levantine politics during the Late Bronze Age and exposed a conflict between a rigid reading of 1 Kgs 6:1 and the Israelite conquest. Joshua 11:11 says that Joshua destroyed Hazor with fire. Joshua must have been at least thirteen years old at the time he was sent as a spy into Canaan (Num 13:2). And if Joshua lived to 110 (as might be suggested from a literal reading of Judg 2:8), then he died no later than ca. 1349 BC. The problem is that Abdi-Tirshi, the king of Hazor, ruled well into the reign of Akhenaten (ca. 1351–1335 BC). Thus, he was not only ruling but also still expanding his territory in 1349 BC.[30]

The early date view does not allow enough time for everything that Abdi-Tirshi accomplished during his reign. Also, the biblical text identifies the king of Hazor as Jabin, not Abdi-Tirshi, and shows that Hazor had completed its territorial expansion by the time Joshua encountered it (Josh 11:1, 10). This indicates that Joshua's life and the conquest took place after the events described in the Amarna letters.

Furthermore, excavations at Hazor show uninterrupted occupation from ca. 1470 BC until around 1200 BC.[31] This archaeological fact has lent important credence to the late exodus view. Without a credible early conquest, an early exodus view is also not credible.

The discoveries at Avaris further complicated matters. Avaris was possibly the largest Semitic city of the ancient world. And because of its proximity to the city of Ramesses (Piramesses), most views hold that this is the city where the Israelites originated. This again proved to be a problem for the early date when it was discovered that most of the city was abandoned during early Dynasty 19 (ca. 1305–1194 BC).[32]

Even though movement of the Pelusiac branch of the river is often blamed for the city's abandonment, cities do not often undergo rapid abandonment as a result of the gradual movements of a river. We can reasonably conclude that the movement of the river was not responsible for the abandonment of Avaris, because the port at Avaris, called Peru-nefer, remained in operation into Dynasty 20 (ca. 1194–1073 BC).[33] It seems likely that if the port at Avaris remained in operation after the rest of the city was abandoned, then Avaris was abandoned for reasons other than river sedimention or the river's gradual movement.

An additional problem with the early exodus view is that the capital of early Dynasty 18 (ca. 1538–1305 BC) was located at Thebes in Upper Egypt, over three hundred miles from the Asiatic settlement in Goshen/Avaris. Moses's meetings with the Israelite elders living in Goshen/Avaris and the king in Thebes would have been entirely impractical. However, during his eventful reign Ramesses II (ca. 1288–1222 BC) moved the capital to Piramesses, only two kilometers from Avaris, making Moses's encounters with the king of Egypt possible.

Despite the clear challenges to the early date view posed by these archaeological findings, we should not dismiss the early date view as merely a problem of history and chronology. This view's interpretive method for the Bible is also highly relevant and is in fact the crux of the controversy. Supporters of the early date believe there is only one way to read the "480 years" of 1 Kgs 6:1, which is as 480 literal calendar years. This practice of reading all numbers in the Bible in exactly the same literal way is an example of a "one-meaning fallacy," which states that words always or nearly always have the same technical meaning.[34] This hinges upon a "false assumption about the technical meaning," as it is described by Grant R. Osborne in *The Hermeneutical Spiral: A Comprehensive Introduction to Biblical Interpretation*.[35]

For example, numbers in biblical Hebrew can be written in either ascending or descending order. Let's say we have the number 123, that number could be written as "three and twenty and one hundred" (ascending order) or as "one hundred and twenty and three" (descending order). Now, some early date defenders say that, when numbers occur in ascending order (like the 480 in 1 Kgs 6:1), these numbers are always "intended to be a technically precise figure."[36] But this only applies with some numbers in ascending order.[37] The meaning of culturally important fixed numbers and sacred figures depends upon context, and there is an established range of ways that numbers in the Bible can be understood.[38] Numbers that should not necessarily be read literally are numbers with special significance, such as seven, twelve, forty, and their multiples, and thus would include the 480 of 1 Kgs 6:1.

Moreover, the text of 1 Kgs 6:1 is remarkably similar to other dedication formulae across the ancient Near East. Assyrian King Tukulti-Ninurta I (ca. 1228–1201 BC) said 720 years had elapsed between his own reconstruction of the temple of Ishtar and its foundation by King Ilu-shumma.[39] The number 720 approximates the distant past using twelve multiplied by sixty, numbers which are highly significant in the sexagesimal system of Assyrian mathematics.

In Egypt, the *Year 400 Stela* of Seti I was a dedication stela given to the Temple of Seth at Avaris, heralding the 400th year, 4th month, and 4th day of a Hyksos King Nebti.[40] Could this get any more numerological? The problem with the "400 years" is that the Hyksos had not yet reigned for 400 years. In fact they had only reigned for about 360 years by the time the stela was erected. Again, the number was used in a non-literal way in order to approximate the distant past.

Yet another example is the *Mesha Stela* (erected by the Moabite King Mesha, a contemporary of King Joram [ca. 852–841 BC]) that ascribes a reign of forty years to King Omri (ca. 882–874) of the Northern kingdom of Israel.[41] But how can this be, since the Bible claims Omri reigned twelve years (1 Kgs 16:23)?[42] This should not come as a surprise since "40 years" was used to indicate an unspecified amount of time.[43] Second Samuel 5:4 says King David ruled forty years, but the text also says that, after Absalom's return and "at the end of 40 years," he approached David (2 Sam 15:7). Second Samuel 5:4 and 2 Sam 15:7 cannot be read as a literal forty years at the same time. The best explanation is that multiples of forty marked important milestones. For the Israelites, the 480 of 1 Kgs 6:1 is twelve multiplied by forty, sacred figures multiplied to mark a new epoch in Israelite history, the foundation of the Temple of the Lord.

We can see that the "480th year" of 1 Kgs 6:1 does not need to be read in a modern, literal sense. And by reading this according to its context, other historic portions of the text—such as chariot use in Gen 41:43 and 46:29, place names in Exod 1:11 and Num 33:3–5, and the events of Josh 11—are preserved without resorting to theories that change the biblical text.

Moreover, the late exodus view is supported by archaeology. The Bible presents a list of towns that the Israelites pass through, including Ramesses (Piramesses), Pithom, and Migdol (Exod 14:2; Num 33:7). Piramesses was founded by Seti I (ca. 1303–1288 BC) and was expanded to become Egypt's capital by his son Ramesses II.[44] The city was abandoned near the end of Dynasty 20 (ca. 1130 BC). Pithom, from the Egyptian "House of Atum," was named by Ramesses II when he rebuilt the fortifications and a temple to Atum.[45] And the fortress Migdol was constructed by Seti I.[46] In order for the Israelites to pass by or through those cities, they had to exist. And since we know from archaeology that these cities were founded during the reigns of Seti I and Ramesses II, the exodus could not have occurred any earlier than the accession of Ramesses II.

This makes Ramesses II the best candidate for the pharaoh of the exodus. Moreover, Ramesses II's reign is connected through treaties and diplomatic correspondence to other contemporary kings in the ancient Near East: Hittite kings Muwatalli II (ca. 1299–1276

BC) and Hatusili III (ca. 1271–1241 BC), Assyrian King Adad-Narari I (ca. 1301–1268 BC), and Babylonian King Kadashman-Enlil II (ca. 1264–1255 BC). Ramesses II went to war with Muwatalli II (ca. 1284 BC) and cut a treaty with Hatusili III in Ramesses II's twenty-first regnal year (ca. 1268 BC),[47] and Hatusili III exchanged diplomatic letters with Kadashman-Enlil II.[48] This gives us solid chronological information about Ramesses II's reign, which gives us additional chronological evidence narrowing down when the exodus took place.

All these data points come together to support a later date for the exodus. (1) Ramesses II is the best candidate to be the pharaoh of the exodus, and he has been definitely placed in the thirteenth century BC. (2) The abandonment of Avaris during Dynasty 19 (ca. 1305–1194 BC). (3) The foundation/renaming of the cities of Piramesses, Pithom, and Migdol during the reigns of Seti I (ca. 1305–1194 BC) and Ramesses II (ca. 1288–1222 BC). And (4) the Merneptah Stela, which tells us the Israelites must have arrived in the promised land by ca. 1218 BC and probably left Egypt years prior accounting for the "40 years" that they wandered in the wilderness (Num 32:13; Deut 2:7; 8:2; 29:5). All of this information taken together points toward the thirteenth century BC as the most likely time period for the Israelites' exodus from Egypt.

Furthermore, the destruction of Hazor can be reliably dated to ca. 1200 BC, which we know from the Mycenaean IIB, IIIA2, and IIIB ware that was found in its destruction layer.[49] If Jericho and Hazor were destroyed as a result of the Israelite conquest under Joshua, we should find destruction layers at the two cities that occur within no more than 100 years of each other. The only possible matching destruction layers date to the late thirteenth century BC.[50] We can thus conclude from the evidence that the date of the exodus must have occurred during the reign of Ramesses II, probably after the Battle of Kadesh in his fifth regnal year (ca. 1284 BC) and no earlier than the year his firstborn son, Amenhirkopshef died (ca. 1265 BC).[51]

## The Importance of Context

In the story of Bezalel above, we got a glimpse into how the Israelites lived before they left Egypt. When Bezalel created the ark, he intuitively understood its form and function. His training immersed him in the mythology and ritual of ancient Egypt. We, however, lack that same understanding that people had 3,300 years ago. The modern reader must cope with multiple alien worlds: the physical and geographical reality of the ancient Near East, the spiritual mechanics of early Israelite belief, and the cryptic world of ancient Egyptian ritual.

For example, the Israelites escaped the clutches of Pharaoh's chariots but took none of the shorter routes to Canaan. This has perplexed some people who have read the exodus account. But the Israelites avoided these shorter routes for good reasons.

Figure 7. Map of the exodus route with a Late Bronze Age coastline (illustration by author; map data from NASA).

First of all, they avoided the shortest route along the Way of Horus. The Way of Horus was a heavily fortified road along the north coast of the Sinai Peninsula that led to the five major Philistine cities (Exod 13:17). They would have encountered both the Egyptian and Philistine military if they had gone that way. They also shunned the major caravan route, the Way of Shur, which was an infamous death trap because it lacked water (Gen 16:7). Instead the Israelites hugged the west coast of the Sinai traveling southward. They then cut eastward across the Wadi Feiran, where they stopped and made camp for an extended time at Mount Sinai. The Israelites essentially made their way hopping from oasis to oasis, ensuring that they would neither run right into foreign military forces nor die of thirst. Finally, the Israelites took the extended route in the wilderness to create cultural change. The generation that left Egypt rejected the land that the Lord provided, and that generation died in the wilderness to raise up a generation acculturated in the pastoral lifestyle (Num 14:7–10, 33).

This example demonstrates that once we learn to see these perceived problems from the ancient viewer's perspective, things start to make sense. This entire book is my attempt to peel back the understanding that the ancients had intuitively. This understanding is important in order to navigate the difficult nature of the ark. The biblical text is silent on anything like the ark before the exodus. And no craftsman replaced the ark after King Nebuchadnezzar II sacked Jerusalem and hauled off the treasure in 587/586 BC. The ark arose abruptly and then vanished suddenly, tempting modern readers to believe God sent the ark as a divine anomaly. However, the Israelites recognized the ark as an object requiring a response of deference and respect. This shows that the Israelites coming out of Egypt possessed a cultural understanding for items like the ark, an understanding that is missing from our modern knowledge of the ark.

When we read a sentence, the writing before and after it affects that sentence's meaning. We call this the *context*. Writing is not meaning in isolation but chains of consciousness, each link held in place by what comes before and after. Material objects also have a context. The use of a material object affects how we understand and perceive that object. That cultural understanding gives us the context that helps us to understand the ark's purpose.

With the incense altar, the Israelites built their altars in a four-horned style. This style is similar to the horned altar of King Thutmosis III (fifteenth century BC) at Karnak temple. By the ninth and tenth centuries BC, horned incense altars were a normal occurance in the Levant. As such, we can readily establish the use and ritual function of incense altars. The altars of burnt offering and offering tables have a similar history.

Yet, archaeologists know of no Levantine antecedent, successor, or contemporary for the ark. We are, therefore, not dealing with a material phenomenon that Israelites co-opted after establishing their presence in Canaan. Instead, the ark likely emerged from a ritual understanding brought from their place of origin: Egypt.

In addition, when we engage the ark narrative, we do so with the knowledge that we are working with a received history of the exodus, which makes things more complicated. As such, past events were written in a way as to make them understandable to an ancient reader, but this adds complexity for the modern reader who may not be familiar with the original context. Maximalist scholars, who believe the Hebrew Scriptures are mostly historically accurate, are plagued with the biblical text offering few details and a poorly preserved archaeological context. And minimalist scholars, who doubt that anything in the Hebrew Scriptures is historically accurate, cannot simply dismiss the exodus as the invention of a Babylonian writer in the sixth century BC. Too many details give it credibility: Egyptian vocabulary, Dynasty 19 place names, and the problems and reality associated with mud brick construction. Some portions of the exodus narrative are exceptionally ancient and contain details that would have only been known to someone living during the thirteenth century BC.

Religious beliefs and practices are seldom cut from whole cloth. Those who weave new religions together seldom sew from abstract theological imperatives that they invented. More often, they patch together ideas and customs from religious concepts that already existed in the quilt of cultural ideas.[52] Israelite religion, even if rooted in the culture of the Mesopotamian ancient Near East, unambiguously claims an extended sojourn in Egypt. If one reads the biblical exodus account alone, no other historical setting than Ramesside Egypt fits the evidence of the text. And it would be strange indeed if the Israelites emerged from an Egyptian context and then built a tabernacle without antecedent or ritual trajectory.

Although ancient authors wrote more about the ark than any other artifact, there's little reliable information about it apart from the biblical text. All considering, the ark is an artifact no one has seen for over 2,500 years. Yet, despite the revolution of biblical studies caused by archaeological and technological developments in the past two hundred years, modern writers have produced relatively little of a serious nature on this subject. And they have said even less about the ark's context and background.

This gap in the literature presents an opportunity for us to ask exciting new questions. Is there Egyptian ritual processional furniture that is similar to the ark? In what ways did the symbols of ritual iconography develop over time? What can this furniture tell us about Egyptian ritual and by extension the underlying religious language of Israelite ritual? In the next leg of our journey, we are going to discover that the ark is in fact an ordinary object that makes sense within its context: the strange and foreign world of Egyptian ritual furniture.

# CHAPTER 2

# Getting Comfy with Ritual Furniture

Let's say you win (or inherit) a really large sum of cash. And overnight the balance in your checkbook balloons by seven figures. What would you do with all that money? Pay off your debts or invest it in sensible exchange traded funds? Not likely. According to a survey of national lottery winners in the UK, winners purchase property most often, followed by a fancy car.[1] Car purchases often follow a large windfall even if the winner already has a sensible vehicle. But why? In our culture, the automobile is the preeminent status symbol. The Late Bronze Age also had its status symbols. But instead of buying a hot cherry Ferrari, ancient people bought beds and chairs.

## Furniture as Status Symbol

Beds and chairs were the luxury items of the ancient world. They were expensive and tricked out like any modern luxury item. Wealth disparity is nothing new, and the ancient world had more than its fair share of the poor. Putting this into perspective, the typical farmer in Egypt died with no more than a bowl and a spoon.

Figure 8. The workers' village at Deir el-Medina (photo by author).

Much of what we know about the Egyptian economy comes from the New Kingdom village of Deir el-Medina near West Thebes. This village housed craftsmen whose job it was to build the tombs and funerary furniture for the kings and nobility of Egypt. These workers built the famous tombs in the Valley of the Kings, including the famous tombs of Seti I and Tutankhamun. And importantly, they paid each other with worthless receipts. At least, it is important for archaeologists because those receipts have survived and have given us a wealth of information about the Egyptian economy and how the craftsmen class lived.

These craftsmen were not permitted to leave the village when not working because they were the custodians of tools and materials belonging to the king. Day and night, the people of the village were guarded by Medjay to prevent them from leaving the village. Despite being under constant guard, the craftsmen engaged in open commerce. They built tombs and tomb furniture for outside customers as well as for other workers in the village.

Egypt was a barter economy and did not exchange coinage until the Ptolemaic period (ca. 325 BC). People exchanged goods based upon their perceived value relative to a *deben* of bronze. Like many currencies of the ancient world (e.g., the Hebrew shekel), the *deben* started out as a unit of weight (about 91 grams during the Ramesside period).[2] Over time, the Egyptians standardized that unit of weight into a unit of exchange. Bronze ingots weighing a *deben* did exist, but people rarely exchanged these ingots for goods. Records indicate that a gold *deben* also existed, but this measure was rarely if ever used except as a weight.

Figure 9. A three *deben* weight (Louvre Museum) (photo by author).

The *deben* was further divided into eight *oipe*.[3] Another unit, the *ẖar*, was based upon a sack of grain and worth about four *oipe*.[4] A large unit of currency sometimes used is the *seniu*. The *seniu* seems to be based upon the value of silver and is worth approximately five *deben*, although this value probably fluctuated over time.[5] Thus, one *seniu* ≈ five bronze *deben* = ten *ẖar* = forty *oipe*.

At Deir el-Medina, a donkey was worth seven *seniu* (about thirty-five *deben*) and a sheep or goat was worth between one and five *deben*.[6] The discrepancy in value between a sheep and a donkey was because anything that could reduce the burden of labor was highly prized. Given the arable land surrounding Avaris and the population of the city, the typical Asiatic household probably had no more than five sheep, a net worth of less than twenty-five *deben*.

For most Israelites, beds and chairs were out of their income brackets. However, that would not always be the case. During the reign of Jeroboam II (ca. 782–753 BC), Samaria became a wealthy city. The elite of Samaria deprived themselves of nothing, which is referenced in Amos 6:4: "Woe to those who lie on beds of ivory and stretch themselves on their couches."

As we discuss furniture, it is important to remember that these objects reflected status. Only the middle or wealthy classes could afford a basic box. And furniture fit for the gods was among the highest quality of goods. Ancient peoples recognized that religious service required the best of the best (Exod 12:5).

## Ritual Processional Furniture

At some time in our lives, most of us will participate in either a wedding or a funeral. And we usually participate without ever consciously realizing that these ceremonies are ritual processions.[7] These ceremonies serve an important cultural function that allows us to recognize change in our society. A marriage marks the birth of a family unit that can bring forth new children. Conversely, a funeral marks the end of a life once lived.

With these modern examples, each ceremony is performed in a certain order. The officiator performs each ceremony or *ritual* with a kind of parade or *procession*. At a wedding, a minister and a nervous groom wait by an altar for the bride to show up. The bride walks slowly down the aisle escorted by bridesmaids and her father before the minister reads the vows. The minister does not begin the ceremony until the bride arrives.

Even though we don't have evidence for a marriage ritual in ancient Egypt, Egyptologists have discovered ample evidence for funerary and religious ritual processions. And many ritual processions accompanied the celebration of temple festivals. Any given temple could have dozens of festivals and feasts. For example, the Abydos festival calendar had no less than fifteen feasts during the four months of inundation alone.[8] During these processions, furniture accompanied by large groups of priests played a significant role.

Figure 10. Funeral procession from the tomb of Ramose (TT55) (photo by author).

Figure 11. Thoth writing on a tree the name of King Seti I (Karnak Temple, Hypostyle Hall) (photo by author).

Many of these festivals and ritual processions were illustrated on the walls of Egypt's great temples. The Egyptians believed that writing and drawing gave magical power substance and presence. Writing and magic were tied together in Egyptian metaphysics, and both were thought to come from the god Thoth.[9]

To give you some idea of how the Egyptians thought this all worked, let us say I was to write a mild curse on a piece of paper: "May there always be one less step than my nemesis expects." The Western mind would think nothing of this other than to maybe crack a smirk because something written on paper has no more power than a bitter tweet or a nasty greeting card. In the West, separation exists between the agency of the writer, the object of writing, and the mechanics of the world.

With the Egyptian mind, that separation did not exist. They had a phenomenological view of writing. A mild curse on paper created an object of writing that affected the mechanics of the world. The written form changed the fabric of reality. So, my mild curse would cause my nemesis to trip at every set of steps he climbed.

Temple reliefs of rituals created a ritual in writing. This perpetually reenacted ritual for the benefit of their gods—a performance of ceremony done over and over. This was done so the gods received praise day and night even when human beings could not be there to perform the ritual acts.

The idea that the gods required continuous ritual or a perpetual offering was not unique to Egyptian religion. Levantine and Israelite religions had something similar. The offering table of the tabernacle had the "bread of the presence." And the altars had horns, which showed a perpetual presence of offerings (Exod 30:1–2; Num 25:30).[10]

With Egyptian temple rituals, processions and iconography were a key part of the drama of the divine. Priests carried a god's statue out of the temples to mingle with the common people. The Egyptians believed the real presence of their gods resided in a statue's physical substance, similar to the Catholic understanding of transubstantiation. Even though the superimposition of the divine upon the material may seem like a simple metaphysic, we have to remember that these ideas developed over more than a thousand years and make perfect sense when understood.

For example, Atenism worshiped the sun as its deity. The sun is an object of pure power. The sun's surface outputs as much energy as a trillion 1-megaton nuclear bombs every second. It is the most powerful object for 38 trillion kilometers in any direction and affects us all. The heat of the sun kills in the desert, and without it crops wither and die and humans starve. There was nothing at all unreasonable about worshiping the sun, even if this concept of divinity was too small.[11]

Since the earliest days of Egypt, ritual processions used various kinds of furniture. While some Egyptologists believe that the Egyptian priests manipulated objects in the presence of the deity through the ritual act,[12] this theory treats ritual processional furniture as passive objects without their own significance. Far from being foils, these objects were essential to Egyptian ritual and magic. Without the presence of ritual furniture, there would be no ritual. This idea is important because this understanding underpins the use of the ark of the covenant.

Figure 12. Aten shining down on Akhenaten and the royal family (Egyptian Museum) (photo by author).

## Introducing Ritual Furniture

Few of us ever stop to think about what makes a chair a chair, or what defines a chest. Most of us intuitively recognize furniture because form and function are inextricably linked. We see a chair and we sit in it. Nevertheless, before launching into an examination of ritual furniture, we need to set out some common characteristics for these objects. The reason is because, while furniture is normally pretty common-sense stuff, when religious use is involved, the basic ideas that define furniture are expanded.

At its simplest, *furniture* is a piece of large movable equipment that makes a space suitable for living or working.[13] But for ritual furniture, this becomes an object that prepares a unit of space for an encounter with divinity. Generally, these objects can make space usable in one of two ways. These objects can separate or encapsulate one space from another—that is, divide one space into two or more. This is a bit like modern room dividers. Or they can add a new quality to an already sanctified portion of space—that is, change one type of space into another. For example, adding a chair turns an empty room into a sitting room.

Figure 13. A *kar* shrine being carried with neck straps at Edfu Temple (photo by author).

For its part, ritual furniture serves a primarily religious function. This purpose can perform a variety of tasks, such as presenting an offering or providing protection for a deity. And when used for processions, craftsmen often modified this furniture with repeated use in mind. This means that the ritual processional furniture was carried or moved as a part of its normal use.

Another characteristic used consistently is carrying poles placed below the item's center of gravity. While this pole placement gives an object maximum visibility by making it ride as high as possible, the disadvantage of this arrangement is that it makes the transportation process less stable. This particular pole orientation was used for most processional furniture in Egypt.

With ancient Israelite ritual furniture, the poles could also separate porters from the sacred, thereby preventing accidental defilement. Unlike Israelite religion where ritual defilement was contagious (Hag 2:13), once Egyptian priests underwent the purification rituals, they were free to handle holy objects.

Even though carrying poles can identify furniture used for processions, an object lacking this feature could still be used for this purpose. Shrine cabinets portrayed in later period temples are an important example where the priests carried them using neck or shoulder straps (fig. 13). Therefore, carrying poles are a diagnostic rather than prescriptive feature.

Additionally, ritual processional furniture was typically dedicated to a person, either a human being or a god. For example, the "chest of Anubis" was associated with the Egyptian god that escorted the dead into the afterlife. Tying furniture to a person became, in Egyptian religious use, the way that the dead influenced the affairs of the living. The barques of deceased kings influenced onlookers into obedience to the now divine monarch.[14]

Moreover, ritual furniture could serve as a kind of container or vessel. Chests and boxes are an obvious kind of storage, but this characteristic also applies to sacred barques because barques are shrines holding votive images in cabinets, as well as to palanquins (vessels made for holding and carrying humans or the statues of gods).

Finally, ritual furniture was often decorated with religious symbols and iconography. Commonly used symbols include the *ankh* 𓋹, *djed* 𓊽, *neb* 𓎟, scepters 𓌀, *tjet* 𓎬, *maát* feather 𓆄, and *wadjet* eyes 𓂀, but could include special purpose iconography such as the uraeus, Nekhbet vulture, and the images of deities. Each symbol had a specific connotation. Religious iconography served the purpose of making otherwise ordinary furniture suitable for use as a religious object.

Figure 14. Statue of Anubis (Egyptian Museum) (photo by author).

## Christmas Presents and Ritual Boxes

As a Western secular culture, few examples of rituals are front and center in our daily lives. Fewer still involve ritual furniture. But one ritual in western culture does involve something similar to ritual processional furniture: the Christmas present.

For families that celebrate this gift-giving winter festival, the process is pretty much the same. Usually, it involves a plastic or dead pine tree. Yet in most homes, plopping a gift under a tree unceremoniously in a brown paper bag simply does not cut it.

Figure 15. Chests from the tomb of Sennufer (photo by author).

No. Instead, you find a box. Lovingly place the gift inside the box, and wrap the box in brightly colored paper. And tie it all together with shiny bows and sparkling ribbons. Once you wrap the gift, only then is it ready to be a gift. And if you have a mother like mine, she saves the box and wrapping for reuse the following Christmas.

Even though the custom of gift-wrapping at Christmas has largely lost its religious meaning, the ritual lives on. So too do the arguments over whom Mom and Dad love more because expensive Christmas gifts remain an indication of status. Thus, although the ancient Egyptians did not have Christmas, they packaged items for other reasons. Most notably, they packaged goods that were buried with the deceased for the dead to enjoy in the afterlife.

The box was the most common type of furniture used for grave goods. And while many of these were little more than storage boxes, some were quite elaborate.[15] Jewelry chests from the tomb of Sat-Hathor-Ant (ca. Amenemhat III of Dynasty 12, 1875–1832 BC) had canopy-shaped lids, were made of ebony with ivory inlays, and had sides of wood sheathed in silver, knobs of bronze, and feet clad in gold.[16]

Moreover, goods enjoyed while alive could be sacralized so they could be enjoyed in the afterlife. Several items owned by Queen Hetepheres bearing the cartouche of King Senefru (ca. 2613–2589 BC) were boxed for her use in the afterlife. Her mourners boxed the curtains for her bed canopy in a long wooden box covered in gold mountings.[17] This storage box was probably made specifically for interment to take everyday items and prepare them for the afterlife. Boxes from her tomb also contained pottery, ointment jars, jewelry, and linens.[18]

The practice of packing favored possessions in boxes for the afterlife or as preparation for a temple foundation deposit shows the versatility of boxes in performing ritual blessing. This was important for the Egyptians because expensive goods and packaging for funerals meant a higher status and more opulent afterlife.

Ritual boxes originally began as everyday storage that was elevated to a religious purpose through the use of *analogical thinking*. Analogical thinking takes mundane items—pots, doors, knives, boxes—and mythologizes and idealizes them. This elevated their use to become fit for participation in the drama of the gods.[19]

The Egyptians used analogic thinking to express complex ideas. The tomb builders of ancient Egypt frequently carved false doors into the walls. Why add a door that did not lead to another room? They were asking the question "How does one move from this world to the next world and the afterlife?" The Egyptians likened moving into the afterlife to walking through a door. They took something familiar and used it as an analogy to express something divine. Religious ritual then engaged what was perceived to be real in the world of the divine.[20]

So ritual chests were idealized into something special through extraordinary use. The earliest of these special uses was to bury grave goods. Many Egyptian tombs portray wooden chests being transported and used to store goods for the afterlife. The earliest iconography of storage chests for grave goods comes from the tomb of Hesyre (ca. Djoser of Dynasty 3, 2667–2648 BC) at Saqqara.[21] This example from a wall painting shows grave goods in a variety of boxes. Yet, storage chests for tombs would have occurred even earlier.

Containers that initially served to protect food and clothing from the elements, animals, insects, and mold were even regarded as having magical properties. Grave goods were stored in boxes that were thought to be empowered by magic to protect and preserve their contents. Through the application of magic and cultic symbolism, such chests became perfectly adapted for a ritualized environment.

Figure 16. False door from the Mastaba of Idut (photo by author).

Figure 17. Philae Temple (photo by author).

Alongside ordinary storage chests, dedicated ritual chests appear in the archaeological record as early as Dynasty 5 (ca. 2498–2349 BC).[22] Chests for ritual use continued through the history of Egypt well into the Roman period.[23] On the Hadrian Gate at the Temple of Philae (ca. Marcus Aurelius), Osiris-Sokar was portrayed carrying a chest for ritual purposes. The transition from reused utilitarian chests probably started from storing clean linen garments for the afterlife.[24] The dead needed clean linen garments to appear before the gods. This is similar to priests wearing clean linens after ritual purification.[25] Why take a bath if you are only going to put dirty clothes back on? Chests that stored linens became idealized and ritualized along with the linens.[26] Ritually pure garments were stored in ritually pure containers for the ritually pure deceased, all to prevent the dead becoming ritually defiled.

Another early usage for a ritual chest was as a container for votive statues. Early stone ritual chests from the Giza Necropolis held wooden votive statues.[27] The Egyptians believed that the dead required proxy bodies for the afterlife. Proxy bodies allowed the spirit of the dead to return to interact with the physical world. And more importantly, embodying a statue allowed the dead spirit to accept food and drink offerings.

Perhaps the greatest fear of the ancient Egyptians in the afterlife was not divine punishment but starvation. Thirty percent of mummies show signs of "episodes of intermittent disease or malnutrition."[28] Since mummification was restricted to the upper classes, we can conclude that the Egyptians lived by subsistence agriculture. Because most people ate within fifty kcals of their nutritional needs, famines killed within weeks. And this fear of famine was passed along as a possible concern in the afterlife.

Although archaeologists today find most storage chests in funerary contexts, ritual offerings provide another source of chests. A foundation deposit at the Temple of Montu at

Tôd produced a set of four copper chests containing items of silver, gold, and lapis. Of all the varieties of ritual furniture, chests and boxes were the most diverse. They were large and small, ornate and plain. They could be made of wood, stone, or metal. Some had carrying poles, and some didn't. And many examples have survived into modern times, making them useful as a basis for comparison with the ark.

Figure 18. The Tôd Treasure showing a bronze chest (Louvre Museum) (photo by author).

## Sacred and Profane Space

The next step on our journey involves a discussion of sacred space. Egyptian religion maintained a strong separation between *sacred space* and *profane space*. They divided the natural order into two distinct realms. Profane space is the ordinary physical world tainted with impurity. Sacred space was set apart from profane space and is defined by purity.

Sacred space is an important concept for understanding religious structures, such as temples. The boundaries of sacred space define the holy from the profane. Sacred space sets apart the physical areas in which the divine can act as intermediaries between heaven and earth.[29] These sacred spaces had a "'cosmographic' function" that the Egyptians thought mimicked the structure of the universe.[30] Sacred areas were like the heavens, and profane spaces reflected what was on the earth.

We see this in the layout of tombs. Egyptian tomb architecture repeats notions of creation separated out into sacred and profane spaces.[31] The antechambers of tombs were public areas that people frequently visited. Those public areas often contained the biography of the deceased and had scenes from the physical world such as hunting, fishing, and nature motifs. On the other hand, the burial chamber was sacred.[32] And the artists who decorated burial chambers used motifs (such as starry skies) that reflected the divine. The burial chamber was nothing less than a gateway to the heavenly realm.

Figure 19. Layout of the Temple of Khonsu at Karnak (illustration by author).

Large freestanding structures, such as temples and palaces, also reflected the cosmic order of creation as sacred space. Columned courts (the peristyle halls) were places where non-priests may have gathered during festivals. Beyond these public places was a set of "Great Doors." The Great Doors isolated a sacred inner court from the rest of the temple. Only priests who completed the purification ritual were allowed to enter the inner court.

Within the inner court was the *set weret*, "the Great Throne." The Great Throne was the holiest place in the temple. It was a shrine, complete with its own roof, inside of the temple. It was a temple within a temple, a bit like Russian matryoshka dolls. Even today, one can visit temples where the Great Throne is still preserved and see that this inner shrine is qualitatively different from the rest of the temple. Take, for example, Luxor Temple, where the entire temple is built from limestone except the Great Throne, which is black granite. And unlike Greek and Roman temples where the holy place is located at the back of the temple, the Great Throne is normally located near the center of the temple.

Thus, when we discuss the normal natural order as perceived by the Egyptians, there was a hierarchy of consecration. Ordinary humans live in profane space. Because of ritual impurity, the religious establishment did not permit uninitiated humans to enter a temple's holiest places. Gods live in sacred space because they are pure by definition.

Figure 20. The goddess Sekhmet from the Temple of Mut, ca. Amenhotep III (Museo Egizio) (photo by author).

Because of their need for ritual purity, the gods did not tolerate the presence of impurity.[33] So to prevent offending a god who might flee and become vengeful in response to irreverent handling, the priests sequestered their gods in sacred space. The ancient Egyptians believed that the gods were capricious and dangerous. The goddess Sekhmet was believed to be able to cure disease because she and her hordes of demons inflicted people with disease in the first place. She cured illness by withdrawing the sickness she inflicted.[34] Hapy, god of the Nile inundation, brought produce to the field but also caused strife and danger and forced farmers to relocate on an annual basis.[35]

## Egyptian Expressions of Sacred Space

The Egyptian concept of sacred space proved to be highly pliable. Sacred spaces could be manipulated, miniaturized, and intensified. These qualities made Egyptian sacred space robust enough to produce several interesting effects. This expression goes beyond even what modern anthropological theory can normally address, giving the Egyptian application a nuanced virtuosity. The Egyptians could express notions of space almost as a kind of language. And this plasticity of sacred space was a quality common to Egyptian ritual furniture and the ark.

Figure 21. Lapwing birds from the Chapelle Rouge (photo by author).

As mentioned above, writing could convey magical power. As such, several iconographic devices could define sacred space. Some suggest that the lapwing bird, 𓅚, was marked on temple walls to indicate that it was an area open to the public.[36] But this is unlikely because the lapwing bird is also found in the Chapelle Rouge, the Great Throne of Hatshepsut—a place that a commoner would never be allowed. More likely the lapwing bird symbolized worshipers giving everlasting adoration. This is an example of a phenomenological icon (see p. 27), a drawing that was believed to have spiritual substance.

Figure 22. Kheker frieze from the Abydos Temple of Seti I (photo by author).

Perhaps the most common and easily recognizable non-architectural device used to mark sacred space was the frieze. A frieze is a decorative horizontal border with a repetitive pattern along the upper section of a wall, column, or object. Decorators often used friezes as an architectural or design element.

We commonly find friezes in tombs and temples and on funerary objects, where its importance goes beyond mere decoration. Friezes contributed to the greater language of larger architectural units, such as tombs, by adding a vertical dimension to symbolic cosmology. For example, the kheker frieze 𓐍 (Gardiner Sign AA30) was used in tombs to show a division between oasis and desert or a horizon that separated the earthly realm portrayed on the walls from the stars and heavens portrayed on the ceiling.[37] This provided an artificial horizon to an architectural element and defined an area of importance.

Figure 23. Uraeus frieze on the Mortuary Temple of King Djoser (photo by author).

Decorators adapted the frieze to other contexts. Friezes could convey a sense of architecture even when used on smaller objects, such as pavilions (which have architectural attributes but are not temples). A particularly common choice was a frieze of uraeus 𓆗 (Gardiner Sign I12), a cobra goddess that was a protective deity.[38] She was also a solar diety, representing the power and fire of the sun. The uraeus frieze even inspired the hieroglyphs 𓉪 and 𓉩 (Gardiner Signs O17 and O16).[39]

An example of multiple friezes and pavilions comes from the Amarna period anonymous tomb 226.[40] This scene contains a total of three concentric pavilions and five rows of uraeus (fig. 24). The outer canopy has a frieze of uraeus wearing *shuty* crowns 𓋛, a symbol of royal power. Hanging from the roof is a row of date palm clusters. These date clusters are a fruit associated with the sun god.[41]

The Amarna period is best known for the reign of Akhenaten and his religious reforms in the form of Atenism. Atenism taught that the only true god was the sun, the Aten, and that everything and every other god was a manifestation of the Aten. And yet, Atenism was often intolerant of other deities that claimed to be the sun god, for example, Amun-Re. Despite Atenism's monolatry and its antipathy towards competing forms of deity, the Amarna royal family was shown with both the Aten and the uraeus (protective cobra and sun goddess).[42] The uraeus had no formal temple, nor an established cult of worshipers. And even though

Figure 24. A pavilion with five concentric uraeus friezes from TT226 (Nina de Garis Davies, 1915).

the uraeus was considered to be fully divine before the New Kingdom, by the Amarna period, the status of the uraeus had drifted from its original identity as an independent solar deity to a lesser divine being, making it palatable to Atenism.

Ultimately, the uraeus frieze defined sacred space through a repeating sequence of divine images. By using one uraeus frieze within another, the Egyptians could define ever smaller units of ritual space. Craftsmen worked these friezes onto smaller objects such as coffins and boxes.

Figure 25. Nested uraeus friezes from canopic shrine of Tutankhamun (Carter no. 266a) (photo by author).

But friezes within friezes could also amplify holiness. The innermost rings had the greatest holiness. Although uraeus friezes can be found on large units of sacred space, ritual spaces were not limited to architecture. For example, the canopic shrine of Tutankhamun (ca. 1334–1324 BC) used a shrine within a shrine (fig. 25). Each shrine was topped with a frieze of uraeus carved from wood and gilded. The practice of decorating canopic shrines continued into the Greco-Roman period, where an example was adorned with both uraeus and kheker friezes.[43]

The Egyptians also used uraeus friezes on coffins and biers.[44] New Kingdom coffins perform many of the same functions as tombs. They define sacred space with the purpose of resurrecting the dead.[45] The spirits of the dead, once made sacred, require a space that they can return to. Coffins even had many of the same cosmographic architectural features, including solar friezes. An example of such a coffin is that of Henettawy (Dynasty 21, ca. 1073–947 BC). This coffin had a uraeus frieze running along the side of an anthropoid coffin.[46]

We also find uraeus friezes defining the sacred space upon royal thrones. In the tomb of Nakhtamun (TT341), a uraeus frieze adorned a pavilion with a deity seated upon a throne.[47] The "golden throne" from the tomb of Tutankhamun had two sets of uraeus: one set along the inside of the throne in hammered foil relief and a second set of four uraeus statues behind the throne watching the king's back (fig. 26).

Figure 26. A pair of uraeus from the Golden Throne of Tutankhamun (Egyptian Museum) (photo by author).

As early as the Third Dynasty (ca. 2686–2613 BC), the ureaus gained sway as the most important symbol of sacred space. This happened because the underlying tenets of Egyptian religion held that each god had a good and a bad personality. *Pyramid Text 534* mentions that the gods have a "good" and an "evil coming."[48] Offerings given to deities were meant to assuage the "bad coming" aspect of deity and turn the "good coming" toward the adherent. The adherent offered back to a god an aspect of the god. This offering fueled and energized the deity.

Offerings were based upon a notion of *reciprocal economy.*[49] Reciprocal economy is a common concept in ancient Near Eastern religions. The worshiper offers bread to a god. The god accepts the bread, multiplies it, and gives abundant bread back to the worshiper. Thus, protective deities were dualistic beings with their personality properly oriented. The god's "good coming" protected the adherent, and the god's "bad coming" inflicted harm upon his enemies.

Similarly, the uraeus had a good coming that protected sacred space and a bad coming that spat fire on the enemies of the king.[50] The uraeus deity reared up in an offensive posture as cobras in nature do. Whoever stood behind the uraeus cobra was protected.

Giving a god the things he or she creates or causes to thrive is called *sympathetic worship*. The goddess Maat was believed to create order and balance. The king presented to Maat voice and symbolic offerings of order and balance, hoping Maat would accept them and make Egyptian society orderly and give the king a stable reign.

We see reciprocal economy in the Bible as well. The artifacts kept with the ark were items resulting from the miraculous acts of God. Such items included a piece of Aaron's budding staff, the golden jar of manna, and the red heifer's ashes. Like the staff and manna, the Israelites believed an appearance of a red heifer to be a miraculous divine event. Such heifers were believed to be a sign that only appeared when needed for ritual purification. The works of God were placed near the divine presence to please God and to promote similar divine acts.

## Materiality and the Ark

Ritual is a repetitive act that occurs in space over time. All the components of the ritual (the performance, the physical object, and the presumed interaction of the divine) are necessary to complete a ritual. Without any one of these components, the ritual would be incomplete. And while any repetitive act could be a ritual, a religious ritual allows people to interact with the divine.

We can analyze any ritual as being either horizontal or vertical. A vertical ritual attempts to interact directly with the divine. Such rituals include the use of offerings directly to a spirit. With vertical rituals, the adherent stays stationary in physical space while addressing the transcendant reality.

But ritual can also be done horizontally. With horizontal rituals, the repetitive act moves items in physical space, but the act does not necessarily attempt to directly address a spiritual being. Horizontal rituals are often used to prepare items for vertical rituals.

I should note that rituals of either kind require the use of physical objects. It is safe to say that ritual cannot be done without physical objects. Even among minimalist Protestants who officially eschew ritual, most of these groups ritually perform either communion or baptism or both. In these cases, physical things are used to perform the ritual. Bread, wine, and water are essential to these rituals. But also required are the ritual implements to hold the elements: cups, bowls, baptismal founts, or even natural features like the River Jordan.

Ritual requires not only a space or place to perform the act, but the physical items that make it possible. Physical items are essential to the act. Without physicality, there would be no ritual. The ritual and the physical items that facilitate the repetitive act are synonymous. Some items could be regarded as so sacred that their use outside of specific rituals is prohibited, for example, the holy anointing oil (Exod 30:31–32).

Ritual objects were specific for the kind of ritual they were expected to perform. For example, the altar of burnt offering was used exclusively with vertical rituals (Exod 29:25). The altar incinerated food offerings, converting them to smoke that would provide "a soothing aroma before the LORD." The altar converts sacred items into something that reaches up to the divine.

While many kinds of ritual and processional furniture are specialized for horizontal or vertical rituals, the ark was used for rituals in both dimensions. As a reliquary, the ark transported holy items from one sacred place to another (horizontal ritual). The Israelites wandered in the wilderness and then entered Canaan with the ark. When the tabernacle was moved, the ark transported the tablets of the Ten Commandments in the chest compartment through profane space. As the focus of the sin offering ritual, the ark was used with a vertical ritual. The blood of the sacrificed bull and the goat was sprinkled upon the mercy seat (Lev 16:14–15). The high priest offered the blood before God's presence above the mercy seat, which was seen as covering the people's sins.

Ancient Egyptian furniture thus gives us insight into how ritual furniture functions. Furniture adds something material for a ritual to interact with, without which there would be no ritual. We have seen furniture used for preparing offerings in both temple and mortuary rituals. Ancient Egyptian furniture could act as a sacred vessel (or reliquary) to hold a votive or cult statue. In the same way, the ark stored the two tablets of the Ten Commandments.

Egyptian furniture used for presenting offerings worked with the ritual notion of reciprocal economy, where something is offered to a god to get more of the same in return. Similarly, other artifacts were placed in the tabernacle in the presence of God "before the testimony": the golden jar with manna, Aaron's budding rod, a small amount of sacred incense, and the book of the Law that testified to the deeds of Israel's God (Exod 16:33; 30:36; Num 17:8; Deut 10: 2, 5; 31:26; and Heb 9:4). That reciprocal economy was the ultimate sign of God's status, giving God the things of God and praising God with the direct acts of God.

# CHAPTER 3

## Boxes and Chests and Arks! Oh My!

Let's imagine you are a fig farmer. Your harvest is ripe and you had a bumper fig crop this year. And you want to thank Amun-Re for such a bounty. So you harvest your figs and bring a bag of them to Karnak temple. Smiling with bag in hand, you approach the pylon. But a lector priest stops you at the gate.

"What do you think you doing?" the lector priest growls.

"I'm going to offer these lovely figs to Amun-Re," you reply. "I want to take these figs and set them before the plinth of the barque of Amun-Re." You are indeed proud of your figs.

"You are not entering this *holy* temple with those figs *tainted with ritual impurity*." The lector priest holds his hand up to you. "If you try to enter the temple, guards with spears will kill you before you make it anywhere near the plinth."

Your smile drops to sadness. "I have traveled miles to offer these figs. And these are the best figs I have ever seen in thirty years of farming. What am I going to do?"

The lector priest, eyeing your figs, says to you, "Well, we wouldn't want those tainted figs to go to waste. I have some friends who might be able to help." He disappears into the temple, and moments later he returns with a group of purification priests carrying a *pedes* chest. The purification priests set the chest down and lift off the lid. The lector priest takes your bag of tainted figs and places them in the chest. The lid is closed.

The purification priests pick up the chest and slowly carry the chest back into the temple. All the while, the lector priest chants and reads out magic spells. When the priests arrive at the offering table before the plinth of Amun-Re, they open the lid of the *pedes* chest. And the lector priest reaches into the chest and pulls out sacred figs to present before Amun-Re.

Essentially, the priests would place offerings tainted by profane space into the *pedes* chest. The priests would then perform their liturgies and carry the *pedes* chest from profane into sacred space. And upon opening the chest, those mundane offerings were ritually transformed into sacred items fit for service to the gods.

## Introducing the Simple Box

As part of our journey, we are going to explore all the various types of chests and boxes that the Egyptians used in their rituals. There's a lot of detail here. So, do feel free to skim this section. I promise, you won't hurt my feelings . . . much.

The Egyptians used at least twenty-four different kinds of chests and boxes. Perhaps the most basic was what they knew as the *debet* (also spelled *tebet*), 𓂧𓃀𓏏. The *debet* is a common term that appears in the Deir el-Medina texts (ca. 1513–1073 BC) among other words for boxes and chests.[1] The term also appears in Semitic literature. Noah's ark and the container used to hold baby Moses (Exod 2:3, 5) use this term.[2] This word continued into the Greco-Roman period as a kind of shrine for a god, a meaning alluding to a ritual purpose.[3] The word survived into Coptic as ⲧⲁⲓⲃⲉ, "chest, coffin."[4]

Figure 27. A large *debet* basket (Egyptian Museum) (photo by author).

Confusing matters, the word *debet* also has a homonym meaning "basket" (fig. 27). But the Egyptians seemed aware of this ambiguity and often specified the material used in the *debet*'s construction. For example, "75 wood *debet* of wood" was placed into the tombs of a necropolis.[5] The "wood" is repeated to show these were wood chests, not baskets.[6]

A box from Tutankhamun's tomb was labeled "wooden box (*debet*)" that contained thirty-nine pieces of linen.[7] So, it seems the *debet* chest could extend to possibly any storage container.

Figure 28. A basic wooden chest (Louvre E 32225) (photo by author).

At Deir el-Medina, several pot shard ostraca mention *debet* chests. Amennakht son of Rashpeteref had a contract to make wooden goods. This agreement was an order to build a table and a *tebet* for the price of ten *deben.*[8]

Moreover, another transaction priced a white-washed wood *tebet* at eight *deben.* This text also included an *áfdet* box costing two *deben* and a wood coffin and a wood bed costing fifteen *deben* each.[9] This puts the value of the *tebet* below that of the *gati* shrine. So, we can figure that the *debet* is a box that has a mid-range value typically between eight and ten *deben.*

## Round Topped Box

The *daben,* , is a wooden box or chest found often in Old and Middle Kingdom texts. The determinative used with this word indicates that it was a box with a round top. They look a bit like classic pirate chests from the movies.

Determinatives are important in the Egyptian language. Determinatives are hieroglyphs that are added to determine the sense of the word. They are characters that have no pronunciation but are written to help the reader know the meaning. Unique pictographic spellings helped the Egyptians keep the many homonyms of their language straight. These pictures (determinatives) frequently look like the physical objects that they represent.

Figure 29. The furniture list from the *Stela of Seker-Kha-Bau* with the determinatives in the lower register (illustration based upon Murray, 1905, Part I, pl. II).

A *daben* box appears in an early offering list from the *Stela of Seker-Kha-Bau.* The stela (ca. Dynasty 3, 2686–2613 BC) was discovered at Saqqara.[10] This stela is important to our knowledge of ritual processional furniture because each word has phonetic letters contained within a bounding box. Bounding boxes were common in lists and accounting. More importantly, each determinative was separated out and stylized to represent the actual object (fig. 29). This list mentioned other important boxes besides the *daben*, including *djeser*, *henu*, and *áfdet* boxes.

From the tomb of Irenessen (Dynasty 4, ca. 2613–2498 BC) at Saqqara, we find *daben hen(u)* in a offering list.[11] The list was also organized by bounding boxes. The *daben hen(u)* is a redundant spelling and not two chests, because the author wrote the term inside a single bounding box. Because the term is redundant, we can conclude this is a container like a *henu* chest.

A papyrus fragment dating to Dynasty 13 (ca. 1819–1673 BC) found in a tomb beneath the Ramesseum contains the phrase “thirty boxes (*daben*) [of] figs.”[12] This appears to be part of a food offering that was interred with the deceased and is the inspiration for our “fig farmer” story at the chapter’s beginning. Thus, the *daben* was among the boxes used to package items for the afterlife.

## Offering Coffer

The *mehen*, , “coffer,” was a vessel used for grain offerings to the gods.[13] Compared with other types of containers, this box appears to be small.[14] The word seems restricted to the New Kingdom and had mostly a utilitarian purpose. For example, a pair of *mehen* was used as stable equipment.[15] A debt of the Medjay Pasderety to Penniut itemized goods that included a wood *mehen* sold for three *deben.*[16] The same document mentioned a wood *tjay* box sold for six *deben.*[17]

Figure 30. A round-topped chest from the tomb of Tutankhamun (Egyptian Museum) (photo by author).

## Luxury Chests

The *pega*, “chest,” was used during the New Kingdom period. The Egyptians prized *pega* chests as expensive works of high craftsmanship from the Levant. These chests were made of exotic woods and decorated with precious stones.

During his thirty-fourth regnal year, Thutmosis III ventured out on his ninth military campaign. He campaigned for a season in the Levant and brought back fabulous objects as trophies of his conquests. The war booty included “wooden goods and *pega* chests” and a *qeniu* palanquin worked in bronze inlaid with costly stones.[18]

The Late Egyptian Miscellanies are a collection of administrative documents used to train student scribes. They date to the Ramesside period. One Miscellany refers to a *pega* among the goods of foreign lands.[19] This scribe described a fine *pega* of Amor (the Amorites) having carrying poles (*maut*) made of *mery*-wood and inlays of the work of Kedy. A red cloth covered its top. From this description, we can infer that the “work of Kedy” is a metal (or wood) into wood inlay craft. Inlays were commonly used in Egyptian furniture.

Another Miscellany described preparations made in anticipation of Pharaoh's arrival. This letter described *pega* chests similar to those found in the first Miscellany. The text reads, "Fine *pega* chests of Amor having their *maut* poles of *mery*-wood inlaid with the work of Kedy, their tops of red cloth."[20]

Figure 31. The ebony throne of Tutankhamun with ivory inlays (Grand Egyptian Museum 378) (photo by author).

Compare the red cloth used to cover the *pega* to the scarlet cloth and porpoise skin coverings that were placed over the ark when it was transported: "And they will spead over them a cloth of scarlet and cover the same with a porpoise skin cover, and they will insert its poles" (Num 4:8). In Israelite religion, scarlet thread together with cedar wood and hyssop were used in cleansing rituals (Lev 14; Heb 9:19). Scarlet was associated with luxury and was the color of the warrior (2 Sam 1:24; Jer 4:30; Nah 2:3).

## High-End Chests

The *gaut*, 𓎼𓄿𓅱𓏏𓆱, was a "box (with lid) made of wood" used as linen chests or for storing precious items.[21] Jac. J. Janssen maintained that a *gaut* box is similar to an *áfdet* coffer but larger given its higher price.[22] A Tomb Robbery Papyrus (ca. Ramesses IX, 1131–1112 BC) recorded precious items tied to the robbery, among which were two *gaut* boxes "full of clothes."[23]

At Deir el-Medina, the Medjay Mentumose used a *gaut* box as partial payment to the scribe Hori.[24] The *gaut* box in this transaction was valued at ten *deben*. This is more expensive than many of the chests already examined and is similar to higher-end goods. These high-end goods included a bronze bowl for twelve *deben*, a bed for twelve *deben*, and a footstool for fifteen *deben*.[25] The total cost of this transaction totaled 127 *deben*,[26] making it one of the largest transactions recorded at Deir el-Medina.

Figure 32. Calcite chest from the tomb of Tutankhamun (Grand Egyptian Museum) (photo by author).

Another ostracon from Deir el-Medina mentions a *gaut* box along with leather goods and linen sheets.[27] This was a list of goods from a shepherd, perhaps the tender of goats and cattle from one of the estates near Deir el-Medina. The shepherd's goods included five *deben* and four *oipe* of leather from the "cow of Ptah." The *gaut* box mentioned is priced at ten (*ḫar*), and the text adds, "which to me equals a live goat."[28]

The *Will of Naunakhte* bequeathed some *gaut* boxes.[29] Even though the word appears early on in the will as a "wood box," later in the will a *gaut* box appears with the stone determinative ▭.[30] Stone chests are not out of the question when we consult the archaeological record. Stone chests for wooden statuary are found among Old Kingdom burials.[31] And a painted calcite chest was found in Tutankhamun's tomb (fig. 32).

Ramesses III's offerings list papyrus to the great temples of Egypt mention *gaut* boxes several times. The king gave thirty-one large silver *gaut* boxes containing coverings for the Theban triad.[32] The papyrus's accounting section includes ninety-two whitewashed wood *gaut* boxes made in the shape of cartouches.[33] A cartouche was an oval-shaped ring (representing eternity) containing a royal name (usually the king's) inside.

Figure 33. Cartouche chest from the tomb of Tutankhamun (Grand Egyptian Museum 242) (photo by author).

Cartouche boxes were used in both divine temple and mortuary contexts. We find a relief of the cartouche box at Medinet Habu,[34] and it is possibly the same kind of cartouche-shaped box found in the tomb of Tutankhamun.[35] The cartouche as a ritual container is important to our understanding because a cartouche was more than simply a name. The cartouche represented the name of the king who was to become, or had become, a god. As such, the king's name conveyed a power not unlike that of a frieze.

Overall, the evidence points to the *gaut* as a box on the highest end of the durable goods spectrum. A *gaut* box could be made of wood, stone, or even silver. The *gaut* box had a ritual function that drew its blessing from the power of the king's name.

Figure 34. A *djeser* from the tomb of Yuya and Thuyu (KV46) with a cartouche of Amenhotep III (photo by author).

## A Table Chest

The *djeser*, , is a chest that drew a wider association from its utilitarian use. Several of these chests are extant from archaeological excavations and no other chest is quite like it. This chest resembles a small table, with tall legs and hinged lids that opened from the top.

The *djeser* is among the oldest forms of furniture in ancient Egypt. The tomb of Hesyre (ca. Dynasty 3, 2686–2613 BC) depicts these chests on the wall paintings.[36] These early chests are comparable to the Dynasty 18 (ca. 1538–1305 BC) chests from the tombs of Yuya and Thuyu (fig. 34) and Tutankhamun.[37]

The etymology for the word *djeser* comes from the same root that means "holy, sacred."[38] However, *djeser* has a broad range of meanings including "private," "secluded," "costly," or "splendid." The *djeser*'s tall legs elevated the container off the ground, which protected its contents from insect or rodent damage. Even though these chests did not begin with a special use in mind, *djeser* chests were eventually used for setting apart special or precious items and for rituals.

## The Box Body

Our next box raises questions as to how ancient Near Eastern people personified inanimate objects and their perceived volition. The *áfdet* (also spelled *áfdjet*), , is a small or medium rectangular box not exceeding three *deben* in cost.[39] The earliest mention of an *áfdet* box appears on the *Stela of Seker-Kha-Bau* of Dynasty 3.[40] The determinative shows a rectangular box lacking distinct features.

But the *áfdet* box was no means limited to the Old Kingdom. Several *áfdet* boxes were among the goods made at Deir el-Medina. Three ostraca mention simple *áfdet* boxes selling for the meager price of two *deben*.[41] The prices suggest that the *áfdet* box was small.

However, *áfdet* boxes appear to have a ritual aspect. A priest of Khonsu was recorded bringing an *áfdet* box to a temple.[42] Ramesses III donated a silver *áfdet* box. Even though wood *áfdet* boxes were normally inexpensive, a silver *áfdet* box was quite lavish.[43]

An interesting *áfdet* box tells us about a man who tried to communicate with his dead wife Ikhtay, the chantress of Amun, using an *áfdet* box buried above her.[44] In this somewhat sad letter, the man asked his dead wife for permission to buy a carrying pole to make his labor easier. This would lead us to conclude that an *áfdet* box could be an intermediary between the living and the dead.

Another ostracon mentioned an *áfdet* box, which reads "an *áfdet* box that is on its body."[45] Any vessel having a votive function could be said to have a "body." Shabti figures, small anthropoid coffers, and even canopic jars had "bodies" (fig. 35). These objects could be substitute bodies for the deceased. In the case of the chantress' husband, he was talking to the *áfdet* box in a personified manner, asking it to pass his message along to his dead wife.[46]

Figure 35. Canopic jars from the tomb of Hori-Re (Dynasty 26) (Louvre N. 2988, N. 2989, N. 2972, N. 2974) (photo by author).

## Demons and the Magical Lockbox

The locked box provides us with a glimpse of the intersection between religion and magic. Many chests were used for ritual purposes, but few were incorporated into daily magical practice. The Egyptians strongly believed in magic and that they could influence the world with spells, incantations, and curses written papyrus and clay figurines.

The *mekhetmet*, [hieroglyphs], and *khetemet*, [hieroglyphs], boxes functioned as receptacles for libation and incense offerings. *Mekhetmet* is the older form of the word originating in the Old Kingdom and often has a determinative that represents a "wickerwork box or hamper."[47] The etymology of *khetem* denotes a box that is a "'closed' or 'sealed receptacle.'"[48] The word is derived from a common verb meaning "to lock, close."[49] This also has a connotation of sealing something magically. For example, these boxes could seal up or consecrate a blessed offering to prepare it for delivery to the gods.

An interesting use occurs in *P. Westcar* related to magical practice. The story tells of a maid who heard an unearthly sound coming from a room. Instead of being spooked, she tracked the noise down to a sack of grain. An evil spirit had taken up residence inside the bag. But a bag couldn't contain an evil spirit. So the maid placed the sack of grain inside a *pedes* box. She then placed the *pedes* box inside a *khetem* box, .[50] Then she bound the outermost box in leather.

The maid imprisoned the demon using the magical power of the *khetem* box.[51] This understanding is particularly important, and easy to miss. The maid's understanding of magic is a two-way street. Magic thinking not only elevated common boxes so they could participate with the god's rituals, but that same thinking empowered ordinary items to physically limit evil spirits in the everyday world.

The Egyptians believed that the material and spirit realms overlapped. They interacted with the divine on a daily basis. Magic spells were cast to protect mothers in childbirth, to protect from dangerous creatures like snakes, to grow the crops, and to protect the dead into the afterlife. The Egyptians walked the world alongside gods, demons, and the unseen. Their daily walk was with one foot in this world and the other stepping next to the spirits.

## Jewelry Boxes

The *seḥdjet*, , is a kind of jewelry box. A list of objects from the Middle Kingdom city of Lahun that were appropriated by the scribe Het included a *seḥdjet ketet*, "a small box," and its contents.[52] The contents of this particular *seḥdjet* box were a gold "master" (*tep ḥer*), perhaps a small gold idol; an amethyst bead; and possibly a silver diadem.[53]

A *seḥdjet* box was illustrated in a tomb located at Beni Hasan.[54] This box was labeled a "*seḥdjet* box of clothing." Contrary to the small boxes mentioned in the Lahun papyri, this box was probably the size of a chest. The relief indicates that the box was rectangular with short legs. An inscription on the side dedicated the contents to Amenemhat, the tomb's owner. Furniture with a ritual purpose often shows this kind of dedication.

A magical papyrus from a collection in Berlin mentions a *seḥdjet* box used in a ritual to protect a child. This papyrus has a list of praises making up a magical incantation with the phrase "*seḥdjet* box of pure bearing of Heliopolis."[55] This phrase occurs after a list of gods who act as subordinate deities to the god Re, for example, "Horus is your [Re's] arm." The box was linked to the ideas of being carried, ritual purification, and the gods of Heliopolis. Thus, this *seḥdjet* box appears to have had a processional and a ritual function.

## Pulled Chests

The *setjet*, , is among the more unusual chests of the Old Kingdom. These containers appear to be roughly the height of a man, although iconography is often an unreliable source for size information. The relative size of these containers sets the *setjet* apart from the related *meret* chests from Dynasty 18 (ca. 1538–1305 BC) onward. The term has a unique determinative that is a pictograph of the *setjet* chest. The chest shown in the determinative has two feathers and a tree on the lid.

The tomb of Niankh-khnum and Khnumhotep, located near the Pyramid of Unis (Dynasty 5, ca. 2498–2349 BC), has a labeled relief with a pair of *setjet* chests dedicated to Thoth.[56] A second example of a *setjet* comes from the tomb of Tepemankh (Dynasty 5) from the Abusir necropolis.[57] This chest is squatter than the previous example. The chest is wrapped with strapping or cloth around the middle. The mastaba of Ptahhetep and Akhethetep (Dynasty 5) shows a similar chest with an enlarged base and narrow top.[58]

The *setjet* resembles the grain heaps seen in harvest scenes and probably contained loaves and grain.[59] The *setjet* most likely was part of a resurrection ritual that involved sprouting grain, as indicated by the "tree" growing from the top. A priest prepared the *setjet* by filling it with wet grain and then allowed the grain to sprout. This ritual is used with other furniture such as the *ḥanu* barques.

## Beating Your Chest

The *meret*, , "chest," is the New Kingdom successor to the *setjet* chests of the Old Kingdom. Painted cloth strips wrapped these chests, and those offering them pushed or pulled them on sledges. Even though the *setjet* chests appear to belong to a ritual practice of the Thoth cult, New Kingdom *meret* chests are connected to other cults: Amun-Re, Min, Montu, and Hathor.[60] And though the *meret* developed from *setjet* chests and look similar, differences in the construction exist between the two. The *meret* chest was generally shorter than the *setjet* but retain the feathered lids and sledges.[61]

An interesting ostracon lists a large number of painted pieces that included a *meret* chest.[62] A decorator appears to have requested this receipt for work he had completed. His job was to paint the illustrations laid out by scribes and master artists who sketched out preliminary drawings in red ochre on tomb walls and objects. This exchange included painted coverings, a painted *meret* chest, and a painted sarcophagus. Since the text mentions the decorator's work, we may infer he painted the *sheqer* and *tebet* chests also mentioned. This shows that carpentry and decorating were separate labor specializations, and that carpenters did not necessarily decorate or finish their furniture.

*Meret* and *setjet* chests often were used to present offerings. Scenes show these chests before a sacred barque or a box shrine, or as part of a funeral procession. For example, paintings from Queen Tausret's tomb (KV14) show *meret* chests as a portion of her funeral goods. The *meret* chests seem to be particularly common with rituals that emphasize resurrection. For example, the chapel of Paser had reliefs of *meret* chests going before the *ḥanu* barque at the Feast of Sokar, a god of rebirth and resurrection.[63]

Figure 36. *Meret* chests accompanying the Barque of Amun-Re at the Chapelle Rouge (photo by author).

*Meret* chests, despite being linked to resurrection, could be associated with gods not typically associated with funerary cults. The Opet festival illustrated on Hatshepsut's Chapelle Rouge shows several *meret* chests in the procession of the barque of Amun-Re (fig. 36). A "beating" ritual act accompanied the *meret* chest.[64] This act is shown being done before the cult statue of Amun-Re. Perhaps beating helped the grain germinate as it forced air pockets to form between the wet kernels.

## Chests for Impure Offerings

The *pedes*, , "box, chest," is a piece of furniture that helps explain much about ritual processional furniture. Already, we've seen *P. Westcar* mention a sack of grain holding a demon being placed inside a *pedes* box.[65] The story of the wax crocodile, from the same papyrus, told of the wife of Ubainer (a chief lector priest) possessing a *pedes* chest full of clothes.[66] In this story, Ubainer had an unfaithful wife who was having an open liaison with a commoner. Ubainer crafted a wax model of a crocodile. And when the commoner went down to the river to bathe, Ubainer walked backwards to the river and threw the wax crocodile over his shoulder. This magical act summoned a crocodile that ate the commoner. Ubainer proves his wife's infidelity to the king by changing the summoned crocodile back into a wax model, and the king had the unfaithful wife burned alive and her remains thrown into the river. The *pedes* was mentioned in the story to show that the unfaithful wife lacked for nothing.

A *pedes* chest can also be a document box similar to some *henu* chests.[67] For example, a letter of Amenemope from the Late Egyptian Miscellanies contains the command to build a *pedes* chest for carrying documents.[68] From the same letter, one man defends his right to the titles of scribe and army officer. The man claimed the evidence he needed was in a day book register found in a scriptorium *pedes* chest.[69]

Figure 37. *Pedes* chests on procession at Luxor Temple (photo by author).

The *Dialogue of Ipuwer*, a Middle Kingdom wisdom text, talks about *pedes* chests. This text suggests that slaves could not afford a *pedes* box, despite its being a low value possession (thus showing how little resources the slaves had). Ipuwer compares the *pedes* box against the more expensive *atep* chest.[70] He says that a slave who could not afford a *pedes* box (think Ford Pinto) now owns an *atep* chest (think Porsche 911), something that should never happen, so the world was going to Hades in a handbasket (think *debet* basket).

This chest had a domestic use for the storage of clothing. Given that most Egyptians owned only one set of clothes per year, the *pedes* chest was by no means an item for the masses. A *pedes* chest was not something the poor of Egypt would have ever purchased. The Amherst fragments mention *pedes* chests along with offerings of lapis and turquoise, silver, and gold.[71] In the *Victory Stela of King Piankh* (Dynasty 25, 747–664 BC), messengers arrived with gifts including gold, costly stones, and clothes in a *pedes* chest.[72]

The *Annals of Thutmosis III* showed a pair of chests with poles labeled "gold and a *pedes* chest containing resin." Thutmosis III used these chests as part of his offerings to Amun-Re at Karnak.[73] The pair of chests was equipped with full-length poles. The Karnak *pedes* chests are practically identical to the Amenhotep III offering chests presented at Luxor Temple (fig. 37).

These *pedes* chests are similar to both *henu* and other portable chests in form. They had carrying poles and a uraeus frieze on a flat lid and were used to transport offerings tainted by the profane world into sacred temples.

Uraeus friezes protected the sacred space of the *pedes* chest, keeping the status of ritual purity even in profane space. The chest functions as an intermediary across different spatial contexts. Empowered by the ritual, the chest overcame the taint by converting ritually impure objects into something sacred (p. 138). Without ritual furniture, no ritual and no offering would be pure enough to be brought into sacred space.

Figure 38. *Henu* chest from the tomb of Kagemni (photo by author).

## The Classic Chest

Does this journey seem like canoeing down the winding narrows of the Blue Nile River? Well, things are about to get crazy as we approach the first cataract. The *henu* chest is important because it is incredibly diverse and highly relevant to the ark.

*Hen(u)*, , is the generic word for chests, boxes, shrines, and even coffins and biers. The word can appear with chest , coffin , and various shrine cabinet determinatives. A *henu* can be large or small with a variety of shapes. It can be a storage chest, a chest for offerings, and used for foundation deposits. The *henu* chest can be a focus of worship and a metaphor for a coffin. And *henu* chests appear with and without carrying poles.

They ranged in size from small cases for writing implements to large storage chests for regular linens. However, the *henu* chest had forms used in ritual and mortuary practices. The word is common in the Old and Middle Kingdoms and remained extant in monumental inscriptions as late as the Ptolemaic period. A *henu* chest appears on the *Stela of Seker-Kha-Bau*, shown as a chest with short legs and a lid with a knob on top.[74]

A painted wood panel (ca. Dynasty 22, 947–713 BC) mentions a list of wood furniture.[75] That list includes an *áfdet* coffer, *henu* shrine, and a *mehen* chest. The *henu* has the shrine determinative  while the *mehen* has no determinative. This shows that *henu* and *mehen* are not synonymous terms during the Third Intermediate Period (ca. 1073–664 BC). The term *henu* is found as a label for ritual chests on the Dynasty 20 (ca. 1194–1073 BC) reliefs at Medinet Habu, even though it was elevated out of common use.[76] So it seems that during the New Kingdom, *henu* chests took on a primarily ritual purpose.

## Chests for Precious Metals

Archaeologists discovered the earliest indisputable instance of a *henu* chest in Queen Hetepheres's tomb (Dynasty 4, ca. 2613–2498 BC). They found this chest along with pottery inside a larger wooden chest. The chest had an inscription on the lid which read *henu ḫer dabenu*, , "a box holding bracelets."[77] The box contained large graduated silver bracelets (9 to 11 cm in diameter) intended to be worn up the arm arranged on rods held up by wooden supports.[78]

The silver alloy in the bracelets consisted of 90 percent silver, 9 percent gold, and 1 percent copper. Butterfly-shaped inlays on the bracelets are of carnelian, turquoise, and lapis lazuli. Beneath the box's gold lining were small toilet items. These items included three small gold dishes, two badly decayed ivory bracelets, and a copper needle. Other items included a gold manicuring tool, thirteen copper and gold bracelets, and a silver vessel probably for cosmetics. But perhaps more interesting is that this box is lined with gold both inside and out like the ark (Exod 25:11; 37:2).

The treasury at Medinet Habu (ca. Ramesses III, 1191–1160 BC) has reliefs showing *henu* chests containing precious items for temple ritual practice. This round-topped lid is shown with a handle on the top of the lid and a handle on the end panel of the box[79] and is remarkably similar to a ritual chest recovered from the tomb of Tutankhamun that was made of ebony and painted white.[80] Writing on the side of the chest from the tomb of Tutankhamun suggests it contained "17 garments making 14 sets of garments."[81]

Figure 39. A *henu* chest with bracelets from the tomb of Queen Hetepheres (Egyptian Museum) (photo by author).

Figure 40. A pair of *henu* chests from a talatat brick at Amarna (Luxor Museum) (photo by author).

The storage of sacred and precious items often included *henu* chests. In particular, bronze, silver, and gold were offered up in ritual *henu* chests.[82] An inscription at the Speos Artemidos (ca. Hatshepsut) says that a *henu* chest of clothing was among the offerings of silver, gold, and "every enduring vessel (*henu*)."[83]

Precious metals were considered to be inherently ritually pure, so bringing them into an Egyptian temple required no special preparation. The Israelite concept of ritually pure metals differs slightly from the Egyptian notion. The Israelites regarded metals used to create pagan images or coinage (which bears a foreign king's image) as ritually defiled. Because of this problem, money changers during post-exilic times traded foreign coins (at a premium) for ritually pure metals acceptable for offerings. Melting precious metals was often sufficient to overcome ritual impurity.

However, much of the ark was cold formed by hammering, so the metal needed to start out ritually pure (Exod 25:18). Exodus 25 states that the metal used to make the ark and its lid was of *ṭahôr*, "pure, ceremonially clean" gold (Exod 25:11, 17).[84] The idea is not that gold being used was 24 karat, 100 percent "pure" gold. During the Late Bronze Age, metalsmiths in Egypt refined gold by cupellation, which removed the copper but not the silver. Gold with an excess of 90 percent purity was rare prior to the Late period (ca. 664–332 BC).[85] Therefore, "pure gold" either meant electrum, an alloy of gold and silver highly desired by the Egyptians, or, more likely, gold not previously used in a cultic idol.

## Packaging the Dead

Sometimes *henu* was synonymous with "coffin." After all, aren't coffins just boxes packaging dead people? The *Biography of Weni* mentions a delivery from Nubia. That delivery included a "*henu* chest of life," that is, a sarcophagus; an *áa*, "coffin lid"; and a *benbenet*, "capstone of a pyramid" for King Merenra (Dynasty 6, ca. 2349–2185 BC).[86]

A stela from the tomb of the solder Ramose mentions a "*henu* chest of Osiris."[87] The text goes on to say that the arms of the lord of the necropolis embraced the chest. This is a euphemism for Ramose's coffin. Even though we find examples of *henu* meaning a coffin, the expression is not very common. This usage is more poetic than more literal terms for coffin, such as *wet*.

The mastaba of Kagemni (ca. Teti) contains a reference to a "chest of cleansing,"[88] which held natron for the ritual purification and preservation of a dead body. The tomb of Djehutinakht at El Bersheh, a site dedicated to the burial of regional governors during the Middle Kingdom, also records a "chest of natron."[89] Natron was a naturally occurring mix of sodium carbonate decahydrate, sodium bicarbonate, sodium chloride, and sodium sulfate that was important for the mummification process.

Mummification used large amounts of natron to preserve the corpse of the deceased. As part of the process, the priests eviscerated the body, removing all the internal organs (except the heart) and the brain. The priest packed the body cavity and covered the entire body with natron. Over the next seventy days, the body would purge fluid and the priests replaced the damp natron with dry until the natron completely desiccated and salted the flesh, not unlike beef jerky. In this state and done properly, a corpse could survive millennia without risk of decomposition. Of course, if the mummy ever got wet, well, that's a whole different story.

These chests with items for ritual purification were important because they were likely an antecedent for chests where ritual purification was achieved by magical warding alone.[90] Mummification was a practice limited to the upper classes and was expensive. This means that these *henu* chests, from the coffin to the chest of natron, were also status symbols.

## Classic Chests with Poles

Reliefs from the tomb of Ankh-Ma-Hor (early Dynasty 6) show several chests being carried to the tomb. Each chest was brought to the tomb with carrying poles set below the center of gravity. This had the advantage of raising a chest up so that is could be seen. But stability was a known problem.

From this tomb, two porters carried a large chest with tall legs and a peaked lid tied with ropes.[91] The purpose of the ropes was to provide a kind of security seal. When packaging items for the afterlife, the packer tied a string around the box and then sealed it with a clay bulla to prevent tampering.[92] In this relief, one porter carrying the chest steadied the box with a single hand. This shows that stability was a problem when the poles were at the bottom of the chest.

Figure 41. A chest being carried by poles with flanges (photo by author).

However, one unique solution to the stability problem used a pair of flanges, one on each side of the box pointing to the floor (fig. 41). The flanges increased stability by preventing the poles from rolling during transport. The disadvantage of flanges is that the carpenters would need to carve down these poles from larger—and significantly more expensive—sections of wood. This disadvantage, and perhaps limited usefulness or reuse, may be why the innovation was not repeated.

The ark would have similar stability problems. The command to carry the ark by the use of the poles would have placed a burden on the Levites (Exod 25:14; 30:4; 37:4–5). As they carried the ark on their shoulders (1 Chr 15:15), they would have to always concentrate to keep the ark upright.

## Chests as Religious Shrines

Some chests served as processional chests or small religious structures. The Treasury at Medinet Habu depicts a number of chests that served a cultic function. Two chests have a statue of a sphinx on the lid. Another has a statue of Re in leonine form. And the fourth one has a statue of Amun-Re in leonine form.[93] These chests were used to present offerings of gold and precious stones to the gods.

Similarly, the tomb of Neferhotep (TT257) (Dynasty 19) shows the deceased and his wife.[94] The couple worships a simian statue of Re-Horakhty mounted upon a chest. These chests served a storage or presentation function, and they were also the objects of worship.

The Medinet Habu treasury showed another *henu* chest with a flat-top lid. On the lid are two sphinx statues facing each other and between the sphinxes is a lid handle. The chest is displayed end on. The sphinxes on the lid are side by side in parallel, not facing each other. And so this decoration could be similar to the two sphinxes that are on the sides of the throne palanquins.[95] This is comparable to the mercy seat on the ark of the covenant, which had two cherubim (Exod 25:20).

Denderah Temple has a reference to a *henu sheta*, "chest of mysteries."[96] The term *sheta*, meaning "secrets" or "mysteries,"[97] refers to religious mysteries. Religious mysteries included the ceremonies, rituals, texts, and even objects associated with cultic service. These are the religious things that remained hidden from all but the uninitiated.

These rites were often done in secret underground chambers deep at the back of the temple. Some of these chambers were elaborately decorated, like the alabaster lined chamber of secrets at Denderah. A "chest of mysteries" is a chest with a sacred image. But with the *henu*, such chests served as a focus of worship with a votive element, such as a cult statue, built on its lid.[98]

Figure 42. The chamber of secrets beneath Denderah Temple (photo by author).

Figure 43. The ceiling from Denderah Temple depicting a shrine (bottom left) (photo by author).

Another instance from Denderah is similar to what we have seen already with the religious phrase "chest of mysteries" with the goddess determinative .[99] This *henu* shows a piece of furniture dedicated to a deity, a characteristic typical of ritual processional furniture. This quality applies to the ark, which has the full name the "ark of the covenant *of the Lord*" (Num 10:33). The ark, like other kinds of ritual processional furniture, was dedicated to a deity.

## Anubis Chest

A special form of *henu* chest, the so-called "Anubis shrine," is probably the most important to our inquiry. Strictly speaking, the Anubis shrine is not really a shrine but a chest for temporary transport. Most Anubis chests that archaeologists encounter were in circulation from the New Kingdom onward.

In its hieroglyphic form, Gardiner Sign E16 depicts the Anubis chest. A dog or jackal lies on the lid of the shrine, respresenting either Anubis or Wepwawet.[100] By itself, the ideogram reads *inpu*, "Anubis." When used as a determinative, the Anubis chest glyph is found in the word *ḥery-sesheta*, "he who is over the secrets." The Anubis chest often mimics cult shrines (chests that serve as shrines). However, this chest was not typically venerated as a religious shrine because it served a different purpose.

An important witness for the Anubis chest is the tomb of Kha-em-hat (TT57) (ca. Amenhotep III). The tomb mentions a set of four titles that includes *henu inpu*, , "chest of Anubis."[101] The chest appears abbreviated in his title "master of the *henu* chest of Anubis, the king's scribe."[102] A *henu* chest is also in Kha-em-hat's title, , "the greatest seer of the chest of Anubis."[103] A variant appears on the ceiling, 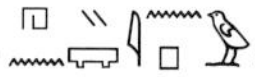, "servant of Osiris, greatest seer of the *heny* chest of Anubis."[104]

Kha-em-hat's duties as a lector priest and his titles were synonymous with the Anubis chest ritual. This implies that the Anubis chest belonged to an entire community and the rituals associated with it were carried out by a special priest. Kha-em-hat's emphasis of his titles shows us the importance of the position.

Some Egyptians regarded these chests as a powerful icon. The burial chamber in the tomb of Userhet (TT51) (ca. Seti I) has a frieze with a repeating sequence of Hathor faces and Anubis chests interspaced with kheker symbols .[105] The Anubis chest is the only piece of ritual processional furniture to have its image used as a frieze.

The tomb of Neferronpet (TT336) at Deir el-Medina (Dynasty 19) has an image of an Anubis chest. A wall painting shows a man standing beside the mummy of the deceased. He carries a chest with a false door and a jackal figure.[106] Bruyère suggested that this was the canopic box for Neferronpet.[107] Canopic chests typically have four compartments for canopic jars and are frequently found on a sledge.[108] The iconographic evidence supports the idea that Anubis chests were a special kind of canopic chests. The vaulted tomb of Pedneit (Dynasty 26, 664–525 BC) has a relief of the Anubis chest, revealing an interior view with canopic jars.[109]

While canopic chests are common in funerary contexts, surviving examples of Anubis chests are rare. One Anubis chest from the burial of Nodjmet (ca. Herihor) is unlike that found in other portrayals. It has a canopy-shaped lid as opposed to a flat lid, a sledge without carrying poles, and lacks a false door.[110] This example is comparable to the Anubis chest painting found in the tomb of Roy (TT255), which has a canopy-shaped lid but was carried on poles and lacked a sledge.[111]

The most famous of these chests is the Anubis chest of King Tutankhamun (fig. 45). The chest was built upon a sledge with two sturdy carrying poles permanently attached. The interior had five compartments: four small compartments at the front and a large compartment at the rear. Gold foil completely covered the wood chest, poles, and lid. The Anubis statue on the lid was wood and painted with thick black paint. The craftsman gave the statue gemstone eyes with gold eyelines. The craftsmen made the statue as one piece with its flat, corniced lid. The lid simply lifted off the top of the chest. This design is similar to the ark, which had the mercy seat resting as a lid on top of the box.

However, the greatest mystery about the Anubis chest of Tutankhamun is its use within Egyptian mortuary ritual. There is no reason to doubt that the Anubis chest once held canopic jars. The deceased's internal organs were held in canopic jars after mummification. The four jars stored the stomach, intestines, lungs, and liver. Each of the sons of Horus guarded the organs: Hapy, the lungs; Duamutef, the stomach; Imsety, the liver; and Qebehsenuef, the intestines. A key fact is that only one set of internal organs for the deceased exists and as a result only one set of canopic jars is used per burial.

Figure 44. Anubis chest from the tomb of Nodjmet (Egyptian Museum, Temp. 20.12.25.11) (photo by author).

Figure 45. The Anubis chest of Tutankhamun (Carter no. 261) (photo by author).

Even though the Anubis chest had four compartments for the canopic jars, Howard Carter discovered that Tutankhamun's canopic jars were not inside the Anubis chest. Besides the Anubis chest, Tutankhamun also had a canopic shrine and inside that was an alabaster canopic chest with the canopic jars.

Priests carried the canopic jars in the Anubis chest to the tomb. They then interred the canopic jars into a canopic chest at the tomb. In Egyptian mythology, the role of Anubis was to escort the dead to the afterlife.[112] The ritual procession ensured the safe transport of the dead to the afterlife, after which the Anubis chest was no longer needed for the deceased.

Most Egyptians would not have commissioned an Anubis chest for their burials. Priestly titles, such as "master of the chest of Anubis," imply that the Anubis chests were multi-use items. Some burials may have had modest Anubis chests or canopic chests decorated with an Anubis motif, but one-off pieces of furniture not included in the burial itself were only affordable for the most extravagant burials.

Among the hundreds of furniture mentions in the Deir el-Medina ostraca, the Anubis chest is never mentioned. The middle-class craftsmen traded funeral crafts to give each other a greater level of burials. The absence of Anubis chests from the trade goods probably means that they already had a dedicated Anubis chest inside the community.

## The Mercy Seat

We've seen from our journey that the history of chests and boxes in ancient Egypt is extensive and complex. And yet, qualities from the ark are reflected in these items. We have seen chests with carrying poles, chests dedicated to gods, chests made of wood and gilded in gold foil, and chests with red cloth covers. Lids made as a single piece with cult statues are in the archaeological record and include the Anubis chest, which is comparable to the mercy seat of the ark.

The Hebrew for the mercy seat is *kapōret*, which comes from the root word *kpr,* meaning to "propitiate/smear." When we convert the verb to a noun, the etymology doesn't make a lot of sense. I noticed, however, that in Egyptian the word *kap*, "lid," exists, and refers to a lid used with a coffin. Late Egyptian transforms and drops final *r*'s, which makes *kap* a good option for the context, especially given that the meaning of *'ărôn* can be a "coffin." The ark as a coffin (or canopic chest) is an evocative image given the complexity of its Egyptian context. Coffins in the Egyptian context served as a proxy bodies that could house the spirit of the dead when it returned at night. This is the same function that the idol served—to act as a body to house a god. So, to refer to the ark as a kind of coffin may allude to its role as a portable temple or shrine housing a deity, not unlike the *áfdet* boxes discussed earlier.

Bezalel made the mercy seat from ritually pure gold. He fashioned the two cherubim of hammered gold and permanently attached them to make one unit. The biblical text says "he made the lid from the two [cherubs]," strongly implying that they were combined into one piece (Exod 25:19; 37:8). The cherubim and the holy presence dwelled above the tablets, providing a cover over the law. The religious ideas communicated in chests and boxes, such as packaging rituals and ritual purity, led the way to other more complicated kinds of furniture and even more complex religious ideas.

CHAPTER 4

# Shrines, No Tent like Home

After a long day on the job, nothing seems better than coming home, eating a hearty dinner, and taking a long nap. However, when the Egyptians wanted to kick back in style, they did not retreat into their homes. They would go outside, pitch tent poles, and put up a canopy. Egypt being a hot country, they would enjoy the cool evening breeze that blew along the Nile from the Mediterranean.

So, when the Egyptians eventually fashioned images of their gods, priests were appointed to clothe the images, and they would feed their gods with *ḥetep di nesu*. The *ḥetep di nesu* offering is a voice offering. The priest says "beef" and that becomes the metaphysical substitute to actually offering some beef. A complete Egyptian offering consists of a large selection of essentials and luxury goods. Rather than everyone giving every kind of offering, a worshiper gives one kind of good. And the priest covers the difference by saying every kind of offering. These offerings included bread, beer, oxen, clothing, and every good and pure thing—the things every Egyptian wished they had in their pantry. And when they began to build homes for their gods (temples), they did so with all comforts of home.

However, the relationship between temples and ritual furniture creates a bit of a chicken and egg problem. The earliest stone temple in Egypt was built by King Djoser (Dynasty 3, ca. 2686–2613 BC) as a funerary temple for the stepped pyramid (fig. 46). But, the first ritual furniture is seen on the Palermo Stone, which records docket tags that predate the first temple by hundreds of years. I wrote above that the purpose of ritual furniture was to make sacred space usable. That is, if you have an empty room, you make it usable by adding a chair and a table. But if you have no room, what need is there for furniture?

Prior to the Middle Kingdom, Egypt did not use permanent temples to house their gods. It is possible that temples could have been constructed of perishable materials, such as reed, wood, and mud brick, and did not survive in the archaeological record.[1] But it is more likely that, for private cults and minor divinities, a tent (or tabernacle) may have been used.

Figure 46. Mortuary temple of King Djoser (photo by author).

While major royal pyramids were built with mortuary temples, lesser pyramids may have had a tabernacle that protected a piece of ritual furniture that could have held a cult statue. A suggestive example is the Seila Pyramid to the east of the Faiyum Oasis.[2] The pyramid is one of the smaller pyramids and possibly dates to the reign of Senefru (Dynasty 4, ca. 2613–2498 BC). A paved processional causeway was built up to the pyramid. But where the causeway stops, there is no evidence that either a mortuary temple or even a smaller chapel stood there. The sloping area from the end of the causeway to the pyramid is only a couple of meters, too small for a temple. However, the leveled area has four post holes four feet apart, forming a perfect square. These post holes suggest that a tent of some kind was most likely pitched there. A tent of that size would not have been large enough to provide much shade to a human, although it technically was large enough to be a cover for a kiosk, a tent under which a living person would sit. However, since this was adjacent to a pyramid (a tomb), we would expect a structure to have a memorial function for the dead, not a place for a living person. It seems more likely this tent functioned as shade for a shrine cabinet with a cult statue. In addition, the remains of a wooden cult statue were found near the site, suggesting that it was used for a religious purpose.

## Origins of the Shrine

The upright cabinet (or shrine) began as a utilitarian container with a simple box construction, and eventually developed into a specialized chest with a sloping top. Even though the Egyptians used regular chests for storing both sacred and mundane objects, they reserved box-shaped shrines for holding the images of gods or things they considered divine. These shrines developed over centuries and became integrated into more complex forms of furniture, as we are about to demonstrate.

Figure 47. Chests under a chair from the Mastaba of Ipi (Dynasty 6, Egyptian Museum) (photo by author).

The canopy-shaped top (e.g., fig. 47 right) appears to be a vestige of the tabernacle structure that came to be identified with divine space early in Egyptian religion. Evidence for these tabernacle-type tents goes back to at least the reign of King Khufu (ca. 2589–2566 BC). Two outer tents have been recovered from this period, which include the tent that surrounds the cabin on the Khufu's solar boat and the canopy found in the mastaba of Queen Hetepheres. Chests with canopy-shaped tops first appear in the iconographic record in Dynasty 5 (ca. 2498–2349 BC),[3] becoming a common iconographic feature by Dynasty 6 (ca. 2349–2185 BC). The lids from Dynasty 5 appear flatter and less curved than in the iconography of Dynasty 6. For example, artists painted a chest with a canopy top and knob handle on Mena's sarcophagus alongside other chests with peaked lids.[4]

As opposed to regular chests, early shrine cabinets had a flat corniced top, a style of cabinet that continued into Dynasty 12 (ca. 2029–1819 BC).[5] The difference between a chest and a shrine cabinet is that a chest opens from the top while a shrine cabinet has doors that open on the sides. Shrine cabinets continued to develop and reached their final form with the canopy-shaped lid during the Middle Kingdom (ca. 2099–1673 BC).[6] This latter form persisted through the New Kingdom (ca. 1538–1073 BC), for example, the shrine cabinet before the dancers in the tomb of Kheruef (ca. Amenhotep III to Akhenaten, ca. 1389–1335 BC).[7] The canopy shaped lid on a shrine or chest served no practical purpose that we are aware of. It is quite impractical, in fact, when compared to chests with a flat top. But it does serve a mythological purpose.

So far we have discussed canopies (or tents), shrines (or upright cabinets), and shrines with lids shaped as canopies. Being able to recognize the difference between the canopy and shrine (see fig. 51) will become important for our study because each of these serves a different function in the scope of Egyptian ritual. These functions have an analogous role in Israelite religion when we compare the ritual purpose of the ark when placed within the tabernacle.

Howard Carter found several examples of wooden shrine cabinets painted black in Tutankhamun's tomb.[8] These black shrines were the vessels used to transport the statues of gods for interment with the dead king. The fact that they housed divine figures is what makes them relevant to our ongoing discussion of the ark's context. The ark was a chest-like object that transported God between the cherubim, so it helps to place the ark among other contemporary furnishings that were also used to transport gods.

These shrines varied in shape and size according to the contents, which usually held the figures of deities on standards, stands upon which the gods were enthroned (fig. 48). Egyptian craftsmen even built a particularly tall and slender shrine cabinet for holding a cubit measure.[9] This particular example retained all the features of a shrine cabinet (sloped lid, hinged door, and sledge), even though it cannot be dragged because of its proportions, making the sledge only ceremonial.

However, when it comes to identifying shrines versus canopic chests, the two can be difficult to distinguish in iconography because canopic chests are chests in the shape of shrine cabinets that held canopic jars. Both shrine cabinets and canopic chests could be equipped with carrying poles.[10] And both can have canopy-shaped tops.

Nevertheless, sometimes we can easily distinguish between the two. A relief in the shrine section of Huya's tomb (Amarna Tomb 1) shows two shrine cabinets among other chests and grave goods.[11] Because canopic chests do not come in pairs and other grave goods are surrounding the depictions, context makes it obvious these shrine cabinets are not canopic chests.

Then again, some shrine cabinets do not have sloped lids but have a uraeus frieze fitted with a canopy.[12] Even though canopic chests are often found with a sledge, no extant examples of a canopic chest with a canopy have so far survived the archaeological record.[13] Yet, we do find examples of canopies on model boats.[14]

Figure 48. The god Sopdu enthroned on a standard (Carter no. 283b) (Egyptian Museum) (photo by author).

Shrines served as homes for the gods shielding them from profane elements. The gods were enthroned upon standards within these shrines. These containers enclosed areas of sacred space. And no god was adequately provided for without a shrine to shelter it. When a shrine is placed inside of a tent or canopy, the combination forms a complete tabernacle-like religious structure that can stand independently as a sacred place.

## Tents and Canopies for Shrines

Regarding the vocabulary of canopies and tents, one term is *ḥeta* (variant *ḥeti*), 𓎛𓏏𓄿𓊡 / 𓎛𓏏𓄿𓅱𓉿𓏥, and is related to the sail of a ship. The term is relatively rare, but the evidence shows that the Egyptians associated the word with large swathes of cloth. In the story of a *Dispute between a Man and his Ba*, the term appears in the line "like sitting under a *ḥeta* canopy on a windy day."[15] It also appears in *Pyramid Text 260*, where a spell is said on behalf of the deceased, who "has sat in the canopy of the Two Courtyards."[16] While this term is rare in literature, canopies commonly appear in iconography. From the tomb of Ramesses III (d. ca. 1160 BC), a tomb painting shows the king burning incense to a statue of Ptah under a canopy (fig. 49).

Figure 49. Ramesses III burning incense before the shrine of Ptah (photo by author).

Other terms related to canopies are quite common in comparison. The term *seḥ*, , "booth/tent," is associated with *seḥ-netjer*, / , "the god's pavilion," a tent used for embalming that was removed at the end of a ceremony.[17] For example, *Book of the Dead* spell 148 states "you should do (it) inside a *seḥ* tent of cloth."[18] Renowned Egyptologist James Hoffmeier surmises that *seḥ* is "more closely linked to ritualistic functions than the *im*."[19]

In *Pyramid Text 183*, the lector calls upon Atum to restore the king to the afterlife. The spell states "in the name of he who is in god's pavilion (*seḥ-netjer*), who is censing, who is in the *daben* chest, who is in the *tjeset* litter, and in the sack."[20] This reference is interesting in that the god is not only dwelling in a pavilion, but we also see a magical use for a *daben* chest, and there is even a sack similar to the maid trapping the evil spirit in *P. Westcar* (pp. 57–58). And depending upon the Pyramid Text variant, *tjeset* can appear with either the chest or litter determinative. The spirits of gods could inhabit both chests and palanquins so this ambiguity may not be accidental. This is because the Egyptian language could be used to suggest two different concepts at the same time, a literary device called *amphiboly*.

In addition, the Egyptians believed that, when the dead were restored, resurrection came from a vicarious association. A vicarious association is when the spellcaster or recipient is in the place of a god to take on the attributes of the god or derive a benefit from the god. In Christian theology, theologians often talk about the "vicarious atonement" of Christ, where Christ takes the consequences of our sins on the cross. In Egyptian magic, spells often make vicarious associations with Osiris so that the dead can benefit from his resurrection. These vicarious associations with the gods are frequently found in the pyramid texts. In *Pyramid Text 535*, we read "your eyes have been given to you as your two uraeus for you are Wepwawet who is upon his standard and Anubis the one before the god's booth."[21] The eyes of the dead become two uraeus (solar goddesses) because the person becomes as Wepwawet (a fox goddess) and Anubis (the jackal god). Egyptian magic often has the caster stand in the place of a god to solicit the god's power. And here in this text, both Wepwawet and Anubis are shown to be enthroned and in positions of influence. This theme of Anubis sitting before the god's pavilion (*seḥ-netjer*) is amplified in the Coffin Texts, e.g., "Anubis makes your savour sweet before your seat in the divine booth."[22]

One might be tempted to concede that the *seḥ-netjer* is the embalming tent based upon the numerous associations with Anubis. But we should note that other gods also had an association with the *seḥ-netjer*. In the *Contendings of Horus and Seth,* Re-Horakhty resided in a *seḥ* tent while his court lived in *im(a)u* tents.[23]

A third term is *im(a)u/iamu*, , and this was a "tent" held up using *wekha*, , "poles." These terms seem to refer to a canopy and vertical poles combination used around some portable shrine cabinets, including some sacred barques. Both terms appear together in the *Annals of Thutmosis III* where they appear as war booty. The *wekha* poles belonged to an *imau* tent and were made of *mery*-wood and worked with silver.[24] These terms also appear in the later annals listing the booty from Retennu (Syria) where they were worked in bronze.[25]

Figure 50. A votive shrine to Wepwawet from the Abydos Temple of Seti I (photo by author).

Figure 51. A canopy and shrine from the Barque of Ramesses II at the Ramesseum (photo by author). The shrine is highlighted in blue and the canopy is highlighted in green.

Ancient craftsmen eventually adapted the canopy for use with practically every kind of ritual furniture. They illustrated canopies covering biers, shrines, barques, and palanquins. And even furniture that did not have a canopy could still have a canopy-shaped lid as we see for chests, biers, and shrines.

For example, a canopy on poles was used with sacred barques. The Barque of Ramesses II from the Astronomical Room of the Ramesseum had a canopy attached to poles placed over a shrine cabinet with a canopy-shaped top (fig. 51). Tops shaped like canopies on chests, shrines, barques, and even biers simulated tents. This suggests that tents had a historical use as part of Egyptian ritual culture.

And the reason for this ubiquity may be the association with cool breezes and comfort. It is a bit like the association Americans have with air conditioning—no office work environment is complete without air conditioning. Likewise, no sacred space is truly home-worthy for a god without a tent for ritual comfort.

## The Generic Shrine

*Kar*,  , is a generic term for a chapel, shrine, or *naos* (permanent shrines made of stone). The word appears in a Late Egyptian Miscellany *P. Anastasi IV* where an unknown author writes a letter to a scribe taken to public drunkenness.[26] The author makes the scathing remark, "You are like a *kar* shrine absent of its god," implying that a shrine is worthless without its god. And elsewhere, some coffin text spells mention Re inside his *kar* shrine, which makes it clear that the *kar* shrine was used as a vessel for a sacred image.[27]

The word *kar* appears prominently in mortuary and religious texts, for example, in *Pyramid Text 627*, which discusses the rebirth of the king. The spell says that the king's *kar* shrine opens up when Re shines, perhaps alluding to a ritual were a king's votive figure was exposed to direct sunlight.[28] In *Pyramid Text 255*, the king rises up and assumes the power and authority of "the Great One." This "Great One" rises up from his *kar* shrine and lays his insignia on the ground.[29] In this same spell, a fiery flame from Horus of Nekhen is directed to those who stand behind the *kar* shrine.[30]

The meanings of these acts are uncertain. Given the religious context, *Pyramid Text 254* suggests that enemies of the deceased such as demonic spirits may have hid behind the shrine. And a blast of fire warded against these enemies.[31] Hiding behind religious structures was a tactic of the fugitive and the guilty. During Solomon's time, Adonijah clung to the horns of the altar to avoid justice (1 Kgs 1:50–53). However, when Joab tried the same stratagem in 1 Kgs 2:28, Benaiah killed Joab beside the altar (v. 34).

*Book of the Dead* spell 130 uses the term for the dead king confined to his coffin, "pure as the *kar* shrine of Horus."[32] Another use shortly after mentions a *nuweḥ*, , "cord," that is wound around the *kar* shrine.[33] This cord may have been used to ceremonially seal the shrine once a set of rituals were performed.

Some shrines from Tutankhamun's tomb had seals using cord. These seals were little more than twine passed through a set of metal loops with a clay bulla (fig. 52).[34] These cord and clay seals could even be used alongside the *khenes* sliding bolt (p. 93).

The *Great Dedicatory Inscription* at the Speos Artemidos (year one of Seti I) mentions a *kar* with the shrine determinative, 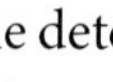.[35] In that text, Seti I claims to have rescued temples that became engulfed in sand and to have replenished the daily offerings and enriched temples. The text says the king caused "the *áshemu* images to be satisfied in their *kar* shrines."[36] An *áshem* was an image of a god and is related to *áẖem*, "image" or idol of a god.[37]

Figure 52. Cord and clay used to seal the third inner shrine (Carter no. 238a) (Burton photo 0631 [1923], color by author).

In *P. Chester Beatty I*, the god Re-Horakhty says to Baba (another name for the evil god Seth) that Baba's *kar* shrine is empty.[38] The implication in the text is that Seth has been made impotent. By removing his idol from its shrine, Seth cannot receive worship or food, and he lacks a physical presence from which he can assert influence on others.

The gift papyrus of Ramesses III (*P. Harris I*) makes a number of references to *kar* shrines. The section concerning Medinet Habu describes Ramesses III fashioning (literally "giving birth to") the cult statues of Ptah-Sokar, Nefertem, and all the Ogdoad. He states that he installed each god into its *kar* shrine.[39] So just as removing an idol from its shrine deprived a god of its power, creating a cult image and installing it into a shrine was perceived as empowering the god and establishing its influence.

Later in that document, Ramesses III records that he made a "statue of the lord" of "beaten" gold.[40] In the section discussing his Memphis temple, Ramesses III states, "I worked into your images that are installed in their shrines in gold, silver, and valuable stones firmly set."[41] The idea of stones being firmly set refers to the age-old jeweller's problem of stones becoming loose in their settings and falling out, just as when a wife loses the diamond from her engagement ring. And as is true for ancient craftsmen and jewellers today, the best solution for this problem is prevention.

At Denderah Temple, a different kind of *kar* shrine is mentioned with priests carrying shrine cabinets.[42] These shrines are portrayed near priests carrying boxes similar to *gati* shrines (p. 90). The orthography uses the shrine determinative 𓉱 similar to what is seen in the reliefs. These *kar* shrines were carried without poles using shoulder straps (fig. 53).

Figure 53. Priests carrying *kar* shrines at Denderah Temple (photo by author).

The Temple of Seti I at Abydos has a relief in the staircase that relates the *kar* shrines to divine barques.[43] This inscription mentions votive images placed on standards and installed into the "*wia* barque and *kar* shrine."[44] The text infers that the *wia* barques and the *kar* shrines were functional equivalents. Both furnishings served in the temples of the gods. We can see that the Egyptians had an order to enshrining: the god's image was placed on a stand, and the stand was placed inside a shrine cabinet. The stand enthroned each god inside its shrine.

At the temple of Thoth at Hermopolis, Ramesses III restored the temple and its *kar sheta*, "shrine of mysteries" of the Lord of All.[45] Per the king's instructions, the reconstruction was made to resemble the splender of Amun-Re's chapel. The rebuilding of the temple makes it probable that this *kar* shrine was not a piece of furniture but an architectural section of the temple. Permanent shrines made of stone, called *naos*, were often installed in temples. Stone *naos* were often made of black granite and overlaid with gold and other fine materials (fig. 54).

The *Annals of Thutmosis III*, found in the Chapel of Amenhotep I and Thutmosis III at Karnak, mentions a stone *kar* shrine with great doors of cedar.[46] Cedar wood was a much-valued commodity in Egypt and was typically imported from the region of Lebanon. Tyre supplied much of the ancient Near East with cedar wood and even supplied the wood that was used in the construction of the Solomonic temple, in which the altar was overlaid with cedar, and then with gold (1 Kgs 6:20–22).

Legendary Egyptologist Alan Gardiner translates the *qeniu*, 𓈎𓈖𓇋𓏲𓉐, as a "portable shrine."[47] It is etymologically related to the *qeniu* that means a "palanquin." We can tell the two terms apart by their determinatives: the former uses a shrine or house determinative 𓉐 (Gardiner Sign O1) while the latter uses a branch determinative 𓆱 (Gardiner Sign M3).

Figure 54. Stone *naos* of Osiris of the Shore, discovered at Kôm al-Ahnar (Dynasty 26) (Louvre D29) (photo by author).

Figure 55. Shabti figurine from the tomb of Tutanhkamun (GEM 4096) (photo by author).

Dhutmose, a scribe of the Theban Necropolis, wrote about the tax collection for locations south of Thebes. His writing dates to the reign of Ramesses XI[48] and makes two references to *qeniu* shrines. The first appears as part of a place name, "the *qeniu* shrine of King Ramesses III."[49] The second appears when Dhutmose mentions that thirty sacks of grains were collected under the authority of "the master of the *qeniu* shrine."[50]

We find a slightly different use in *P. Berlin 3050* (ca. Takelot I, 891–876 BC). This text describes the procession of the barque of Amun-Re-Horakhty and the god hearing his followers' recitation around his *kar* shrine. This joyful noise gave a "happy heart" to his *wia* boat's crew.[51] These phrases show a ritual procession with priests as followers and small votive figures as the "crew" placed on the deck. The Egyptians believed small votive figures could be proxy servants for the gods. They would bury *shabti* figures (fig. 55) with their deceased in the belief that the *shabti* would serve the dead person in the afterlife. The *kar* shrine, then, would be the cabinet on the barque that held the cult image of the god. The *kar* shrine, even though it is a generic term for a shrine cabinet, can also be used in a more specific way. Words that are used both generically and specifically are not uncommon in language. We tend to use some trademarks as both generic terms and as specific kinds of products. For example, people tend to use "BAND-AID" to mean both a generic bandage and a specific brand of bandage.

This use of a *kar* shrine can be found in many temples. An earlier example of a shrine cabinet is located at Ramesses II's Abydos temple (fig. 56). This *kar* shrine had a canopy, a uraeus frieze, and votive statues of worshipers. Four priests carried the shrine on poles in a presentation ceremony to the god Thoth.

Overall, *kar* is a broad term that can refer to the stone *naos*, a portable shrine used in ritual processions, or a palanquin carriage. The *qeniu* could refer to either a portable shrine or a palanquin. These shrines could be adorned with gold and gemstones and priests could use them to hold divine statuary. And once put into service, these items maintained a continuity of sanctified space appropriate for cultic service.

Figure 56. Four priests carrying a *kar* shrine on poles at the Abydos Temple of Ramesses II (photo by author).

## Shrine Cabinets

Most shrine cabinets were built as containers for either mortuary purposes or for housing idols in temples. From Seti I's Abydos temple, three examples of shrine cabinets exist with a ritual processional function. These cabinets had carrying poles and sledges and contained the cult statues of Heket and Hathor.[52] The use of these shrines was antecedent to notions of *localism*, the idea that a god only resided in one place at a time.

While localism may seem incongruent with Israel's notion of God, during the Late Bronze Age, most people believed that localism characterized the nature of divinity. God behaves as if he were a localist deity as people interact with the ark. God's shekinah glory follows the ark, and dwells and interacts with the physicality of the ark. This is remarkably similar to Egyptian notions of shrines that held divine images.

Besides furniture like the *kar* and *qeniu* shrines, other shrine cabinets existed with the specialized purpose of transporting deities. Some shrine cabinets were used to house statuettes or divine images, such as the the *qeref*, and .[53] For example, a vizier's statue was made with an accompanying *qeref* shrine.[54]

An ostracon that dates to Ramesses III's seventeenth, eighteenth, and nineteenth years, mentions a *qeref* shrine twice in the foreman Khay's property list.[55] The consistency of items from year to year suggests that the property remained in Khay's possession. Yet, the foreman did not actually own the property. The scribe organized the list by year and without monetary values. It is possible that this list was a custodial account, that is, property kept by the foreman for safekeeping.

Another ostracon mentions a *qeref* shrine that was used with a divine image (*tut*).[56] The first item mentioned is a religious image or idol made of wood, and the second is a *qeref* shrine. This text seems to confirm that the *qeref* shrine was normally paired with some sort of divine idol or votive image.

## Outer Shrine Cabinets

The *gati*, , or *get*, , is a kind of shrine often built around another item. Even though it was similar to the *ga/gaut*, "chest/box," the Egyptians used the *gati* shrine differently. *Gati* shrines were used to surround coffins, sarcophagi, or other shrines. The *gati* shrine was an example of shrine within a shrine, and the importance of this to biblical studies is that nested shrines are a part of the biblical record. The tabernacle and the temple both had nested forms of enshrined holy space.

One Deir el-Medina ostracon mentioned an outer coffin that the craftsmen altered by attaching a *gati* to it.[57] These outer shrines were elaborately decorated, and this ostracon states that the craftsmen decorated the *gati* shrine with three sacks of fine lapis. When Howard Carter discovered the granite sarcophagus in the tomb of Tutankhamun, the sarcophagus was surrounded by four nested wood *gati* shrines covered in gold foil (fig. 57).

Figure 57. Front view of the inner golden shrine of Tutankhamun containing his sarcophagus, showing the double doors with two sliding bolt locks (photo by author).

Besides their funerary use, *gati* shrines are interesting because they attracted thieves and tomb robbers. This has proven to be a boon for archaeologists because many of these thieves were caught and criminally prosecuted. Several court reports from these criminal proceedings have survived and given us an abundance of details about ritual furniture that we would not know by any other means.

One tomb robbery papyrus recorded the deposition of purification priest Penwenhab in year eighteen of Ramesses XI.[58] Penwenhab confessed he robbed "this god's" *gati* shrine, who happened to be Ramesses II. The robbers stole four *khenes* items of silver.[59] He replaced the items with wood replicas so that their absence would not be noticed. Silver was a rare metal during the Egyptian New Kingdom period, a metal that was rarer and more valuable than gold. So, silver was only used in very special circumstances or as accents to larger gold pieces.

Silver remained more valuable than gold until the beginning of the Iron Age, which is roughly the time of Solomon (ca. 969–930 BC). While we know that gold, silver, and bronze were collected in the contributions for the creation of the ark and tabernacle (Exod 25:3), silver was reserved primarily for making sockets on the planks of the tabernacle (Exod 26:19). Door hinges found in Egyptian contexts would have served a similar function, but extant examples were made of bronze, not silver.

Figure 58. The small golden shrine of Tutankhamun, showing the silver bolt locks (Carter no. 108) (photo by author).

Early Egyptologists believed that a *khenes* was a gold ox or double-headed lion amulet from the rare determinative .[60] However, we have no reason to assume that the *khenes* described in these definitions is the same as that in Tomb Robbery Papyri given the thief above replaced the *khenes* with wood replicas. The thief needed to restore the appearance of the *khenes* to cover up the crime. Amulets were normally placed inside furniture out of sight, whereas the *khenes* seems to have been an external feature.

In an inscription at the temple at Deir el-Bahari, Hatshepsut was described as accompanying the gods on procession as they *khenes*, "transverse" the lands.[61] When used as a verb, *khenes* means "to tread/wander." But with a two-headed ox determinative, the word means to move in two directions.[62] An inscription to the Hathor cow at Deir el-Bahari reads "going to Buto, travelling (*khenes*) in marshes, backwaters, and the ways of Horus," [63] indicating that *khenes* is a verb of motion.

An inscription found at the Speos Artemidos also dating to Hatshepsut's reign reads, "the great (goddess) Pakhet transversed (*khenes*) the eastern valley."[64] The *Poetical Stela of Thutmosis III* likewise states, "let them see your Majesty like an Upper Egyptian jackal, lord of speed, a runner who transverses (*khenes*) the two lands."[65] The idea behind *khenes* is not the idea of traveling in one direction, but back and forth at will.

Since it has a back and forth action, the *khenes* in the tomb robbery papyrus is neither an amulet nor a decoration, but a sliding door bolt on a shrine cabinet door (fig. 58). Large shrine cabinets used with sacred barques may have had two sets of doors, one set on the front and one on the back of the shrine, or perhaps a shrine within a shrine. Each set of doors had two metal bolts that keep the doors shut. Door bolts made of silver have been found on the smaller shrine cabinets in Tutankhamun's tomb, and were not ebony as was reported by Carter (fig. 59).[66]

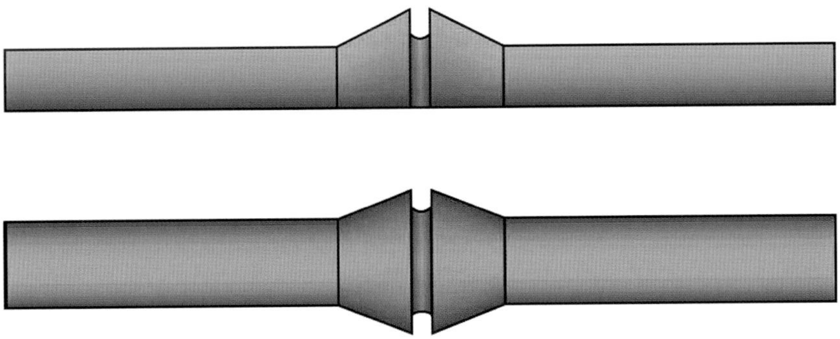

Figure 59. Diagram of the lateral and dorsal views of a sliding door bolt (illustrated by author).

Overall, we find that *gati* shrines can refer to any shrine cabinet used to contain another item. That item could be a coffin, canopic box, or even another shrine. Moreover, *gati* shrines were built with double doors and at least one pair of *khenes* sliding door bolts, and they could be covered inside and out with gold foil.

## God as a Local Deity

As a continuation of the Egyptian tabernacle tradition, shrines were vessels of sacred space. They sheltered divinity from the contamination of profane space. But their function goes beyond just sacred space. The combination of canopy and container alludes to the early history of cultic worship in Egypt. That combination is used in the funerary boats of King Khufu. And it is probable that a tabernacle was used instead of a funerary temple at the Seila Pyramid. Egyptian iconography associated shrines with canopies and tents. This pairing of ritual equipment and its meaning within ancient Egyptian religion is highly relevant for understanding the Israelite pairing of the ark with the tabernacle.

The Israelite tabernacle was a tent that the law only permitted the priests to enter. Clearly, the tabernacle was more than just a mere tent. It enclosed sacred space for the purpose of housing a shrine (the ark), and together, they functioned as a complete, self-contained sacred estate. The shrine housed and sheltered the deity. The tent provided a boundary between what was sacred and what was profane.

Bezalel, Oholiab, and others built the tabernacle with its own precinct of sacred space decorated with cherubim (Exod 26:1; 36:1–2). From an Egyptian perspective during the New Kingdom, the true presence of a divinity was only in one place at a time (localism). This was prior to the development of transcendence as a theological concept. So, ancient Near Eastern people viewed the gods as powerful spirits that traveled the land, but only resided in refuges of sacred space.

Thus, to keep a god with the people, the ancients felt that only a shroud of holiness could compel a god to stay. They believed the gods were aloof. Gods had to be coerced to stay, that is, held captive in an idol often against their will. That captivity held a god to service. If the gods fled, they took with them any blessings and protection they might have provided.

The ark of the covenant was thus a radical departure from the idolatry model of divine blessing. Instead of a god forced to stay and bless, the Israelite God remained voluntarily and blessed by establishing a treaty (covenant) with the Israelites. And while the maintenance of sacred space was important, the presence of an idol was unnecessary.

The Israelite tabernacle was built with many layers of sacred space. The tabernacle was separated from its most sacred space by the tabernacle curtain, the veil of the Holy of Holies, and the two cherubim on the ark (Exod 25:22; 26:1; 26:31). When the tabernacle was completed, the glory of the Lord filled it as a cloud so that Moses was unable to enter the tent of meeting, the inner tent of the tabernacle complex (Exod 40:34–35). While the children of Israel used the religious forms and conventions they were familiar with, the Lord manifested himself in a way unfamiliar to the inhabitants of the ancient Near East.

# CHAPTER 5

## Barques, Art with a Message

Have you ever come home only to find a delivery notice pasted to your front door? You snatch the notice and read it only to find that it has no helpful information other than that it is a registered letter and your signature is required. Of course, the postal carrier has come and gone, so you will have to wait till the next day to receive it. You have no idea who the letter is from or what it is about, but it has to be important—only important letters are sent by registered mail, because special delivery service isn't cheap.

So, immediately, your mind races as to what this letter could be about. *Am I being served with legal papers? Did my well-heeled aunt die and cut me out of the estate? Is my publisher congratulating me on my recent New York Times best-selling book? Has a wealthy benefactor read my work and decided to fund a university chair where I can pursue my research without ever having to worry about funding again?* (A fellow can still dream.) The point is that the mystery letter contains a message that you cannot understand until you actually read it.

In modern times, we live in the afterglow of the Protestant Reformation. If a religious group wants to say something about its beliefs, the group explains their beliefs by writing about them in a book or a long confessional statement. Suffice it to say that when we talk about religious beliefs, we tend to use carefully chosen words. But religions of the ancient world did not construct their theological statements in such a way. However, they did communicate their message in other ways, and one common way was through works of art.

In this chapter we are going to look at some of the most influential ritual furnishings that preceded the ark. So, if in the last couple of chapters we crossed the border of the hinterland, this leg of the journey will plunge us into the deepest, darkest jungles of the unexplored. And we will now begin to see the big picture of what the ark is trying to tell us. And if we can place the ark in its context, perhaps we can gain the understanding that was intuitive to the ancient Israelites when they saw the ark at Mount Sinai.

When they arrived at Mount Sinai, the ancient Israelites understood what sacred barques meant because many of them had participated in Egyptian religious practice (p. 115). These barques communicated a specific understanding about what it means to be a god. This idea of divinity suggested that gods resided in one place at a time (p. 94), and that an idol was the physical, material presence of divinity (p. 100). In this chapter, we are going to flesh out the ways these ideas developed in Egypt through barques, and ultimately how the ark borrowed that understanding and turned it on its head.

## The Origins of the Sacred Barques

The subject of sacred barques is incredibly rich, and the details of barques can be rather overwhelming. Sacred barques are replete with history and pregnant with symbolism, and they have been used in temple rituals since Egypt's earliest days. Little of this evidence has been brought into the conversation regarding the ark. With that in mind, please understand I am only scratching the surface of what could be said of barques.

Let me begin by clarifying that the history of barques is important because it tells us much about the ark. The visual language that went into the ark was not cobbled together overnight. It was a slow development that took place over a thousand years of religious practice. And learning about the course of that development helps us to understand the overall message that the ark was used to communicate within Israelite religion.

Figure 60. The Step Mastaba of King Djoser, Egypt's first pyramid (photo by author).

The history of sacred barques begins in the Old Kingdom (ca. 2686–2185 BC). In the previous chapter we discussed a ritual practice using shrines and tents as *ad hoc* religious structures. However, when the kings of Dynasty 3 built the first pyramids (fig. 60), they also built the first temples in Egypt to accompany these massive monuments of stone and mud brick (fig. 46). These temples were not dedicated to worshiping the gods, nor even worshiping the kings as would be done later in Egypt's history. These mortuary temples serviced the king for a single purpose: to provide the king with food and drink offerings so he would not starve in the afterlife.

As mentioned previously, the greatest fear of the Egyptians, including the king, was starvation (p. 35). Fear of starvation was the single driving imperative of ancient Egyptian culture and religion. The elaborate burials of the middle and upper classes were done to feed the dead in the next life. The coffin texts are full of references to food, drink, food-offerings, bread, and hunger; for example, CT 604:

> To bring an offering of bread and beer in the realm of the dead. Hail to you, you lords of food-offerings, who grant provisions, who bring food and convey provisions; may you bring to me food and convey provisions to me, for I am a living soul, a follower of Osiris. Come to me and bring me the food-offerings and provisions of Osiris, for I am a "son-who-loves."[1]

This complete coffin text had no other religious concern than feeding the deceased spirit. The ancient Egyptian's chief concern was over the next meal, and thus the function of the first mortuary temple was to ensure that the kings would not starve in the afterlife.

Figure 61. Food and floral offerings given by Pentjeny to Osiris (Louvre C. 211) (photo by author).

The feeding of the dead involved presenting offerings of bread, meat, and beer. But there was a problem. To be fed in the afterlife, the deceased needed a body to return to. Yes, the coffin and mummy could act as proxies for the spirit to return to for feeding, but the priests who would feed the deceased king were not permitted entry into the tomb once it was sealed.

Too much distance remained between where the king had to be (buried inside his pyramid) and where the priests were forced to remain (outside of the tomb).

The food offerings had to either get closer to the king or the king had to get closer to the food offerings. The Egyptians chose the latter solution. The early kings built mortuary temples close to their tombs and erected statues of themselves for food to be presented to. But the dead kings were now spirits made ritually pure by the interment process, so they could only go to places where there was a high standard of ritual purity. This means that their cult images had to remain in sacred space, and for this the Egyptians turned to the idea that the gods traveled by boat.

During the Third and Fourth Dynasties, the kings of Egypt elevated the space found in the tabernacle shrines and instead made for themselves permanent stone mortuary temples. Even though the kings of Dynasty 3 were affiliated with the cult of Atum-Re at Heliopolis (a northeastern suburb of modern Cairo), permanent temple architecture at Heliopolis has yet to be discovered, although excavations are currently in progress.[2] In Dynasty 5 (ca. 2498–2349 BC), we see kings start to create special architecture for the gods, notably the sun temples. Sun temples were built upon elevated platforms and had a perimeter wall and a square frustum with an obelisk and pyramidion on top.

Six sun temples are known to have been built although only two have been discovered to date, which belonged to Usarkaf and Nyuserre. The sun temples had offering tables but there is no evidence of ritual furniture use, and worship at the sun temples seems to have been restricted to the private religious practice of the kings. The construction of sun temples did not last beyond Dynasty 5. However, they provided a precedent for the divine temples of the Middle Kingdom.

Religious practice within the sun temples was based upon the myth of the sun god Re. Re was believed to travel across the sky in a boat during his daily voyage. The notion of the gods traveling by boat was adopted for most Egyptian deities. With Egypt being a river nation, the preeminent form of travel was by boat. To show that a god can travel great distances, the Egyptians incorporated boats into their mythology. They elevated real boats to a ritual purpose through analogical thinking. Unlike ritual chests, the elevation ultimately resulted in a complete mythological transformation. This transformation shows the gods using the sacred barque not as real objects but as mythological conventions (fig. 62).[3]

This resulted in many iconographic representations of barques that are not literal portrayals of real objects but are mythological constructs, that is, artistic or abstract portrayals meant to express the myth. We will not concern ourselves with purely abstract barque portrayals because we are primarily concerned with real historical objects related to the ark.

The ritual furniture used with the transport of gods was often designed with mythological suppositions in mind. The barques of ancient Egypt were influenced by the specifics of Nile River culture, which is why boats were such a powerful motif. However, the ark was not bound by river culture and as such did not display any boat-like traits. The ark appears to have been predicated upon a difference theological understanding than barques. Nevertheless,

Figure 62. Stela of Amenemope with a mythical Re-barque in the lunette (Dynasty 18) (Museo Egizio Cat. 1515 = CGT 50043) (photo by author).

the basic function of barques and the ark is the same: to transport the local presence of a deity. For that reason, it is worthwhile to explore the subject of Egyptian barques in detail.

Early barques (the physical shrines used to hold a cult image) originated with solar, lunar, and bovine deities. Any god or goddess could have a barque, and each temple had its own variation of a sacred barque or shrine. A barque is really just a special type of shrine, but a shrine *par excellence*. Unlike ordinary shrines, which had limited surface area that could be decorated, the physical surface of a barque could be decked out with almost limitless religious ornamentation and iconography. This made the barque ideal for communicating religious themes and messages.

## Generic Barque and Boat

The Nile was a large, deep, slow-moving river that divided the country down the middle. The river could be navigated by boat from the first cataract in Aswan all the way to the Mediterranean Sea. Boats were the primary means of travel in ancient Egypt. Boat travel was the only means of long distance travel in Egypt until the wheel was introduced during the Second Intermediate Period (ca. 1650–1530 BC). Thus, the boat was central to Egyptian life and culture. Similarly, Egyptian religion and ritual expressed itself using nautical themes.

So when we broach the topic of barques, we need to start with *wia*, , the generic term for a boat. The term is common and scholars do not contest the meaning. However, a brief examination of the term focused upon divine barques might be useful. A *wia* can refer both to real boats and to processional replicas that function as ritual furniture.[4] The chapel of Hathor at the temple of Deir el-Bahari shows depictions of Hatshepsut's trading fleet as "*wia* boats of the king."[5]

The term is also frequently applied to mythological or idealized barques.[6] The *Contendings of Seth and Horus* mentions the sun god Kheper being content in a mythological *wia* barque.[7] In a similar idealized manner, the *Abydos Decree of Seti I at Nauri* mentions the barque of Kheper when it was set upon its pool.[8] However, the same text mentions a *wia* in a non-mythological sense where Seti I inaugurates his temple and embellishes the *wia* barques with precious stones.[9]

The Qurna temple of Seti I has an inscription on the portico dating to Ramesses II. The inscription mentions the completion of Seti I's memorial temple and the god's *wia* barge. The identity of the god in this text is ambiguous. The Egyptians did not have a problem with ambiguity like we do in the West. The "god" in this case could be either Amun-Re or the deceased king—it really didn't matter to them. The Egyptians even considered the statue of a god to be synonymous with the god itself.

During the Festival of the Valley, the god in a sacred barque crossed the river between Karnak and West Thebes aboard a large boat (called a *wia* barge) propelled using an electrum-covered pole. The Festival of the Valley was a processional festival led by the barque of Amun-Re, which the king's barque would have followed. Afterward, the barque rested in Seti I's mortuary temple "at the head of the kings" before visiting the other mortuary temples in West Thebes.[10]

Figure 63. The Mortuary Temple of Seti I at Qurna (photo by author).

The text *UC 16448* mentions a *wia* barque having "a heavenly (inner) shrine," double doors, *neba* carrying poles, and a uraeus frieze.[11] These features were standard equipment on a Dynasty 19 sacred barque. This suggests that sometimes a *wia* barque was a synonym for a *seshem* barque (see p. 103). We see something similar in the "Stela of Montu" (ca. Dynasty 11, 2169–2029 BC), which mentions the purification priest Montu son of Insi carrying a processional *wia* barque on behalf of the king.[12] Thus, we see that sacred barques were already a fixture of Egyptian religion as early as the Middle Kingdom (ca. 2099–1673 BC).

## Portable Barque Shrine

The *wetjes-neferu*, , "the beautiful shrine," is a synonym for a barque shrine. The term appears only in a limited number of texts. The word was derived from the verb *wetjes*, "to lift or carry"[13] and has a related term *wetjes-netjeru*, "shrine of the gods" found in the inscription of the tomb of Ptahshepses (Saqqara necropolis no. 48) (Dynasty 5, ca. 2498–2349 BC).[14] This text mentions *wetjes-netjeru* with a boat determinative being lifted up for all the festivals of his lord,[15] meaning without doubt a sacred barque.

Figure 64. Beaded collar weight of the god Sobek with a sacred barque (Louvre E. 11520) (photo by author).

A *wetjes-neferu* barque is mentioned in the stela of the Thutmosis I Temple of Osiris. Thutmosis I made monuments to Osiris and furnished his "*seshem* barque of eternity," a euphemism for the barque used in a mortuary or memorial temple.[16] A *wetjes-neferu* barque was made of silver, gold, lapis, black bronze, and every precious and noble stone.[17] This list of materials is typical of religious shrines. The black granite statues of Neferibre-Nofer mention that the deceased had renewed the *wetjes-neferet* barque in precious metal.[18] And the reference to "black bronze" indicates that the Egyptians sometimes used patination to color bronze. Patination is a chemical treatment that colors the metal and protects it from corrosion. An example of black bronze can be seen in the collar weight of the crocodile god Sobek (fig. 64).

The *Stela of Ikhernofret* states, *wetjes en-es neferu-ef,* "lifted its splendor for him," following the reference to the barque bier (p. 144).[19] The text reads, "I caused him to enter into a *weret* barque bier and *lifted its splendor for him*." The phrase is an amphiboly, a grammatical construction that can mean two things at the same time. Amphibolies are frequently found in poetic and prophetic literature, and in this case the phrase alludes both to the king's glory and to a vessel the king's mummy was transported in. We have already come across an amphiboly in the ark narrative, that is, the meaning of "pure gold" (p. 65). The association of the term *wetjes-neferu* with various kinds of barques and biers developed through to the Ptolemaic period where it became synonymous with the barque of Horus at Edfu (fig. 65).[20]

Figure 65. The Barque of Horus at Edfu Temple (photo by author).

## Processional Sacred Barques

As we get into the history of sacred barques, our journey is going to take us into some shallow tributaries. And like explorers probing into unexplored territory, we are going to see a lot of strange things that may not immediately seem connected. I will point out some sign posts along the way. There will be some history, which will be important when it comes to dating the ark. Iconography appears in the historical record at easily datable points in time. And we will see how the Egyptians used barques to engage ideas of holiness.

The barques used in temple rituals are tied to concepts of holiness. The *seshem*, (or *seshem-khu*, ), is a term for a processional sacred barque. The term appears with either a boat determinative or a simplified representation of a barque resting on a plinth . The term is often translated as "idol" or "portable image,"[21] even though it was convincingly shown to be a processional barque.[22]

The term *seshem-khu* comes from two root terms: *seshem* meaning "to lead/conduct" and *khu* meaning "to protect" with the connotation of "setting apart" or "sanctifying," broaching the idea of being "holy."[23] The idea of being "set apart" is close to the biblical definition of holiness. It is likely that the adjective *khu*, "sacred," may be related to word for *khu*, "fan," with the determinative (Gardiner Sign S37).[24]

Figure 66. The statue of general Nakht-Min (CG 00779) (Luxor Museum) (photo by author).

When used with *seshem-khu*, *khu* is written in adjectival position. And though dictionaries treat the word as a compound noun, compounding is unlikely because, when a pronoun appears, the pronoun occurs after the first lexeme (for example, *seshem-ef khu,* lit: "his barque of sacred").[25] A comparable text on the back side of the Dynasty 18 statue of general Nakht-Min (fig. 66) describes the deceased becoming "acquainted" with a *seshem-es djesret*, "its sacred barque."[26] From the sanctuary of the Chapel of Ramesses I at Qurna, Seti I says he made a sanctuary for his father's *seshem* barque.[27]

Figure 67. Sacred barque of Ramesses II from the Ramesseum with a *seshem-khu* label (circled in red). The barque is being carried by three ranks of priests (photo by author).

The Hypostyle Hall at Karnak depicts a *seshem* barque that was transported using a cedar barge built by Seti I.[28] A *seshem* barque also appears in the Temple of Ramesses II at Abydos in room VI of the first Octostyle Hall. The inscription says that Ramesses II made a temple for the *seshem shepes*, "noble barque," of his father.[29] And in the Astronomical Room at the Ramesseum, four barques are portrayed on the eastern wall. The Barque of Ramesses II is labeled with *seshem-khu* (fig. 67).

In the West Chapel of Khonsu at Luxor Temple, the jambs of the façade mention the *seshem-khu* barque of Khonsu. The craftsmen decorated that sacred barque with electrum, lapis, and precious stones, and placed it upon four *neba* carrying poles.[30] The Karnak text (ca. Taharqa, Dynasty 25) mentions the *seshem* barque of Khonsu.[31] Taharqa also states that he improved the *seshem-khu* barque of Amun.[32]

The *seshem* barques, besides having carrying poles and occasionally canopies, also had figureheads. Normally, *ḥeru*, 𓁷𓏤, means "faces" as in the faces of human beings, but with sacred barques and barges the term usually refers to figureheads. Several sacred barque figureheads are extant and survive scattered among museums worldwide. The Egyptian Museum holds a substantial collection of barque figureheads, and the British Museum has a bronze figurehead of the Barque of Re (Ahmose II, Dynasty 26) probably from Kom Firin.[33] The Liverpool World Museum has another figurehead, labeled as "Isis with shield of protection (aegis)." The item dates between Dynasties 26 and 30 (664–343 BC). Another Isis figurehead is on display at the Louvre (fig. 68). The Rosicrusian Museum in San Jose, California, holds at least two figureheads, and the Walters Art Museum has a gold figurehead of Sekhmet dating to the Third Intermediate Period (ca. 1073–664 BC).

Figure 68. Bronze Isis barque figurehead (Louvre N. 3960 [B]) (photo by author).

## The Religious Message of Old Kingdom Barques

Although the history of barques began during the first dynasties of Egypt, few barque images have survived from the Old Kingdom. However, Egyptologists are certain that they must have existed for a number of reasons. Boats played an important ritual role in the king's burial. Surrounding the Great Pyramid of Khufu (Dynasty 4, ca. 2613–2498 BC) are pits that contain boats used in the deceased king's procession. One of these boats has been reconstructed and is on display at the Solar Boat Museum in Giza.

Figure 69. The reconstructed boat of King Khufu (Solar Boat Museum Giza) (photo by author).

Even though most mortuary temples of the Old Kingdom were destroyed by subsequent kings—more out of neglect or as salvage for raw materials than malice—the floor plans for these temples remain. Several of these mortuary temples have long, narrow chapels indicative of sacred barque use. The elongated chapels accommodated the carrying poles used with some barques.

We should note that the absence of elongated chambers does not exclude barque use because the earliest barques used a sledge and draw cord instead of carrying poles. These elongated chapels have not been found in the extant mortuary temples from the time Djoser until Khufu. However, these chambers are evident in the mortuary temple of Khafre onward. And if sacred barques with carrying poles were introduced during mid-Dynasty 4, this places the introduction of sacred barques around the same time as the shrine cabinet. This suggests that developments of the mid-Fourth Dynasty started a period of religious innovation that was formative to Egyptian religion.

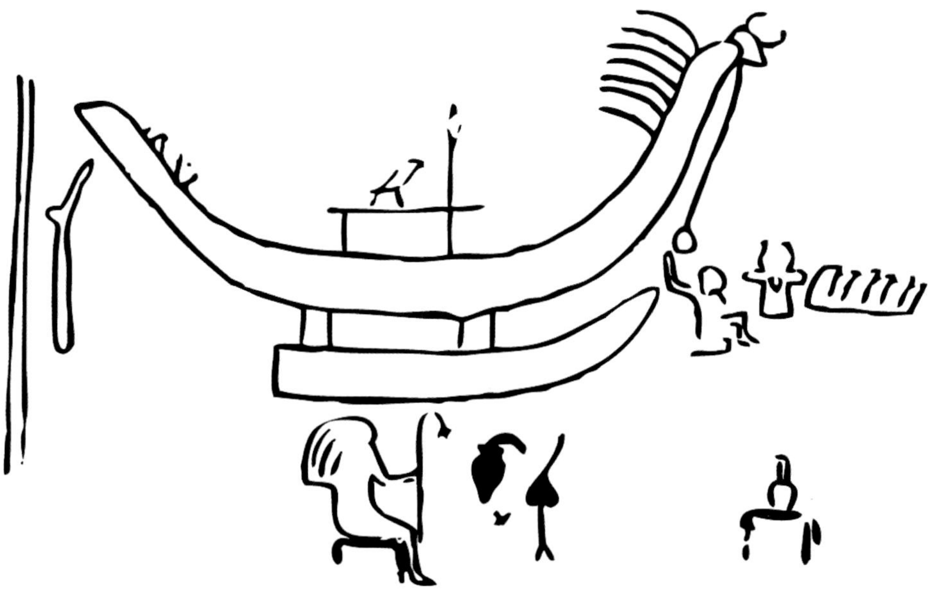

Figure 70. Graffito of a bovine barque from the Wadi Hammamat (Weigall, 1913, pl. VII [17]).

Furthermore, Old Kingdom graffiti portrays archaic barques. These archaic barques are called *ḥanu*,  or , and should not to be confused with *henu* chests. The *ḥanu* barque exists in literature as early as the first couple dynasties. During the early dynastic period, the *ḥanu* barque was common to a variety of local cult contexts and included the Maaty barque and the king's *bik* barque. The primary iconographic attestations of these appear on the *Palermo Stone* (Dynasties 1–3, ca. 3000–2686 BC).[34]

The barque from the Wadi Hammamat is an example of a *ḥanu* barque (fig. 70). It has a basic ship-like form with a deeply curved hull, a figurehead, and a rudder. Wrapped up in the basic boat form are all the mythological presuppositions of Egyptian river culture. And while the ark emerged out of Egyptian religious culture, the river mythos is absent from the ark's design (as noted previously). The barque was crested with a falcon deity and had a bovine figurehead. The figurehead indicates the cult to which the barque belongs, but it also gives the shrine a direction with an unmistakable front and back.

In these early *ḥanu* barques, we find a nascent Bronze Age understanding of divinity. That understanding is that the true presence of a god appears in one place and is enthroned in terms that are cultually contextualized. By contextualized, we mean that the things familiar to daily life would appear as part religious symbolism. For indigenous Levantine cultures, this could mean the gods standing on the backs of horses or bulls. For Egyptians, this meant the gods enthroned upon a boat.

And for early Israelite culture, which rejected agrarian living and river culture and embraced a pastoral lifestyle, the ark became a shrine having all the appearance of localized divinity but without Egyptian mythological trappings. The early days of Israelite culture had a mixed multitude of ethnicities (Exod 12:38): Levantines, Libyans, Nubians, Medjay, and even Egyptians. All these cultures were grafted into Israel and this new nation adopted a common origins narrative that God created the world in six days and rested on the seventh (Exod 20:11). This origins story prompted the Israelites to abandon the Egyptian ten-day week and institute a seven-day week instead.

That origins narrative, which stated that the Spirit of God hovered over the waters (Gen 1:2), is a polemic against other creation myths. The narrative makes no attempt to relate the mystery of the creation in analogic terms of our daily experience and does not explain how God created the world. As such the biblical origin story is anti-myth, a substitute for myth. Thus, it is not quite accurate to say that the ark is aniconic—we know that the ark had cherubim as icons. Instead, the ark communicates the visual theology of this anti-myth. Just as the Spirit of God hovered over the earth, the foundations of which had been established by God (Job 38:4; Ps 104:5; Prov 8:29), so too did the Spirit of God hover over the ark and the tablets of the law.

## Middle Kingdom Cult and Barque Development

The graffito (a scribble on a rock) from Wadi Hammamat had many of the characteristics that we find in later Sokar barques. The early *ḥanu* barques lacked carrying poles, but had a sledge and draw cord which were used to drag the barque on procession. The "dragging of the Sokar barques" became part of the ritual procession of the Sokar cult. Later, when carrying poles were added, the sledge and cord were retained as ceremonial features.

The Festival of Sokar and the *ḥanu* barque appears prominently at Medinet Habu. The Sokar Festival involved the king in procession with a *ḥanu* barque that granted him eternity.[35] This barque is depicted with utterances implying the barque was dedicated to Sokar-Osiris or Ptah-Sokar-Osiris.[36] The compositing of deity reflects that the cults of Sokar, Ptah, and Osiris borrowed from each other's practices. As their cults became less distinct, these cults syncretized into common practice. Think of composite gods (Amun-Re and Sokar-Osiris) as a kind of business merger between two companies serving the same customer base; for example, the Facebook-Instagram and Disney-Pixar mergers.

Figure 71. The name 'Sokar' written with a detailed *ḥanu* barque determinative (Temple of Seti I at Abydos) (photo by author).

During the Middle Kingdom, the Memphite cult of Ptah, a creator god, and the Abydos cult of Osiris adopted ritual practices from the Sokar cult such that the Sokar Festival became linked to the Osiris resurrection myth. In the ancient world, life was short, and death was imminent. People focused upon the brevity of life and anticipated life after death, making the Sokar cult's message attractive.

Unlike the typical barque for divinity, the *ḥanu* barque was made in two pieces: a reusable sledge and scaffold of verticles stakes made of wood, and a "boat" section made of ephemeral materials, particularly ropes and reed thatching. The barque was suspended in a rope cradle attached to the stakes mounted on a sledge with carrying poles. The thatching on the side of the shrine is visible, with rope holding it in place.[37] The ephemeral building materials suggest the builders of the *ḥanu* barques rebuilt them on a regular basis. The temporary nature of these barques accounts for the great variation found in the iconography of *ḥanu* barques.

Figure 72. The Sokar barque made of thatching (Temple of Ramesses III at Medinet Habu) (photo by author).

Festival scenes at Medinet Habu show empty sledges and carriages entering the temple and leaving with the Sokar barques, but not those barques returning as is depicted in other barque scenes, for example, at the Ramesseum.[38] The scene at the mortuary temple of Ramesses III from the east wall of the second court portraying the Feast of Sokar shows five barques on procession.[39] Three of the barques are identical. The fourth is a barque with a recurved stern and a true shrine cabinet with four vertical stakes. The fifth is an "empty" barque with a recurved stern, four vertical stakes, and nothing between the stakes.

The Sokar Festival ritual cycle is similar to the *setjet* and *meret* chests. The festival possibly began with building a *ḥanu* barque of thatching and filling it with grain. Water was then poured into the barque and the barque was carried to a ritual site upon its sledge. This ritual not only germinated the grain but malted it. The importance of malting is that it was a necessary step towards making beer. Unlike in the Levant where the majority of people ate barley, only Egypt's poorest people ate barley. Most Egyptian barley was used for beer production.

Many cultures in the ancient Near East considered fermentation to be a process that involved the divine or, at the minimum, was evidence for the divine; for example, "beer of the beer-god" in CT 21.[40] Some people in Egypt drank nothing but beer because it was healthier than drinking the water. Beer was a necessity of life in ancient Egypt.

Beer making purified the water of the Nile, which was full of deadly viruses, bacteria, and parasites. So when the barley was smitten by the plague of hail during the Egyptian sojourn (Exod 9:31), this exacerbated the water crisis begun by the plague of blood (Exod 7:24) by eliminating one of the only tried and true methods of water purification.

The result of beer production in Egypt is that it became ritualized and elevated into a life-giving resurrection ritual. At the ritual site, the *ḥanu* barque was buried where the grain sprouted in the darkness with the assistance of divinity, demonstrating the cycle of rebirth, and the empty sledge was returned to the temple to begin the ritual cycle anew. Grasses grow, produce grain, and die, and that grain becomes new grass, and so on ad infinitum—that never-ending cycle of life, death, transformation, and life again.

Thus, Sokar barques appear to have functioned similarly to the corn-mummies, another artifact demonstrating cyclic rebirth.[41] Corn-mummies have their origin during the New Kingdom period.[42] But the Sokar ritual long predates corn-mummies, implying that the corn-mummy ritual was borrowed from the Sokar ritual. This suggests that the practices surrounding the Osiris cult were not original to it.

Even though Old Kingdom barques left their indelible style through the *ḥanu* barque, a different kind of barque developed, marking a change in how the Egyptians worshiped the divine. The Middle Kingdom laid much of the foundation of Egyptian literature, culture, and religion, which the Egyptians would view fondly as a "classical" period. And it was during the Middle Kingdom when tabernacle use declined for worshiping the gods in favor of permanent stone temples. Unfortunately, few temples from this period have survived. Most of the stone from these temples was recycled as fill for New Kingdom building projects.

The Karnak temple complex is probably best known today for its magnificent pylons and columned halls from the kings of the Eighteenth and Nineteenth Dynasties (ca. 1538–1194 BC). However, the history of the site extends as far back as the reign of Senwosret I (Dynasty

12, ca. 2029–1819 BC). Blocks found in the construction of Pylon IX show the king presenting offerings to what is probably the barque of Amun.[43] The relief is badly worn, with only trace details surviving, and was not found in its original context, so little can be said except that the relief establishes the use of barques at Karnak during the Middle Kingdom.

Figure 73. Panorama of Karnak Temple from the 1st pylon to the obelisks (photo by author).

While any reading of the following stela would be controversial, I believe that an important example of Middle Kingdom barque iconography was discovered in an unlikely place, Serabit el-Khadim. Serabit el-Khadim was a turquoise mining site located in the Sinai Peninsula that operated during Middle and New Kingdom. The mining operation was active diring the nineteenth or twentieth centuries BC and periodically during the New Kingdom. The mines were worked by Levantine miners and administered by Egyptian overseers. Besides the mining operation, the site is notable for having a temple to Hathor and many votive stelae written in Egyptian and an early Semitic language.

The barque relief was found on HSM 1935.4.7 (Sinai 375a), a small votive stela that dates to the reign of Amenemhat III (Dynasty 12) (fig. 74).[44] In antiquity, the stela was engraved and then painted with red ochre. To date, the stela has generally been recognized as only an early alphabetic inscription.

To read the shallow inscription on the stela, I used specialized photographic techniques to discern between the inscription and subsequent damage to the piece. Separating the image by color channels revealed clearly where the stela had been damaged since its original creation. In sections where the inscription is not degraded, the inscription is clearly readable with the use of strobe lighting.

The text from HSM 1935.4.7 begins at the top center of the stela with two generally accepted characters: the Egyptian character *imy-r*, 𓌸 , "overseer," on the left and an early alphabetic ox-head alef on the right. The Egyptian character is oriented so that it should be read from right to left, even though some epigraphers have chosen to read it in the opposite direction, believing that the author was not fluent in writing Egyptian. I do not accept that assertion given the clarity of the rest of the Egyptian portion of the inscription.

Figure 74. *Stela HSM 1935.4.7* found at Serabit el-Khadim (illustration by author).

The early alphabetic inscription wraps along the top and down the right side of the stela and possibly reads, *ʾḥ bʿl zkr,* "The brother of Baal Zakor." Baal Zakor is common Semitic meaning "Baal Remembers." But the reading of the so-called alef has led to confusion because epigraphers have failed to recognize the neck attached to the ox-head. If one accounts for the neck, the next character is clearly *ḥ*. The next three characters, *bʿl,* are admittedly difficult to see without the assistance of multi-spectral photography but are definitely present. The *zk* have been recognized by other epigraphers and half a final *r* is visibile, alternatives for which are limited.[45] The use of *zkr* is attested in most Semitic languages so its meaning is uncontested.

The Egyption inscription wraps around the edge of the stela and down the left side of the inscription, and reads *imy-r áḥ-n[etjer] . . . seshem ir iaḥ wen,* "overseer of the tem[ple] . . . the barque of Hathor celebrates the festival procession." Only part of the *netjer* glyph ꜧ is visible, as the rest of the glyph is in a damaged area. The relationship between the "overseer of the temple" and "brother of Baal-Zakor" is unclear. Perhaps it is the same person. Perhaps the stela is a dedication by two people. We cannot be certain.

Most epigraphers assume that this leftmost ox-head is a Semitic alef. However, the ox-head is attached to a very long neck (two horizontal lines) attached to other lines of the illustration. Taken in its entirety, this illustration shows a two-thirds representation of a Middle Kingdom barque, making the ox-head a figurehead. This representation is exceptional in that it was found in the Sinai. It is the only picture of a sacred barque found outside of the Nile Valley. It is also a rare example of a barque from the Middle Kingdom period.

Typically, a sacred barque pictograph would be read as *seshem*. And in this text, the *seshem* is an icongraphic element that interacts with the text and is intended to be read as part of the text.[46] We can be certain of this reading since the next word is a verb in the stative tense. The stative tense in Egyptian requires that the subject of the sentence precedes the verb.

The iconography shows elements of archaic and New Kingdom sacred barques. The rounded shrine cabinet is reminiscent of archaic barque styles like those found on some *ḥanu* barques. But the hull is more level than is typical for *ḥanu* barques and is similar to New Kingdom *seshem* barques. Carrying poles are visible, as well as a box stand and a sledge. The fact that only two-thirds of the barque was shown is not unusual. Partial depictions of barques are found on other stelae.[47]

The neck on the ox-head is an important detail that appears on other early alphabetic inscriptions.[48] The neck seems to be a vestigial feature suggesting the alef's origins. The alef character represents a glottal plosive phoneme. But the Egyptian language does not have a true glottal plosive. So when the Asiatics living under Egyptian occupation developed their alphabet, they used what was closest from the writing system they were most familiar with. I would suggest that the alef does not come from the Egyptian ox-head, 𓄀 (Gardiner Sign F1), as is often suggested. Even though cosmetically similar, the Egyptian character is a determinative that has no neck and no phonetic value. I would suggest the alef sign comes from the iconography of the Hathor barque figurehead, not Gardiner Sign F1, sometime during Egypt's Middle Kingdom. Hathor's name in Egyptian, *ḥut-ḥer*, has a natural glottal stop.

The Temple of Hathor was the center of religious life at Serabit el-Khadim, and from this text it appears that both Egyptians and foreigners participated in that religious experience. The importance of religion to the early Semites ultimately led to the development of the modern alphabet. Early Semitic communities outside of Avaris participated in forms of religion similar to their Egyptian neighbors. Moreover, this text shows that the Levantine community would have been intimately familiar with Egyptian religion, including sacred barques and their significance.

## New Kingdom Iconography

The New Kingdom (ca. 1538–1073 BC) was the golden age of ritual furniture. Many temples were built during this period, and many examples of ritual furniture survive from this period. The sacred barque hits its zenith at this time. It was the era when barque use proliferated to practically every cult in Egypt. The New Kingdom was also the period during which the exodus occurred and the ark was built, so it's particularly important to our study, as all the contemporary comparative material comes from this period.

Figure 75. The Barque of Amun of Amenhotep I (photo by author).

Sacred barques of the New Kingdom period, unlike earlier *ḥanu* barques, had a shrine cabinet (see p. 78) that held a divine image. Earlier barques may have contained a divine image. However, we cannot be certain of what *ḥanu* barques contained. On the other hand, *seshem* barques are often shown with their interiors exposed, revealing that they contained the divine image of a god. The main purpose of barques was to provide a throne for a god to assert their power from.

An early New Kingdom example of a divine barque is the Barque of Amun (fig. 75) at Karnak, depicted on a block within the Great Throne (barque sanctuary) of Amenhotep I (fig. 76). The barque features ram figureheads on prow and stern, a figurine of a royal sphinx on a standard facing the prow, and a pair of rudders, but no deck crew statues.

Each item on this sacred barque conveyed its own message. Early barques had a figurehead that lacked an elaborate crown and distinctive solar disk. Many of these figureheads had little more than a uraeus with a Hathor crown. The ram symbolized Amun-Re. And as stated earlier, the ureaus protected the image of the god from outside defilement. It's worth noting that the figurehead on the early Amun barques lacked jewelled collars. It is likely that figurehead iconography had not yet developed to the point where the collars were shown stylized in profile.

The jeweled collar would become an important feature of later figureheads because it signified the god's wealth.[49] The wealth of the gods was important. You can't expect a god with a cash flow problem to provide food or bless your crops, can you? This is even important in Israelite religion. For example, "For every beast of the forest is mine, and so is the cattle on a thousand hills" (Ps 50:10).

Figure 76. The Great Throne (barque sanctuary) of Amenhotep I (photo by author).

Sacred barques were the throne of the gods, but the gods of Egypt had a physical presence in their idols that needed care. So every morning, Egyptian priests would purify themselves so they would be clean enough to conduct the temple rituals. They would ritually bathe, shave their heads, clean their mouths with natron, and wear clean linens and papyrus sandals. These priests would go to the back of the temple to the Inner Shrine with the naos of the god. They fed the divine image with offerings and clothed their god. They then carried the god's image to its barque in the Great Throne, where the gods ruled by day. In the evening, the priests would return the god to the naos where it could sleep. The imagery and symbolism of the sacred barques conveyed notions of a kind of divinity that relied upon human hands. The Egyptian gods were fed and clothed by priests, had to be carried in order to assert their power in the daytime, and needed to be put to bed to sleep at night.

## The Royal Sphinx

A royal sphinx stands on the prow of the Amenhotep I barque. We can find the royal sphinx depicted on the sides of thrones and reliefs, and often in the act of killing foreign enemies (fig. 77). Royal sphinxes normally have the body of a lion standing upright, an upright curled tail, and the head of the king wearing a royal crown. This sphinx wears the double-feathered crown of Amun. The sphinx communicated the message of royal power and might, that is to say, the power of the king was present and in service to the god Amun. This is both an ideological and mythological message.

Figure 77. The royal sphinx from the tomb of Khaemhat (TT57) (photo by author).

In Egyptian mythology, a hierarchy existed for who could serve the gods. Most of the gods of Egypt were not served by ordinary folk. Those filthy commoners were not considered good enough to serve the gods. Only the best people, that is, kings, were fit to serve the gods. Thus, as sacred barque iconography developed, kings, both living and dead, featured prominently upon the decks of the barques in service to the gods.

In contrast, the cults of Hathor and Thoth relished having their god served by a throng of common people.[50] And because of their class appeal, these two cults were among the most popular in Egypt. Hathor, the cow goddess, was the most popular deity in Egypt and the default religious practice. When the Israelites felt they had been abandoned by Moses (and their God) when he ascended Mount Sinai, they naturally fell back into worshiping a golden calf (Exod 32:8).

## Winged Goddesses

The vulture goddess in Egyptian myth symbolized caring, nurture, motherhood, and ultimately became a symbol of holiness. Two vulture goddesses emerged that expressed these qualities: Mut, the mother goddess, and Nekhbet, a goddess that protected and sanctified. Nekhbet's wings were thought to purify sacred space. And it was this connotation of purity that was soon commuted to winged goddesses of every kind.

Egyptologist Henri Frankfort, in his discussion of the coronation of kings, noted that the Egyptian crowns were "charged with power" derived from the twin goddesses, Wadjet (a cobra goddess similar to the uraeus) and Nekhbet.[51] Although he suggested the two ladies were tutelary goddesses because of the geographic locations of their cults, Nekhbet of Nekheb (modern El Kab) and Wadjet of Buto,[52] I would suggest that they held a deeper significance in defining sacred space. This action of a cobra goddess excluding defilement and a vulture goddess including and nurturing holiness transformed the king into a walking, talking temple of holiness. A similar notion is found in the New Testament: "Do you not know that your body is a temple of the Holy Spirit who is in you . . . ?" (1 Cor 6:19).

Complementing the sanctifying wings of the Nekhbet are the uraeus goddesses placed upon the frieze on the top of a shrine, pointing outward with their purifying fire. On paintings and reliefs, the iconography points the uraeus to one side. This is because of the "loaded weapon" effect that the uraeus could have had upon the observer. The nature of the uraeus was to cast fire upon the trespasser in what I liken to a "death ray" effect. *Pyramid Text 256* describes the effect as "the flaming blast of my uraeus is that of Ernūtet who is upon me."[53] Winged serpents spitting fire also had a functional equivalent in Israelite iconography. In Israelite iconography, these serpents were known as *seraphim* from the Hebrew word *śrp*, "to burn," which are mentioned in a couple of biblical texts (Isa 6:2, 6).

And the repertoire of Egyptian religious iconography was once again expanded under the reign of Amenhotep III. Amenhotep III enacted a plan of religious reform that resulted in Luxor Temple being destroyed and rebuilt to face Karnak.[54] He linked the festival calendar at Luxor to the calendar at Karnak, overthrowing the distinct rituals at Luxor and increasing the length of the Opet Festival from eleven days under Hatshepsut to twenty-four days.[55] Amenhotep III built a processional colonnade that was later decorated by Tutankhamun, Horemheb, and Seti I with barque scenes from the Opet Festival. An additional court, a pylon, and barque chapels were added by Ramesses II.

Figure 78. The Colonnade Hall at Luxor Temple (photo by author).

From the second antechamber in the main Luxor Temple, which is the chamber immediately before the barque sanctuary, three barques are depicted on procession. Leading the way was the barque of Amun-Re. The barque of Amun-Re of Amenhotep III retains the uraeus crown of the early Karnak barques. Twenty-four priests carry the barque, twice as many as those who carried the barque during Hatshepsut's reign. In addition to the symbols found on preceding barques, we see the addition of a standing king holding a Kheper, a scarab beetle that represented the sun god. The Kheper was a placeholder for Re that manifested the radiance and glory of the divinity. The king presents an offering of the sun god back to the sun god in a display of reciprocal economy.

Figure 79. Re-Horakhty with solar disk showing a Kheper scarab. The solar disk incorporates the throne name of Tutankhamun (GEM 828) (photo by author).

Perhaps most interesting is that the interior of the shrine cabinet is exposed through both the sides of the shrine and the veil. During the reign of Amenhotep III, the barque of

Amun-Re had only a single compartment. Later on, the shrine would have two compartments: one for Amun and the other for Re.

When the shrine cabinet interiors are exposed, two winged goddesses are seen facing each other with their wings spread out protecting the holy space. With the barque of Amun-Re, these goddesses are manifestations of Maat, goddess of order or balance. In the holy space between the wings, the idol of Amun-Re was drawn as a Kheper.

The Nekhbet vulture on the veil created one layer of holiness surrounding and sanctifying the barque from the outside. But the two winged goddesses created a second holy space within the barque. This created a holy of holies within the barque. Winged goddesses creating holy space was not isolated to religious furniture, such as barques. The iconography is also found on Dynasty 18 funeral equipment.

Figure 80. Winged goddesses on the sarcophagus of Tutankhamun (photo by author).

The red granite sarcophagus of King Tutankhamun has four winged goddesses protecting and sanctifying the body of the deceased king. The sarcophagus has a different winged goddess on each corner: in clockwise order, Serqet (shown in fig. 80), Nekhbet, Isis, and Neith. These four goddesses protected coffins and canopic chests, and together they surrounded the deceased to help him journey to and from the afterlife. Nekhbet and Isis escorted the dead to the realm of the dead, while Serqet and Neith provided the magical power to restore the dead so that he could make his nightly return to this world. Together the four goddesses created a zone of ritual purity allowing the divine king to move freely to and from the afterlife.

And where Egyptian iconography created a holy space using winged goddesses, the Israelites used a functional equivalent in their own iconography, the cherubim. Early Israelite religion regarded the space between the wings of the cherubim as sacred and holy. The curtains of the tabernacle decorated with cherubim limited the sacred space within the tabernacle precinct (Exod 26:1). And the cherubim marked what was holy and provided perpetual praise similar to the lapwing icons (p. 39).

The ark of the covenant too was a holy space within a holy place. The ark was placed in the tent of the tabernacle or within the Holy of Holies in the temple. The Holy of Holies had a veil that concealed the ark within the temple itself. Yet, the ark had its own holy space, not inside the ark, but above it between the wings of the cherubim on the mercy seat.

Even though the ark was meant to be seen when carried because the pole rings were attached to the feet, the mercy seat and body of the reliquary were to be covered at all times when not at rest in a holy space. The ark, when transported, was to be covered with a scarlet cloth and porpoise skin cover (Num 4:8). We should note that it is possible that the ark was carried off without its coverings to Aphek to battle against the Philistines, precipitating the Israelite's disastrous military failure (1 Sam 4:3–4). This is likely since the men of Beth-Shemesh saw the ark and recognized it from a distance (1 Sam 6:13).

Scholars have questioned whether the cherubim were represented as people, lions, or bulls. Taurine (bull) cherubim were commonly found among Mesopotamian religious icons and could either have wings swept backward or multiple wings in both directions. Leonine (lion) cherubim are found in Egyptian and Levantine contexts commonly as sphinxes, but these were portrayed with wings swept backward. With anthropoid (human) cherubim, the wings follow the arms of the human form and are normally swept forward.

The wings of the cherubim were spread upward covering the mercy seat and facing each other inward to the mercy seat (Exod 25:20). This is similar to the goddesses found inside the Egyptian sacred barques. Given the archaeological context, we should expect the cherubim on the ark to be anthropoid for their iconography.

## The Veil and Vulture

When a veil was added to Egyptian ritual furnature and architecture, the veil was quickly coupled with the symbolism of winged goddesses. The vulture and veil would become some of the most important iconographic developments that carried over to the ark. Veils would be incorporated into the tabernacle, and winged goddesses would become cherubim (Exod 26:31).

Figure 81. Interior of the Barque of Amun-Re at Luxor Temple (photo by author).

Between the reigns of Thutmosis I and Hatshepsut, several modifications were made to the divine barques at Karnak.[56] The *tayt*, , was a "veil" or less commonly a "shrine." The word appears frequently with the clothing determinative  (Gardiner Sign S28). *P. Harris I* talks about the city of Memphis and its barque sanctuary being exalted like a royal palace beneath a "veil of gold" like the doors of heaven.[57]

Numerous reliefs show veils being used with barques, likely linen veils with a gold foil Nekhbet vulture.[58] The barques depicted on Hatshepsut's Chapelle Rouge reveal the wings of the vulture imprinted upon the veil. A Nekhbet vulture as part of the veil is seen peeking around the back of the barque. Similar veils are also found at Luxor temple (see fig. 81 upper right). Ramesside versions of the veil could include a trim of uraeus along the edges of the "wings"[59] with each uraeus filling the place of a feather. Vulture iconography on the veil is common enough to reasonably suggest that it was a defining feature.

Veils provided a way to separate the sacred object from the onlooker while preserving a silhouette of the form.[60] However, the entire barque was not covered by the veil. Instead, the veil was drawn under the canopy poles, forming a tight wrapping around the base of the cabinet, leaving the top exposed.[61] Even though the Egyptians viewed the veil as a barrier, it was not a barrier in the same manner as a door or a wall. The veil added a layer of sacredness by magical warding.

Figure 82. Relief from the chapel of Osiris Heqadjet at Karnak (Legrain, 1900, p. 129).

But the veil employed a different kind of protection than was provided by the uraeus. The uraeus provided separation of sacred space by keeping the profane out. The uraeus protects the god with outward radiance while the vulture protects by inwardly focused power and sanctification. This message of sanctification was communicated visually by the embrace of the Nekhbet vulture's wings. This relationship can easily be seen in a relief from the chapel of Osiris Heqadjet at Karnak (Dynasty 23–25, ca. 818–664 BC) (fig. 82), where Nekhbet has her wings extended to sanctify a pair of uraeus: one was wearing the white crown and the other the red crown, representing Upper and Lower Egypt.[62] In this example, the dual uraeus symbolized kingship over the two lands (Egypt), and Nekhbet symbolized ritually cleansed kingship. Nekhbet's good manifestation purifies through her embrace, while her bad manifestation appears in the destructive power of the sun through the power of flame.[63]

Following the addition of the veil, barque iconography developed at an accelerated rate during the reign of Queen Hatshepsut. Additional votive figures were added to the deck including worshipers to the front and back of the shrine cabinet. The figures of two goddesses, Isis and Maat, stood on the prow, between the figurehead and the royal sphinx (fig. 83). And a pair of oarsman were added beneath the barque's rudders.

Figure 83. The Barque of Amun from the Chapelle Rouge (photo by author).

Even the two fan bearers with fans standing above Hatshepsut's barque of Amun-Re added flavor to the religious message. We have already learned that the fan communicated holiness (p. 103). But these fans had other symbols worked into them. The fans are shown with an ankh "life" for a ferule. The fan handle on the left is shown with papyrus stalks while the fan on the right displayes lotus stalks. Both plants were considered sacred products of the Nile River. Papyrus was made into many items: arrows, baskets, writing materials. Blue lotus flowers were squeezed for their juice, which was added to wine for its narcotic properties (fig. 84).[64] Lotus juice was used to induce religious visions and for recreational purposes.

Figure 84. Women collecting and squeezing lotus flowers for their juice (Louvre E. 11377) (photo by author).

## Cryptographic Writing

During the New Kingdom, an important source for barque images was the Great Hypostyle Hall at Karnak that was started by Seti I and completed by Ramesses II. On these barques, the figureheads wore crowns with a solar disk and a uraeus frieze was added to the shrine cabinet.[65]

In Amun-Re barques, the shrine cabinet is split into two compartments. The lower compartment has the image of Re, with a solar disk, seated upon a *men* sign 𓏠. The significance of the *men* sign 𓏠 is part of a cryptographic writing of the throne name of Seti I, Menmaatre 𓍹𓇳𓁦𓏠𓍺.

Cryptographic writing is key to understanding the religious message of the sacred barques. Each sign in a king's throne name could express a different religious principle. With the throne name of Seti I, the *men* sign provided stability, *maat* conferred order and balance, and *re* was the all-powerful sun god (fig. 85).

Figure 85. Cryptographic writing of Seti I on barque frieze at Karnak Temple. King Seti I's throne name alternates with the ureaus (photo by author).

Similarly, the throne name of Ramesses II magically conveyed notions of power, order, and being chosen. The barque of Amun-Re during the reign of Ramesses II includes its own cryptographic rebus. In the upper compartment of the barque of Amun-Re, the goddesses are holding a *weser* (or *user*) sceptre 𓌀 instead of the ankh 𓋹 sign, reflecting the cryptographic writing of Ramesses II's throne name, Usermaatre 𓍹𓇳𓌀𓁦𓌡𓈖𓇳𓍺.

Throne names were more than just a name that a king chose when he took the throne. The king's name characterized a thematic religious program that he may have felt was important, and the name could be used as a magical incantation. For this reason, the king's name was used everywhere. The throne name of the king was worked into the iconographic elements of barques and temple reliefs. And common people wore jewelry and carried amulets with the king's name.

Cryptographic devices also prevented future kings from usurping an inscription. These devices hid the name of the king in the iconography. The cryptography entangled the power of the king with the gods. This did not protect the king as much as it advanced the king's power and royal agenda.

## Other Messages in Iconography

Even though the general configuration of the barques of Khonsu, Mut, and Amun-Re remained consistent with the barques of early Dynasty 19, their portrayal eventually developed subtle artistic changes. Besides the use of royal iconography, portrayals of sacred barques communicated other messages.

Figure 86. The Barque of Mut from the West Shrine at Luxor (photo by author).

For example, the depiction of the barque in the West Shrine of Mut at Karnak Temple reveals an interesting feature of this barque not seen in other barques. In the position of the standing king are two superimposed figures (fig. 86 upper right). One face wears the vulture crown of a queen. It is possible that these figures represented Ramesses II and his Queen Nefertari.

At the Ramesseum, the mortuary temple of Ramesses II, eight barques are portrayed on the southeast wall of the Astronomical Room.[66] Unique to the going out procession as well as unique to the Ramesseum is a highly detailed portrayal of a barque of Ahmose-Nefertari (fig. 87). In my opinion, this is perhaps finest relief of the barque of Ahmose-Nefertari. However, art criticism aside, Ramesses II was communicating a different messege by including the barque of Ahmose-Nefertari in his processions.

Figure 87. Barque of Ahmose-Nefertari from the Ramesseum (photo by author).

Ahmose-Nefertari was the queen of Amenhotep I, the king who inaugurated the royal burials in West Thebes. Amenhotep I created a cottage industry for the craftsmen at Deir el-Medina, and both Ahmose-Nefertari and Amenhotep I were deified by the craftsmen. Beyond her role as a patron for craftsmen, Ahmose-Nefertari was considered the matriarch of kings. She was the mother of the Thutmoside line of Theban kings during Dynasty 18, a royal bloodline that lasted two hundred years and ended with the death of King Tutankhamun.

But Ramesses II was unrelated to the Theban kings. By venerating Ahmose-Nefertari in his mortuary temple, Ramesses II created a tie between the traditional line of kings and his own reign. Ramesses II's predecessor and father, Seti I, did something similar at his Abydos Temple. Seti I wrote out the list of kings from Egypt's earliest days and placed his name in the line of succession.

Figure 88. Astrophotograph of the Great Temple of Abu Simbel (photo by author).

Ramesses II sent a completely different message with the Great Temple of Abu Simbel near the modern Sudan border. The Great Temple was dedicated to Re-Horakhty, Ptah, and Amun-Re. The North Chapel has a partially idealized barque of Re-Horakhty characterized by the recurved stern and a child with lotus flowers on the prow.[67] The barque is shown floating above a plinth. The figures on the deck are enlarged and the kneeling king is shown wearing the blue crown. The blue crown was used for important state functions and symbolized the king victorious at war.

An enlarged figure of Re-Horakhty is shown seated upon a block throne under a canopy. In the columned hall of the temple, several reliefs exist of Ramesses II heroically defeating the Hittites at the Battle of Kadesh—at least that was the official story. The fact is the Egyptians and Hittites only gave each other black eyes, and Ramesses only snatched a stalemate from the jaws of defeat. The Great Temple was intended to deliver a threat to the Nubians, saying, "If you rebel against me, then I will do to you what I did to the Hittites."

Finally, from late Dynasty 19, the iconographic representations of figureheads started to become progressively larger and continued to be exaggerated until Dynasty 25. This began to relate an entirely new message that the figureheads mattered more than the rest of the barque. Late New Kingdom kings emphasized their piety by exaggerating the size of the god's figureheads.

Figure 89. Barque of Mut from the Triple Shrine of Seti II (photo by author).

## Idols and Holiness

The Lord met Moses on Mount Horeb and spoke to him from a burning bush. He said, "Remove your sandals from your feet, for the place on which you are standing is holy ground" (Exod 3:5). At Mount Sinai, God warned the people not to set foot on the mountain. If the people had stepped on the mountain, the anger of the Lord may have broken out against them (Exod 19:21–23).

Even Israelite priests had to consecrate themselves or face the Lord's anger. This is similar to Egyptian priests who performed a variety of purification rituals (bathing, shaving) to consecrate them for holy service. The reason priests had to perform these rituals was to convert or commute their impurity to an acceptable status (p. 117).

But like the rest of the ancient Near East, the gods of Egypt were captive to their statues. In these images, the true presence of deity resided. The idols of the gods at night would sleep in their stone *kar* naos in the inner chambers of the temple. In the morning, the priests would dress the cultic idols with fresh linens and carry them to the Great Throne. There, they would place their gods in the sacred barques. From the sacred barques, the gods exercised their power in the daytime (p. 117).

The sacred barques were the pinnacle of ritual processional furniture. The purpose of the sacred barque was to create a holy place so that the gods of Egypt could assert their influence upon the outside world. The gods ruled from their barque as if they ruled upon the throne of a king. All their divine power and authority was asserted from inside the most holy of spaces. Moreover, the gods could extend their influence from their barques outside in the profane world where defilement resided.

Even though the ark used a visual language common to the ancient Near East, the message of the ark was that the God of Israel was different. Without a cultic idol placed in the center of the shrine, the normal message of this kind of furniture inverted. Israelite theology could not bind their God to an idol. The presence of God moved with the ark from place to place. But without an idol, God was not put to bed at night, nor was he clothed, fed, or cared for by human hands. Without an idol, God was shown to be utterly sovereign. The ark and tabernacle visually communicated that God is holy, never leaves his throne, and never sleeps.

CHAPTER 6

# The Ark and Other Extraterrestrial Vehicles

Let us say that you want to travel to the moon. It goes without saying that it would not be advisable to climb into a cannon and have yourself shot into space. But assuming that you survived the trauma of the explosive force of the cannon and achieved orbit, you would then find yourself without oxygen to breathe, and the lack of atmospheric pressure would burst your blood vessels. You would freeze from the near zero Kelvin temperatures and fry from the solar radiation. In short, the environment in outer space is utterly hostile to human life.

A human being needs air to breathe, heat to stay warm, and protection from the elements. In other words, humans need an Earth-like environment to survive. When astronauts venture into outer space, they travel in a space shuttle and wear special suits to recreate the Earth's conditions. To explore space, humans need to take their environment with them in an extraterrestrial vehicle. Otherwise, they would perish in the hostile conditions.

The analogy of extraterrestrial vehicles is fitting when describing sacred barques and shrines. Shrines are capsules of sacred space that transport an idol through profane space. On the surface, sacred barques are little more than shrines cabinets attached to a boat-like hull.

Previously, we saw chests acting as devices that converted profane objects into objects for sacred use (p. 47). These chests made profane objects usable in sacred space. And we also saw where the gods were enthroned in their sacred shrines, from where they were said to assert their divine authority (p. 132). But the shrine as a throne was only one side of the coin. These gods needed the help of shrines that could act like extraterrestrial vehicles so they could voyage into profane space.

## Between the Sacred and Profane

This concept of gods requiring sacred space to maintain their presence varied among Levantine cultures. Some Levantine cultures had no requirement to maintain sacred space for idols, and any dusty shelf would suffice. This connotes a less rigid understanding of things sacred and profane.

Figure 90. Barque of Amun-Re from the east wall of the Great Hypostyle Hall (photo by author).

However, the Egyptians believed in a strong separation of the two domains, a belief that may have been adopted by the early Israelites. The separation between profane and sacred space created a theological problem where people and items could not cross between domains without resorting to various kinds of rituals. That transitional threshold between profane and sacred spaces is called *liminality*. The problem of moving items from one kind of space to the other is called *liminal inertia*.[1]

Newton's first law of motion, also called the *law of inertia*, says that an object in motion remains in motion and an object at rest remains at rest. Like Newton's inertia, an object in profane space remains profane and an object in sacred space remains sacred unless something in the system overcomes the liminal inertia.

Priests of the ancient world used many rituals to overcome impurity and the perceived taint carried by items from profane space. They believed that their gods reacted to conditions that affected holiness. Thus, their most holy places became sequestered from things and practices that could contaminate those spaces. The ancient Egyptians believed that, without sacred space, a god would object to defilement and flee its idol. If a god fled, the risk for the worshiper was that the god's departure would remove any blessings or protection. Because the Egyptian gods were capricious and vindictive, defilement could provoke the gods to become vengeful and inflict harm upon the devotee.

Figure 91. The *Ta-Wer* fetish of Osiris, Temple of Seti I at Abydos (photo by author).

And even though some gods like Osiris inhabited the realm of the dead and did not need a physical manifestation in the mortal world, some deities needed an image to inhabit so they could participate in the profane world. One of these deities was Maat. Maat was the goddess that brought order to the world. How could a goddess maintain order in profane space if she never left sacred space? If a god has no real presence in profane space, how can a god influence the world? The question might seem seem naïve in the light of a Western view of God where he only needs to command something for something to happen (divine fiat). Yet, questions like this still persist in present times and the debate regarding the omnipresence of God has continued for centuries. The Egyptian answer to this question was that the gods went on procession to influence the physical world.

Temple architecture enforced a strict heaven and earth separation that excluded common people from religious events. The gods would communicate indirectly through priestly intermediaries from inside the safety of sacred space, and the redistribution of offerings provided food for the priests. This was the world as normal.

During the festivals, the normal world turned inside out. The priests carried the gods on procession outside of their temples. The divine expanded across the non-sacred landscape, allowing the common people to mingle with the gods. Gods "talked" directly to people by responding to questions through the movement of their sacred vessels, and offerings were distributed as occasions of public beneficence.[2]

Ritual furniture allowed people to move items in and out of sacred space, overcoming the religious barrier of limality. With these rituals, profane items could be made sacred and be brought into the sacred spaces of temples and tombs. Likewise, sacred idols could be moved outside of temple sacred spaces without becoming defiled by profane space.

## Funerary Biers

Every society has its unique funeral customs. While funerary customs in the West seem logical to us, these customs are distinct to us and our culture. When someone dies in North America, the body is usually first delivered to an undertaker. These days, of course, they prefer the less foreboding title "funeral director." The undertaker's job is to act as a middle man making all the arrangements to prepare a body for burial.

Upon receiving a body, the undertaker drains the body of blood and fluids, and he replaces them with embalming fluid. Normally, upon death, the body of the dead undergoes a process called "marbling" where the skin turns greenish black.[3] Modern embalming arrests this post-necrotic state, which would distress the grieving. The undertaker dresses the body in its finest clothes and applies makeup to give the deceased a life-like appearance.

The undertaker puts the body on display in the coffin for a "viewing." Relatives and friends of the deceased gather together to "view" the body in a ritual event that compels the bereaved to view the death in real terms. This event restructures society in absence of the deceased and acts as a mutual coping mechanism.[4] This ritual is, of course, contingent upon the body not having been dead long. After the visitation and sermons, the coffin is closed and is loaded onto a hearse. The hearse leads a caravan of cars driving slowly to the cemetery in a motorized ritual procession. And after the deceased is buried, people usually gather to eat finger sandwiches and sausage rolls while chatting awkwardly.

In ancient Egypt, funeral rituals were somewhat different. Unlike modern embalming that only temporarily preserves the appearance for viewing, Egyptian priests mummified the body to preserve it forever. The priests placed the mummified body in a box or upon a bed called a *bier*. The Egyptians either carried or dragged the mummy by oxen to the grave using the bier. A priest performed the "opening of the mouth" ritual, done so the deceased could eat and drink again, and then the body was interred in a coffin. A year later, relatives gathered at the tomb to talk to the spirit of the deceased and eat a meal. Unfortunately, the archaeological record does not tell us whether the conversation was awkward or not.

Funeral biers provided special transport for the dead in ancient times. Biers were essentially the hearses of ancient Egypt. Biers were special chests or shrines that transported the deceased from the mummification place to the tomb and its permanent coffin.[5] They were containers of sacred space that transported the already purified mummy to the tomb. As the bier was transported to its destination, the priests would chant magic spells to purify the dead even further, helping the dead cross over into the afterlife.

During the Old and Middle Kingdoms, biers were non-processional furniture, that is, funeral parties originally interred biers with the deceased. But the complexity, expense, and ultimately the scarcity of wood that hit Egypt during the Ramesside period changed the bier from single-use furniture to furniture that was reused for many burials.[6] The scarcity of wood in Ramesside Egypt is suggestive of the plague mentioned in Exod 10:15 where the locusts ate every green plant and stripped the trees. While annual plants will grow back the following season, trees take generations (if ever) to recover once destroyed. However, all biers served the common ritual function of escorting the dead to the underworld.

The bier was also the counterpart to the Anubis chest (p. 69). The funeral party transported the canopic jars to the tomb using the Anubis chest, which followed after the bier. And once they completed the processional ritual, the canopic jars were transferred to the permanent canopic shrine. After the priests placed the jars in the canopic shrine, the dead no longer needed the Anubis chest.

Likewise, they transported the mummy in a bier to the tomb, where they placed the mummy into its permanent coffins and sarcophagus. After the interment of the dead, the deceased no longer needed the bier.

Scenes of the construction of funeral biers showed owners who had enough wealth to build their own. Perhaps the rich designated their biers as communal assets so that they could have ongoing influence in the community. Priests would keep communal biers in the treasury of the local mortuary temple until they were needed again.

## Old Kingdom Box Biers

Biers underwent a lot of change over their history. And there will be a lot of material from biers that compare well to the ark. Even though biers are less important for their iconographic value than barques or palanquins, we are going to find that where they compare to the ark is on the basis of construction methods.

During the Old Kingdom, it is difficult to tell biers from coffins given that both were buried with the deceased. The *itjnet*, , is a type of bier (or maybe coffin) that only appears once in Egyptian texts. The rock tomb of Ibi (Dynasty 6, ca. 2349–2185 BC) at Deir el Gebrâwi shows a relief of this kind of bier.[7] The term appears in a label over an item being worked on by two craftsmen. The craftsmen designed the *itjnet* bier with a flat corniced lid and legs.

In the scene two workers are finishing the chest and the caption that coincided with the iconography reads "beating varnish of the *itjnet* of [. . .] house and hewing of the interior." The iconography of the carpenters shows that they are not so much "beating" as "polishing" (or perhaps "slapping" or "rubbing"). We can observe that the hands of the carpenters are open and palm down.

Figure 92. An *itjnet* being finished by a pair of workers (Davies, Deir el Gebrâwi, part I, 1902, pl. XIV).

The word for varnish in this caption is *senetjer*, "incense." Lab tests have identified *senetjer* with the resin of *Pistacia* trees.[8] This resin is better known as mastic or "Arabic gum." In its softened form, the resin can be used as a varnish, but when hard it can be burned as "incense"[9] and even incorporated in cosmetics as "perfume."[10]

The mastaba of Khafkhufu I (Dynasty 4, ca. 2613–2498 BC) depicts a man preparing a ball of *senetjer* in an incense burner.[11] These burners typically looked like a small bowl with a stand and could even have a perforated lid.[12] The burner was similar to the incense cones commonly used during the Old Kingdom.[13]

## Oxen-Dragged Funeral Biers

During the Old and Middle Kingdoms, ox-dragged biers became synonymous with having a good funeral. However, having something dragged by oxen becomes an important point of difference between Egyptian and Israelite ritual practice. And an incident over the use of an ox-drawn cart was an important point of contention with the handling of the ark.

The *mestjepet*, 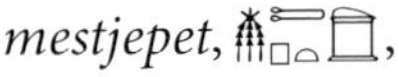, was a funeral bier dragged by ropes. The word is uncommon but appears in the tomb of Djau (Dynasty 6) at Deir el Gebrâwi.[14] Fortunately, the tomb features a relief, depicting a bier on a sledge. The scene depicts several men dragging two shrines by a rope: a larger bier followed by a smaller canopic chest. This arrangement was the normal funerary procession ritual during the Old and Middle Kingdoms.

Another example appears in *P. Berlin 10499* version of *Sinuhe*.[15] The text discusses the time of Sinuhe's death and the details of his burial. His mourners made a procession for him and placed his mummy in a *mestjepet* bier dragged by oxen.

Unfortunately, few burials from these periods remain undisturbed so details are lacking when it comes to burials using *mestjepet* biers. The *mestjepet* establishes a pattern that ties the bier to the processional canopic shrine. But the importance of being dragged by oxen hinges upon the status of the dead with regards to ritual purity. In Egypt, at the point when it was dragged to a tomb, a mummy had undergone a process of bathing, desiccation, and ritual purification. So the mummy was considered to be ritually clean when it was interred. However, in Israelite culture, a corpse was always considered to be ritually unclean (Lev 22:4; Num 19:13). Moreover, it was commanded that the ark be carried by its poles (Exod 25:14). So, while an ox was considered a clean animal, there would always be an association between ox-drawn carts and burial of the dead, which was ritually unclean. The association of oxen that were used to draw a cart with burial customs was without doubt part of the Egyptian context. However, this left open the controversy of whether such oxen were an appropriate offering to give to the Israelite tabernacle (Num 7:3–6). The issue was resolved by not using the oxen that had drawn a cart in tabernacle service, instead giving them to the Levites.

## Middle Kingdom Funeral Biers

The *shefdyt* was a type of box coffin found in Middle Kingdom funerary and prophetic contexts. The *Dialogue of Ipuwer* mentions a *shefdu* coffin: "Look, they were buried as a falcon in the *shefdu* coffins, as what the pyramids concealed fell into emptiness."[16] While *shefdyt* and *shefdu* began as synonymous terms, they become distinct by the New Kingdom (see below). The *shefdyt* coffin is important to the development of ritual furniture because it operated as a box of magical incantations. These coffins were the archetypes for later kinds of biers.

Figure 93. Mourners carrying the *shefdyt* of Antefoker (Davies, 1920, pl. XXI).

The funerary procession from Antefoker's tomb (TT60) (ca. Senwosret I) shows nine men carrying a *shefdyt* coffin with poles (fig. 93). The text found in the Antefoker relief has a bed determinative 𓍱. This determinative has strong connotations with sleep, death, and funerals. In the Antefoker relief, the mummy in a bier is clearly identifiable in the register below the labeled one in question. A team of men and pair of oxen pulled the bier upon a sledge.[17] The bier in the register below and the Dynasty 12 (ca. 2029–1819 BC) context strongly suggest that the object in the top register was a box coffin. The tradition of anthropoid coffins within a box coffin was discontinued after the Middle Kingdom.

The transition to the anthropoid coffins during the Second Intermediate Period (ca. 1650–1530 BC) accompanied a shift in meaning from the *shefdyt* of Antefoker to the *shefdu* of the Tomb Robbery Papyri. Priests stored the *shefdu* in the temple treasury at Medinet Habu where they kept the *per-en-setja*. It is unlikely that priests would store a coffin of any kind in a temple treasury—not even the coffin of a king. Theological reasons demanded that the mummy and its coffin had to remain in a tomb. The coffin was the proxy body to where the spirit of dead returned. And tombs were the gateway to the realm of the dead.

Figure 94. The Great Pyramid of Khufu (photo by author).

By the New Kingdom, the *shefdu* was probably a bier instead of a true coffin. A difference in the two terms is even more likely given the prevalence of box-shaped biers during Ramesside funerals.[18] The significance here is that Ramesside period burials primarily used anthropoid coffins for final interment. Biers developed into elaborately decorated "magical instruments" like their earlier coffin counterparts.[19] But, instead of simply being a coffin, the *shefdu* supplanted the ox-drawn biers, favoring transportation by carrying poles.

This development may have happened because the cost of these boxes was prohibitive for anything other than temporary transport. While Egypt had mostly a barter economy, it was still subject to the problem of inflation. As the Egyptian economy grew over millennia, the cost of items and labor increased. And the cost of funerals became a factor in the production of funerary items. Egyptian kings offset much of this inflation by bringing resources from regions outside of Egypt, like Nubia and Canaan.

We even see this increase in costs in pyramid construction. The kings of Dynasties 3 to 4 (ca. 2686–2498 BC) built their pyramids of stone using skilled labor. These early kings could afford to build with stone because labor was cheap. Some of these efforts, like Khufu's Great Pyramid, were believed to have nearly ruined the Egyptian economy. Later pyramid building used cheap mud bricks and never lived up to the grandeur and permanence of the early pyramids. But as inflation took hold, even these pyramids became smaller and smaller over time.

King Ahmose (ca. 1538–1513 BC), the first king of Dynasty 18, was the last Egyptian ruler to build a pyramid. It was only forty meters high, a shadow of the past glories of the

Old and Middle Kingdoms. Egyptian kings from that point on interred themselves in rock cut tombs or under the foundations of temples.

The *shefdu* mentioned in *P. BM 10043* was covered in copper foil. The inflation of the late Ramesside period dramatically increased the value of all metal, making the copper foil a tempting target for thieves. The relatively thick copper foil means the craftsmen probably fastened the foil mechanically, so the thieves could tear the foil off the *shefdu* bier quickly like tearing wallpaper off of a wall.

The construction method of metal foil over a wood core in ritual furniture is a distinctly Egyptian design pattern seen in the tabernacle furniture. Levantine craftsmen did not typically use this method of construction. The *shefdu* used copper foil over wood like that found on the altar of burnt offering.

Bezalel made the core of the bronze altar from acacia wood. He made the altar body and the horns entirely from acacia, and overlaid the entire structure with bronze foil (Exod 27:1–3). The other three furnishings (the ark, offering table, and incense altar) had a similar design except gold foil was overlaid instead (Exod 25:10–11, 23–24; 30:1–3).

## Barque Biers

We find the term *weret*, , in a single text. The determinative suggests a bier shaped like a barque. The *Stela of Ikhernofret* describes Ikhernofret causing the god (that is, the dead king) to enter the barque bier.[20] The barque bier developed as a way to ritualize the journey to the afterlife. This reenacted the migration between the mythological *henhenu* to the *wia* barque or the night-barque to the day-barque.[21]

Early biers were little more than coffins transported on raised supports or beds mounted on a sledge beneath a canopy.[22] Between the reigns of Thutmosis IV to Amenhotep III (ca. 1399–1351 BC), biers merge with sacred barques. This resulted in a new form of mortuary bier distinct from earlier types, taking a chest coffin with a canopy lid and adding the hull of a barque.[23] These barque biers commonly occur in Dynasty 19 iconography.

A relief from the tomb of Userhet at Sheik Abd el-Qurna shows oxen dragging a barque bier.[24] On this bier, the statues of Nephthys and Isis were placed at each end of the deck of the barque, facing in toward the cabinet. These goddesses escorted the deceased from the place of mummification to the tomb and into the afterlife.[25] This feature is not found on earlier biers.

## House of Dragging

When the Israelites made the furniture for the tabernacle, they used Egyptian design patterns of metal foil laid over a wood base. But once the Israelites entered the promised land, the altars constructed thereafter used Levantine building techniques (Josh 8:31). We do not find the metal over wood construction again in Levantine construction until the Solomonic temple (1 Kgs 6). This Egyptian design pattern is expressed in the construction details of the *per-en-setja*.

The term *per-en-setja*, 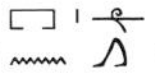 , translates literally as "house of dragging" from the verb *setja*. Alan Gardiner though the term to meant "a receptacle which can be dragged." He based his translation upon the similar term *ḥesmen ákh-en-setja*, which he rendered as a "bronze brazier which can be dragged."[26] Iconography shows that the *ákh-en-setja* had a sledge but no poles. Therefore, to move the *ákh-en-setja*, one must drag it. But the Tomb Robbery texts tell us that the *per-en-setja* had carrying poles, so it is unclear whether the *per-en-setja* could be dragged.

The term *seta* appears in *P. Anastasi II* that spoke in praise of Ramesses II. The author wrote "every foreign land, he dragged away (*seta-en-ef*) carrying their tribute."[27] Given that the tribute is in poetic form, we could expect a colorful meaning to help illustrate the verse. Scribes used the verb *seta* as part of a standard repertoire for conquest passages.[28]

Another use from *P. Harris I* clarifies the meaning: "I caused to deliver (*seta*) libation offerings and geese to your city Heliopolis to the leaders."[29] The translation of "to drag" cannot be applied here. Reliefs show live geese offerings where priests carried them in holding their necks. If this seems like rough handling, we do have to remember that priests were going to kill the geese as sacrificial offerings.

*P. Harris I* also described in a clause of purpose a daily offering of pomegranate wine and grape wine. Priests presented daily offerings such as these to "drag" (read: bribe) the Heliopolitan people to come to the temple.[30] I guess, with many temples to choose from at Helopolis, it seems getting people to come to church was even a problem in the Late Bronze Age. And tasting exotic alcoholic beverages provided a bit of incentive to come "participate" in the religious service.

According to *P. BM 10403*, a *per-en-setja* could be dedicated to either priests or kings.[31] This text describes a *per-en-setja* and a *shefdu* belonging to Ramessesnakht, the chief priest of Amun.[32] This document uses both words in the same way. The *per-en-setja* was used in the memorial ritual but was not necessarily buried with the dead king.[33] The association suggests that these furnishings had a broader use than a single interment.

There are clear parallels between biers and palanquins and the ark when it comes to construction details. The craftsmen that built the *per-en-setja* covered the wood box with copper foil.[34] The description of the ark includes an acacia wood chest overlaid with gold foil: "And they shall construct an ark of *acacia wood* two and a half cubits long, and one and a half cubits wide, and one and a half cubits high. And you shall *overlay it with pure gold, inside and out you shall overlay it*, and you shall make a gold molding around it" (Exod 25:10–11). Moreover, there are examples in Egyptian furniture where items were overlaid inside and out with gold, such as the *henu* box of Queen Hetepheres (fig. 39).

*P. Westcar* mentions prince Hordedef being carried on a *qeniu* palanquin of ebony that had *neba* poles of *sesnedjem*-wood clad with gold.[35] Compare this to the description of the poles from the ark: "Then make *poles of acacia wood and overlay them with gold.* Insert the poles into the rings on the sides of the ark, to carry the ark with them" (Exod 25:13–14).

The discovery of a chest from Tutankhamun's tomb showed pole-rings located under the chest near the feet. Compare this to "You shall cast four gold rings and fasten them on its four feet, and two rings shall be on one side of it and two rings on the other side of it" (Exod 25:12). Placing the pole-rings on the feet under the chest takes the load off the rings. This placement prevents metal fatigue and possible shearing. The bottom of the chest would bear the weight of the ark while the rings held the poles in place.

The bronze altar of burnt offering is also similar: "And you shall make the altar of *acacia wood*, five cubits long and five cubits wide; the altar shall be square, and its height shall be three cubits. And you shall make its horns on its four corners; its horns shall be of one piece with it, and you shall overlay it with *bronze*" (Exod 27:1–2). The *per-en-setja* had bronze pole rings similar to those on the bronze altar of burnt offering.

Both the Israelite tabernacle and Egyptian ritual furniture were constructed using wood overlaid with metal. This construction method is a distinctly Egyptian design pattern. The Egyptians rarely made burnt offering altars from stone. An exception to this is the four-horned altar at Karnak. This altar dates to the reign of Thutmosis III (ca. 1477–1423 BC) and is about three hundred years older than similar Canaanite examples.[36] In contrast, Levantine cultures made the majority of their altars from stone.

## Carrying Poles

We have already touched upon the fact that the ark was made using an Egyptian design pattern and that there are examples of Egyptian chests that attached their carrying poles at or near near the feet. And we also covered that Egyptian carrying poles could be made as wood poles covered in gold (pp. 145–46), just like the ark. But more can be said about carrying poles and the ark.

The Tomb Robbery Papyri tell us that the *per-en-setja* of the high priest Ramessesnakht had six pole rings of copper and six carrying pole-ends.[37] The text mentions pole-ends almost exclusively instead of complete poles. This raises the question of why the ends of the poles were a significant detail.

*Neba,* , is a generic word for carrying poles. This term differs from *mawedj,* used to describe poles that accompanied *debet* chests.[38] A *mawedj* was a single carrying pole used to carry one or more items normally across one's shoulder, whereas a piece of furniture using a *neba* poles could use one or mores poles.

For example, farmers used *neba* poles in agriculture. The tomb of Paheri showed farmers using *neba* poles to carry sacks of grain.[39] In contrast, the *Restoration Stela of Tutankhamun* tells us Amun's sacred image was carried on thirteen *neba* poles.[40] So, in effect, a *mawedj* pole was a *neba* pole, but not all *neba* were *mawedj.* For the barque of Ptah, Ramesses III made *neba* poles overlaid with quality gold and engraved with the name of the god.[41] And a text from the reign of Taharqa mentioned the sacred barques (*seshem-khu*) of Ptah, Khonsu, and Amun carried upon pairs of *neba* poles.[42]

And where there are carrying poles, we often find rings into which poles can be inserted. Iconographic and archaeological evidence of pole rings abounds. In the Egyptian language, the word *shaq* was associated with several types of rings.[43] The semantic range of *shaq* can refer to any metal or stone ring. The *Kahun Papyri*, a list of possessions, used the phrase *ḥesmen shaq* to mean finger rings of amethyst.[44] However, *P. Mayer A*, a Tomb Robbery Papyrus, mentions the theft of "two rings of bronze," rings used for carrying poles.[45]

The Egyptians used *neba* poles with biers, barques, and chests. The author who wrote *UC 16448*, a Dynasty 22 (ca. 947–713 BC) painted wood panel kept at the Petrie Museum, mentions the *neba* carrying poles as part of a *wia* barque.[46]

In ancient Egypt, carrying poles could be removable, or made as a permanent part of the furniture. The craftsmen could construct these poles as part of a sledge. Such poles remained permanently attached and could not be removed from the item even when at rest.

And depending upon the furniture type, carrying poles could be either long or short. Long poles transversed the length of the carried piece. And when porters inserted long poles into their rings, two porters could carry the item from opposite sides using the same pole.

Conversely, short poles typically did not extend across the length of the piece. Only one person held such a pole at any one time. Short poles are often shown with multiple pole-rings per pole or, less commonly, a long socket. With long poles, the craftsmen set the rings so the box's weight rested across the pole. But with short poles, using only one ring creates a pivot point against the edge of the box. Without a second ring, the stress of the box's weight could tear off a single pole-ring.

A chest from the Tomb of Tutankhamun had a pole-ring assembly with bronze rings (fig. 95). Each short pole required two bronze staples driven through the wood box bottom.[47] At least two rings were needed to hold each short pole in place.

Summing up, carrying poles appear in three configurations in both iconography and artifacts: (1) poles attached permanently that could not be separated from the furniture's body, (2) long detachable poles inserted through pole rings or catches, or (3) short poles that could be inserted into sockets or multiple rings.

The *per-en-setja* bier in the Tomb Robbery Papyri had six pole-ends, two more than were needed to carry it. Extra poles were a common addition to sacred barques. For example, the West Shrine of Mut at Luxor Temple shows the Barque of Mut with four poles (eight ends) superimposed (fig. 86).[48] During the reign of Ramesses III, the sacred barque of Amun-Re had ten pole ends.[49] This indicated that the poles served more than just a utilitarian function of carrying the item but were present for processional purposes. More poles meant more people on parade, implying the furniture's owner was of greater importance.

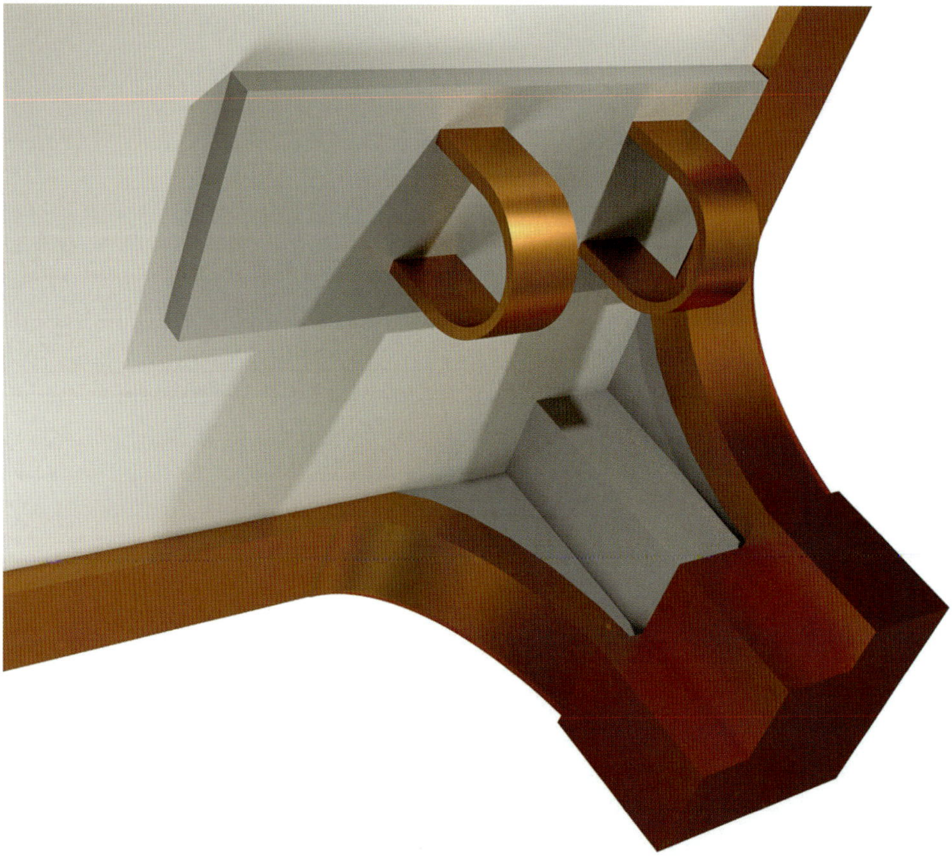

Figure 95. Pole-ring assembly from the chest of Tutankhamun (Cairo, Egyptian Museum, JE 61445; Carter No. 032) (illustration by author).

Recently, a new theory has been suggested that the ark used short poles to resolve an apparent contradiction.[50] Exodus 25:15 commands that the poles were to remain in the rings at all times. But later, the Kohathites put the poles into rings to make the ark ready for moving (Num 4:6). Why would priests remove the poles when they're not supposed to, making it necessary for the Kohathites to replace the poles in the rings? The proposed solution suggests the ark's poles never really left the rings, but the poles were retracted under the ark. And the Kohathites merely extended the poles into place. The theory suggests that these poles were similar to those used on the Tutankhamun Chest (JE 61445/GEM 4881), which retracted to a space under the chest.[51]

While this hypothesis is interesting, it faces a hurdle in the number of pole rings made for the ark. Retracting short poles require two or more rings per pole to keep the poles in place during transport. Archaeologists find these multiple ring assemblies in iconography as well as in the real objects.[52] On the other hand, only four pole rings were made for the ark (Exod 25:10). This is not enough pole rings to prevent metal fatigue and shearing (p. 147).

Figure 96. Ebony and ivory chest of Tutankhamun (JE 61445/GEM 4881) (photo by author).

Furthermore, short poles are normally no more than the length of the chest. In the case of the ark, this would be no more than two and a half cubits (45 inches). However, the ark's poles were so long that they stuck out of the Holy of Holies. Observers from the inner sanctuary of the Solomonic temple could see the poles (2 Chr 5:8). Clearly, the poles used by the ark were long poles.

I do not believe that Exod 25:15 contradicts Num 4:6. Probably, the situation that led to the inserting of the poles in Num 4:6 resulted from mishandling the ark. The separation of the ark from its poles took place when the sons of Aaron were priests. Aaron's sons, Nadab and Abihu, were not good priests and did not do things by the book. They presented an offering of strange fire (Num 3:4) that resulted in summary punishment by the Lord. So the careful reader could conclude that this was not the first offense of Nadab and Abihu.

But this was not the only time summary judgment after a second offense occured in relation to the ark. We find something similar with the striking down of Uzzah. Many presume that God judged Uzzah for touching the ark (2 Sam 6:7). This is only half true. After the Philistines captured the ark, they brought it back to the Temple of Dagon (1 Sam 5:2). It is unlikely that the Philistines treated the ark with the same respect as the Levites, and they not only touched the ark but probably looked inside it too. Some Philistines died but others only suffered from tumors (1 Sam 5:12). However, 50,070 men at Beth-Shemesh were killed after they peered inside the ark (1 Sam 6:19). The punishment at Beth-Shemesh was more severe than against the Philistines. The difference may have been because the men at Beth-Shemesh were not Levites, had no compelling need to touch or look inside the ark, and they knew (or should have known) better (Deut 10:8).

Yet, the Lord's anger burned against Uzzah for two other reasons. The obvious reason is because they put the ark on an ox cart (2 Sam 6:3). The only prescribed method to transport the ark was to carry it by its poles (Exod 25:14). And I'm sure the connotation with oxen-drawn funeral processions would not have impressed the Lord. When the Philistines returned the ark, they showed greater respect by using a cart drawn by dairy cows that had never pulled a load, not oxen (1 Sam 6:7). By using dairy cows instead of oxen, the Philistines took no chance that these cattle would have been used for a funeral procession and avoided any taint or association with anything that could be construed as ritually unclean.

But the less obvious reason was the genealogy of Uzzah. Uzzah was the son of Abinadab, son of Jesse (2 Sam 6:3; 1 Sam 16:8; 17:13). That makes Uzzah King David's nephew and thus a Judaite. Biblical law permitted only Levites who descended from Kohath to transport the ark (Num 4:4–15). Still think genealogies are boring? What can I say? Genealogies matter. Therefore, similarly, I would suggest the Kohathites had to restore the poles to their proper place after egregious mishandling by Nadab and Abihu.

## Iconographic Interchange

Furniture for the dead was decorated or gilded with gold and painted with elaborate iconography, which were thought to contain magic that would protect the mummified remains so the deceased could become a god in the next life. Once transformed into divinity, the deceased no longer suffered from the ravages of decay and demons that preyed upon the dead.

The Egyptians buried the dead using biers and Anubis chests that sanctified and protected their contents. Entire communities used these objects as vessels to convey the dead to their tombs. This furniture ritually prepared the dead for final burial as part of cleansing the deceased and by reenacting the dead's sacred journey to the underworld.

Icons seen as magical became part of religious repertoire. Even though the Egyptians had many symbols with discrete magical effects, the most important icons were used upon sacred barques and funerary biers. Eventually, other kinds of furniture borrowed the symbolism found on barques and biers.

## Palanquins

One of the most important concepts that helps us understand the ark is the dichotomy between sacred and profane. That dichotomy separated what is holy from what is not. We have seen notions of holiness and the sacred reflected in chests, barques, and biers. Palanquins started as purely secular objects and were transformed into sacred furniture by borrowing aspects from other types of ritual furniture.

Figure 97. The Golden Throne of Tutankhamun (photo by author).

A palanquin is a chair, or even a carriage, often covered with a canopy and carried with poles. The palanquin did not begin with a religious purpose in mind. Rather, the palanquin got its start as a status symbol of wealth or rank. As with chests, palanquins developed over centuries until they were idealized. Unlike barques, where the evidence is concentrated in the New Kingdom, the bulk of evidence for palanquins is from Old Kingdom tomb sites.

The earliest palanquin appearing in the iconography was found in the tomb of Nefermaat at Medum from the beginning of Dynasty 4.[53] This palanquin was little more than an upright chair and a footstool fastened to a tray with poles. The design was not stabilized for the seated officials that rode high in the chair. Later designs accounted for this lack of stability, placing the poles near the center of gravity allowing for safer travel.

Unlike thrones, Old Kingdom palanquins were used primarily by court officials. Later palanquins may have implied divine status, but early palanquins conveyed a sense of "moral rectitude and fiscal responsibility."[54] No known iconographic examples survive of kings using palanquins during the Old Kingdom. Yet, a king could have used a palanquin, especially given that *P. Westcar* suggests Prince Hordedef was carried in a palanquin.[55]

Figure 98. Palanquin of Queen Hetepheres (photo by author).

A complete palanquin was found in the tomb of Queen Hetepheres (Giza tomb G 7000X) (fig. 98). Hetepheres was the queen of King Senefru and mother of King Khufu, builder of the Great Pyramid at Giza. Her palanquin was made in a litter style out of wood and covered in gold foil with writing in black paint. Unlike the armchair found in the same tomb, this palanquin lacks religious symbols and iconography.

Several court officials and regional governors from the Old Kingdom were shown being carried in a variety of different palanquin styles. A relief fragment from Khnumhotep's tomb at Saqqara (Dynasty 5, ca. 2498–2349 BC) showed the nomarch holding a flail and seated in a litter-style palanquin.[56] A palanquin from the tomb of Ni-Maat-Re included vertical poles and a sunshade.[57] Tesen's mastaba (tomb G 4810) from mid Dynasty 5 shows a litter-style palanquin with tent poles and a canopy.[58] The mastaba of Snedjem-ib Inti (tomb G 2370) from the reign of Shepseskara had a palanquin in the style of a throne.[59] Overall, the Old Kingdom marked a pioneering phase for the palanquin with various styles being tried and tested.

Toward the end of the Old Kingdom, Egypt's bureaucracy had gathered significant power and influence. These officials arranged burials rivaling the funerals of kings. This rise in status was reflected in their palanquins. The mastaba of Watetkhethor (ca. Teti) at Saqqara showed the deceased in an upright palanquin style that emphasized throne-like aspects.[60] The chair's shape is similar to the block thrones used by deities and the side panel of the chair had the image of a seated lion, a motif reserved for royalty.

Even though many iconographic examples of palanquins from the Old Kingdom exist, examples from the Middle Kingdom are rare. Little further development took place after Dynasty 6 (ca. 2349–2185 BC). Yet, a rich vocabulary exists for palanquins.

## Palanquins for the Great

Besides being used for nobility and court officials, Old Kingdom palanquins were also associated with the king and even divinity. However, that association is different than for officials. In the case of scribes and administrators, scenes with palanquins were often used to decorate their tombs. Kings were buried in pyramids, and most pyramids were not decorated at all until the Fifth Dynasty. When later pyramids were decorated, the pyramid walls were mostly decorated with Pyramid Texts, spells that protected the king in the afterlife. And it is in those spells that we find palanquins connected to the king.

The *sepa*, , is another Old Kingdom palanquin. *Pyramid Text 571* says "he who is in the *sepa* palanquin" provides for the king.[61] Another Pyramid Text similarly says that the goddess Nekhbet commanded he who is in the palanquin to provide for the king.[62] These texts imply a ritual and processional use associated with the supply of food and drink.

The *á*, , and *ḥetes*, 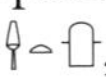, are terms for "palanquin" used during the Old Kingdom. These terms always appear as adjectives with the phrase "great one" (*wer*). And both terms appear in the Pyramid Texts. In a hymn of awakening the dead king, a chorus of women receive the *wer-á*, "Great One of the palanquin."[63] Both terms appear in *Pyramid Text 438* where the king is proclaimed to be immune from death.

A *wer-á* is shown in the tomb of Seneb.[64] The determinative in the text shows the carriage of the palanquin with a person riding within it. Beside the text, Seneb was shown riding in his palanquin. The palanquin in the determinative and the relief differ, showing a difference between determinative and the real object.

In another Pyramid Text, the king proclaims "the great one of the litter (*wer-ḥetes*) and the great one of the *wer-á* palanquin of Hentyimentiu."[65] A different Pyramid Text used *wer-á* to say that the deceased did not make the king "dance" as the great one of the palanquin.[66] One possibility is that the *wer-á* was used to carry people while the *wer-ḥetes* was a shrine for an idol shaped like a palanquin.

## Palanquins for the Sick

The *khudet*, , is a word used during the Old Kingdom. A biographical stela of Washptah from Giza mentions that the king procured a *khudet* palanquin for his servant who had been ill and suffering, so he could supervise the king's building projects—how good of the king.[67]

The tomb of Djau at Deir el Gebrâwi (Dynasty 6) mentioned a *khudet* palanquin of ebony.[68] A scene accompanying the text shows a worker holding an adze working on the carriage portion of a palanquin. The determinative,  (Gardiner Sign Q1), may suggest that the palanquin was a symbol of authority. This was the determinative used with words for thrones and in the name of the god Osiris.

## Palanquins and Chairs

The *qeniu*, 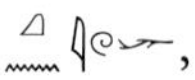, is a general term that means "palanquin" or "throne" but can also refer to simply a "chair." Think of this like grandpa's recliner being called his "throne." The term comes from a root word meaning "to embrace," possibly from the idea that chairs with arms embrace those who sit in them.[69]

The term appears frequently in the Deir el-Medina ostraca. The workers at Deir el-Medina used *qeniu* to mean either stools or armless chairs with backs.[70] The term is mentioned in three of the four annual property lists for Khay, the foreman of the Deir el-Medina craftmen.[71] A discussion of the carpenter's trade mentions *qeniu* chairs among the items taught by a carpentry instructor.[72]

The Medjay Mentumose paid to the scribe Hori "one wood palanquin (*qeniu*) which has its *meryt* upon its *át* pole."[73] Egyptologist Jac. J. Janssen suggests the *meryt* was an upright back support and the át were the poles of the back of the chair.[74] Admittedly, some *qeniu* prices seem low for a palanquin given other New Kingdom commodity prices; for example, the three *seniu* (roughly fifteen *deben*) paid in *O. Gardiner 103*. However, other prices are commensurate with the highest valued goods, such as the thirty *deben* paid in *O. Cairo 23800*.[75] While it seems incredible for a worker to pay fifteen *deben* for a stool (equivalent of three goats), someone paying more for a chair than for a bed is equally incredible since beds were priced between twelve and twenty-five *deben*.[76]

A fascinating document from mid-Dynasty 20 (ca. 1194–1073 BC) mentions a bribe. Now, bribes were—and some argue still are—a common practice in Egypt. A bribe was commonly paid to secure an opportunity to become an apprentice or for a promotion. A group of administrators took a large bribe consisting of a list of goods to secure a promotion for a boy.[77] Among these administrators, the scribe Hor-Shery received a wood *qeniu* chair valued at eleven *deben* and a large folding chair valued at thirty *deben* with a footstool.[78] And the chief of the workmen, In-Her-Khau, received a "one small wooden palanquin and its poles" valued at thirty *deben*.

Figure 99. Footstool from the tomb of Tutankhamun (Egyptian Museum) (photo by author).

The *Annals of Thutmosis III* written upon the walls at Karnak Temple mentions the booty Thutmosis III plundered from Kadesh. This text describes six *qeniu* and footstools (*hedem*) made of ivory, ebony, and *sesnedjem*-wood and worked with gold.[79] During the ninth campaign in the *Annals* (year thirty-four), Thutmosis III brought back from the Levant wooden goods in a *pega* chest and a *qeniu* palanquin inlaid with costly stones.[80]

## Palanquin Thrones

Earlier we mentioned that the ark's most important area of sacred space was not inside the chest but above the box between the wings of the cherubim on the mercy seat (p. 46). The sacred space of the ark was not contained by the physical vessel but exposed to open air, where it could be seen. The ark was not unique in having sacred space exposed for all to see. The palanquin throne had its most sacred area of space exposed and protected by winged goddesses.

The palanquin throne resulted from the stationary throne and the palanquin merging into a single piece of furniture. During the New Kingdom, the portable throne became the symbol of divine kingship. While bills of sale at Deir el-Medina show that palanquins were still being made for private use, iconographic depictions of palanquins were no longer represented in private tombs. New Kingdom palanquin iconography took on two different forms: the king's palanquin throne or a god's idol seated on a palanquin.

The first appearance of a royal palanquin in the New Kingdom is at Deir el-Bahari (Hatshepsut, ca. 1477–1456 BC). An empty throne is shown being carried by twelve servants.[81] Carrying poles ran through rings attached to the throne's seat. The palanquin platform was supported by the poles. And most of the carrying stress was placed upon the throne and not the platform, unlike most palanquins. Both arms of the throne are visible. Each side displays a royal lion, and the chair legs had leonine feet. The throne has no other symbolism.

Figure 100. Bust of Queen Hatshepsut (photo by author).

Another relief of a palanquin throne is at Luxor Temple (ca. Amenhotep III, 1389–1351 BC).[82] Little of this relief, unfortunately, survives except the leonine feet, carrying poles, and a servant carrying the throne. Traces of a uraeus frieze are visible near the seat. The uraeus frieze is possibly the first religious iconography to be added to palanquins.

The reign of Amenhotep III marks an important transition of the portable throne from a carriage carrying the king to a vessel transporting divinity. At this point, thrones became a sacred vessel that enabled Akhenaten, Amenhotep III's successor, to replace some religious imperatives. These imperatives, that is, the processions of the sacred barques, were a necessary part of Egyptian ritual and cultural practice. Amenhotep III's reforms heralded the beginning of a sacred palanaquin throne, which became known as the "Great Palanquin of Electrum."

Figure 101. Leonine foot from a chair from the New Kingdom (Roemer- and Pelizaeus-Museum Hildesheim) (photo by author).

The rock cut tomb of Meryra at Amarna shows a sacred palanquin throne resting on the ground with servants facing the throne from behind holding offerings.[83] The same relief shows a priest thurifying (censing) the empty palanquin throne, indicating the object was sacred. The throne has the royal lion on the side as is typical of most thrones. But it also has the royal sphinx wearing the double-crown standing above it. The royal sphinx was a symbol often used on the sacred barques to show divine kingship (e.g., fig. 77). The lion was a common royal motif in the ancient Near East, and even King Solomon used lions to decorate the arms of his throne (1 Kgs 10:19).

This representation is odd in that the king is not seated in the throne even though servants are presenting offerings, suggesting the throne was a cultic instrument. This raises some interesting questions. Was the sacred palanquin throne a proxy for the divine power of the king? Does an empty throne suggest it was occupied by some invisible deity similar to what was shown in the procession of the architrave at Luxor Temple?[84]

From Huya's tomb, a relief of Akhenaten superimposed with the image of the queen shows the royal couple being carried on the sacred palanquin throne.[85] This image is incomplete but includes a royal lion, a royal sphinx, and a uraeus frieze. Another relief from the same tomb showed Akhenaten and the queen being carried on the Great Palanquin of Electrum by servants. Some servants held fans and sunshades. And the image of the god Aten rode above the royal couple on procession to meet ambassadors from Retennu (Syria), Cush, and other foreign lands bringing tribute.

More than just an important religious symbol, the Great Palanquin of Electrum was an important symbol of the state. The Great Speos at Gebel el-Silsila has a relief of Horemheb being carried on a palanquin throne by soldiers.[86] This throne lacks the religious symbols of the Great Palanquin of Electrum and is a throwback to the earlier thrones of Dynasty 18. This presents a view of Egypt's king as a more secular or military figure. The notion of Egyptian kingship was always tied to concepts of religion. However, in this instance, Horemheb seems to shy away from some of the overt religious symbolism used by previous kings.

But the use of the sacred palanquin did not end with Horemheb. Sacred throne palanquins appeared again with the royal cult images in several Ramesside tombs. The tomb of Amenmosi (TT19) of early Dynasty 19 depicts priests carrying the royal cult image of Amenhotep I.[87] The throne was placed upon a box stand. The image of the dead king wearing the blue crown was seated on a throne surrounded by the wings of a Re falcon.

Khabekhnet's tomb (TT2) at Deir el-Medina shows Amenhotep I wearing the blue crown being carried on a palanquin throne.[88] While the palanquin throne is not appreciably different from non-Amarna Dynasty 18 palanquin thrones, a difference appears in the porters. Dynasty 18 porters were typically soldiers or servants, while later porters were often priests with a high priest walking beside the throne. The priests carried the king's cult image in a manner remarkably similar to the sacred barque procession.

The same tomb shows the cult statue of Amenhotep I being carried on a palanquin throne augmented with religious symbols, that is, the uraeus frieze and the Nekhbet goddess protecting the king with her wings.[89] Over the shoulder of the Amenhotep I statue is an image of Amun enthroned with Maat protecting Amun with her wings. The statue of the king would be visible in procession and not just an artistic convention, just as the king in a palanquin would be open for all to see as a sign of royal power.

Other Theban tombs (Huy, TT14; Piay, TT344; Panehesi, TT16) show cult images of Amenhotep I and his great queen, Ahmose-Nefertari. Amenhotep I held a special place in the hearts of the West Theban people. Amenhotep I was the king that first commissioned a tomb for himself in the Valley of the Kings. Archaeologists have not found the location of Amenhotep I's tomb. But this king was responsible for establishing the workers village at Deir el-Medina and a cottage industry that ensured the livelihood of these craftsmen for generations. These craftsmen revered Amenhotep I as their patron god.

During the reign of Ramesses III, the palanquin takes on idealized significance at Karnak where the king was shown being carried by the spirits of Buto and Hierakonpolis.[90] Inside the palanquin the king was seated on a *ḥeb*, "festival" symbol 𓎰, similar to Amun seated upon *neb* or *men* symbols, implying that what is being shown may not be a real object.

Figure 102. West Thebes at dawn near the Mortuary Temple of Amenhotep III (photo by author).

At Medinet Habu, the sacred throne palanquin is further augmented. The throne has the royal lion, royal sphinx, Re falcon, and image of Buto on its sides.[91] The back of the throne had a pair of Maat goddesses with their wings surrounding the king, and the entire throne assembly was encased in a kiosk with a uraeus frieze, all iconography borrowed from barques. A mixture of priests and soldiers accompanied the throne.

## Decline of the Symbol

The decline of the portable throne is linked to the loss of Egyptian hegemony. Even though Ramesses III was successful in his struggle against the invasion of the Sea Peoples, his successors lost control over both Nubia and the Levant. By the reign of Ramesses IV (ca. 1160–1153 BC), the New Kingdom had virtually lost its entire hegemonic influence.[92] The succeeding kings failed to recover what was lost, even though some evidence exists that Ramesses VI (ca. 1149–1142 BC) made a campaign into Canaan.[93] As the Egyptians lost their foreign holdings, the varnished image of the god-king having divine power over the world became difficult to maintain.

The portable throne was unique in the history of Egypt in that it had a long developmental history but suddenly fell out of favor near the beginning of Dynasty 21. The royal cult that began with the early dynasties of Egypt continued through to the end of the Ramesside period. The tomb of Nebamun (TT65) (ca. Ramesses IX, 1131–1112 BC) at Abd el Qurna shows the royal cult image upon a box stand parked in front of an image of Amun.[94]

The portable throne was not just a chair for the king, but was a significant religious symbol within the processional ritual. The final appearance of the royal cult palanquin appears at the Temple of Khonsu at Karnak (ca. Herihor).[95] The palanquin has the royal lion and sphinx, and Nekhbet wearing the *ḥedjet* crown 𓋑 with her wings around Herihor.

Theban building projects were financed by royal patronage. And this probably dictated the decorative agenda at Karnak. As that patronage declined, scenes of the king riding upon his portable throne gave way to more traditional portrayals, such as the king offering sacrifices. Scenes turned from political to religious priorities.

The trickle-down effect of less spending for temples and memorials limited what reliefs and paintings ended up being used in lesser tombs. The final appearance of a palanquin appears in a double image at Karnak (Shoshenq I, ca. 947–925 BC). However, the image upon the throne is not the king but Amun-Re.[96] Thus, the final throne palanquin did not belong to a king but to the king of the gods.

## The Ark as Holy

When Bezalel completed the ark, no priest carried the glory of the Lord into the ark. When the tabernacle was complete, the Lord's glory moved from Mount Sinai into the Holy of Holies (Exod 40:34; Num 9:15). The Lord by his own volition entered into the tabernacle and dwelt over the ark of the covenant. Unlike the gods of Egypt, the God of Israel expressed perfect judgment and complete sovereignty.

The God of Israel disrupted the normal course of history by creating a sacred space upon Mount Sinai. His holy space enveloped the entire mountain and no Israelite was permitted to go up the mountain or touch its border (Exod 19:12, 23). From there, the sacred space between the wings of the cherubim provided a means from which the glory of Lord moved from place to place. This convention is similar to the sacred barques, biers, and palanquin thrones, and is analogous to a modern space shuttle. The glory of the Lord followed the ark until the priests finally brought the ark into the Solomonic temple (1 Kgs 8:11).

The tabernacle and its furniture were mere reflections of the holy space in the heavenly temple (Rev 11:19). The ark of the covenant that Bezalel built was an imperfect copy of a heavenly reality. Nothing created by human hands would have ever been holy enough to satisfy a God of supreme holiness. The prophet Isaiah says, "Thus says the LORD, 'Heaven is my *throne*, and earth is my *footstool*. Where then is a house you could build for me?'" (Isa 66:1). A statement of supremacy couched in the language of furniture. It was not that the ark was so holy as to be able to transport God, but rather that the God of Israel was merciful enough to condescend to the frailty and ignorance of humankind. God followed the conventions of holy and profane space to show his nature and, as a concession, so that he could establish a relationship with humankind.

7

# CHAPTER 7

## The Over-Arking Context

As we conclude our journey, I hope you have come to appreciate the complexity of the Bronze Age world and the Egyptian context for the ark of the covenant. The ark emerged from a trajectory of visual language and tradition that we can infer from the over four hundred objects and icons that have survived in the archaeological record.[1]

Sacred barques were covered with layers of iconography and magical warding. Each layer (the deck of the hull, the shrine cabinet with its veil and frieze, and the winged goddesses inside the cabinet) provided a distinct, more holy, area of space. This warding created sacred space that could transport a cult statue in a state of uninterrupted purity. The complexity of this religious symbolism was intended to meet the ongoing requirements of the deity anticipating any needs imposed by the ritual cyclic economy: purity, life, dominion, power, and order.

But with palanquin thrones, the separation of these layers is collapsed onto a single plane, which is the seat itself. The religious effects of the motifs had an intensifying relationship that was all focused upon the single area of sacred space. The palanquin thrones borrowed the barque iconography and compressed it to fit upon the physical chair.

When iconography was added to ritual furniture, the nature of iconographic augmentation became a permanent addition to the repertoire. The uraeus prevented defilement from the outside. The vulture wings sanctified the space within them. The Djed pillar added stability and continuity. The lapwing bird symbol provided perpetual worship (p. 39). The Ankh symbol imparted abundance and flourishing of life. Religious symbols added unique magical effects. Some of these symbols, such as the cryptograph rebus of the king's throne name, were only used during the lifetime of the king. Other symbols became a permanent part of the artistic repertoire. When added to the repertoire, these symbols were carried forward cumulatively. Over time, each kind of furniture became heavily loaded with iconography. Some pieces, like the *shefdyt* biers, became so augmented and elaboratedly decorated with iconography that they became cost prohibitive magical instruments (p. 143). Each symbol was added at specific points in time. This allows us to pinpoint when iconography was added and to independently date a piece of furniture (fig. 103).

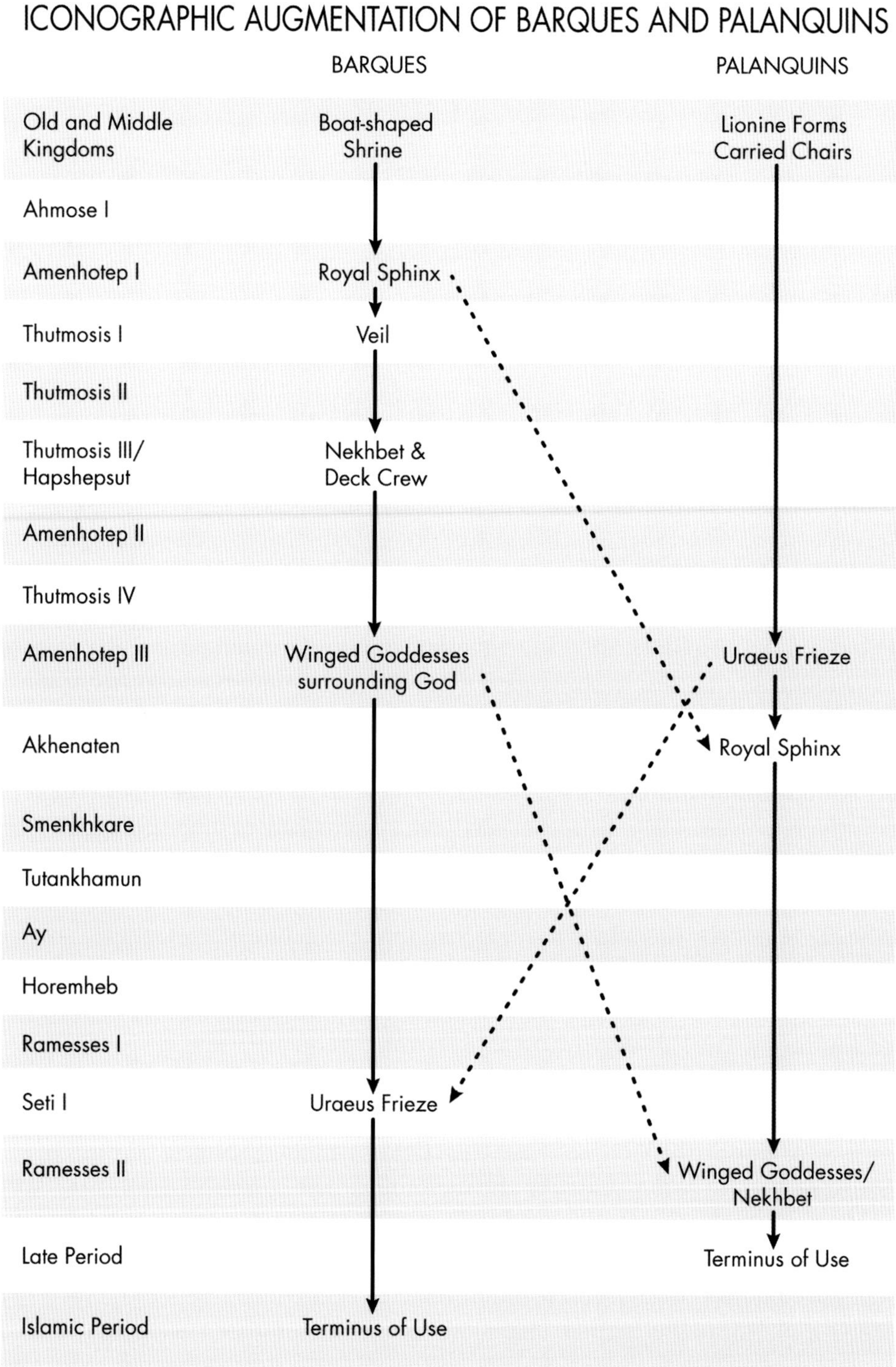


Figure 103. Iconography augmentation chart (illustration by author).

We see that toward the end of Dynasty 18 (ca. 1538–1305 BC), the features that made one kind of furniture distinct were adapted into other kinds of furniture. In trying to appease their gods, the Egyptians piled one symbol upon another. The net effect is that the function of each kind of furniture slowly came to be deconstructed. Chests became shrines, shrines became barques, biers and palanquins became like barques.

The ark shows a similar kind of deconstruction. The reliquary is essentially a chest. It is similar to other cultic chests of Dynasty 19 (ca. 1305–1194 BC), a simple box with an idol or religious element on the lid. As there is no mention of iconography for the ark's chest, the ark's box section may not have been covered with the icons of holiness. Instead, the sides of the ark's box could have been covered with inert writing or nonreligious icons (such as pomegranates) for decoration.

The ark's lid had a pair of cherubim facing toward each other. This is most similar to the sacred barques from the reign of Amenhotep III onward. And yet, the only piece of Egyptian ritual furniture where the sacred space was above the piece of furniture and exposed to the open was the palanquin throne. Palanquin thrones dating to Ramesses II had dual winged goddesses protecting the space in the throne.

The ark's deconstruction and the dating of its symbols suggest the ark was made no earlier than the reign of King Amenhotep III (ca. 1389–1351 BC) and no later than the end of Dynasty 20 (ca. 1073 BC). During the reign of Amenhotep III, winged goddesses surrounding a god first appear in the archaeological record. It is also the period when the palanquin throne first manifests with its sacred space exposed to the open. We also find statues on the lids of certain chests as early as the reign of King Tutankhamun (ca. 1334–1324 BC). The use of palanquin thrones declines toward the end of Dynasty 20 (ca. 1194–1073 BC), indicating a "latest date" limit (*terminus ante quem*) for the ark. The granularity and dating of this visual language suggest that, if the ark had been created even fifty years before the earliest appearance of this iconography, the message of God's identity would have been indecipherable even to the people who lived with it. It would be like sending a flash drive memory stick back in time to Winston Churchill.

Moreover, the ark was a miniaturized portable temple analogically recreating sanctified sacred space. The ark had the characteristics of a shrine, a coffin, a reliquary, and a throne, reflecting the same sort of deconstruction undergone by its Egyptian counterparts. The fact is that, as a chest, the ark was less chest-like. As a shrine, the ark became less shrine-like. As a coffin, the ark was less coffin-like. As it became more and more like other things, the ark also became less of any one thing. The ark is an ideal fit as ritual processional furniture and follows an Egyptian design pattern. Was the ark a barque, a coffin, a chest, a reliquary, or a throne? Yes, and so much more.

Compared to the wonders of Egyptian ritual furniture, the ark was relatively simple. While myth and legend have inflated the grandeur of the ark, we have to keep in mind, when it comes to the difficulty level of the ark's construction, it falls midway in the spectrum of Egyptian furniture. The ark was more complex than a bed, palanquin, or chest, but less complex than a barque, and about the same technical difficulty as an Anubis chest. Any reasonably competent Late Bronze Age Egyptian craftsman would have had the skill to build an artifact like the ark with only rudimentary tools and supplies. Thus, a craftsman having the plunder of Egypt available with the Sinai's acacia trees would have had all he needed to set up a basic workshop, make his tools, and build the ark.

And once the ark transferred the shekinah glory to the Holy of Holies in the Solomonic temple and the artifacts carried with the reliquary found their new home, the ark's purpose was fulfilled. Afterwards, the ark continued to represent God's presence and to receive the blood on the Day of Atonement to cover over the penalties of breaking the law contained on the tablets within the ark, until finally the Solomonic Temple and the ark ceased to be. "They will no longer say, 'The ark of the covenant of the LORD.' And it will not come to mind, nor will they remember it, nor will they miss it, nor will it be made again" (Jer 3:16). With the message of the ark delivered, the old order of things passed away. But the real treasure of the ark has never been in its gold, wood, or artistic merit. The treasure of the ark resided in the God who met humanity above the cherubim, who moved with the ark in holy space, and who set the stage for something greater.

# Epilogue: Where Is the Ark Today?

Probably the most common question that I get is, "Where is the ark today?" Or the similar questions: "Is the ark in Ethiopia?" and "Wasn't the ark found under the Temple Mount?" The book that you (hopefully) just read shows that the ark is important because of what it meant to people in the past. And I hope that what you have learned gives you confidence in the historical nature of the ark's story.

But for a handful of people, encounters with snakes spitting fire, entrapped demons, and gods wandering the land are simply not enough. Ignited by the fantasies of other writers on the subject, some readers will still want to know where the ark is today. I have intentionally not made this topic a part of the book because the answer will likely disappoint those readers.

The last recorded sighting of the ark was during the reign of King Josiah (2 Chr 35:3). This means that the ark was not whisked away to Ethiopia during the reign of Solomon. The story of the ark being in Ethiopia was concocted in the thirteenth century AD to prop up Aksum's (modern Ethiopia) failing monarchy and includes an anachronistic mishmash of famous figures that interact with no respect to real history.

This also excludes the possibility that the ark was taken by King Shoshenq I when he came up against Jerusalem (2 Chr 12:9). Even though he took the treasures of the house of the Lord and the palace, these seem to be a ransom preventing an Egyptian conquest of Jerusalem, as opposed to an actual conquest. And the ark's attestation during the reign of Josiah seems to indicate that Rehoboam held the ark back from being handed over to Shoshenq I three hundred years earlier.

When Egyptian King Neco II (610–595 BC) marched through Israel to help his ally King Ashur-Uballit II (612–605 BC) of Assyria, Josiah tried to interfere in regional politics. He tried to stop Neco II from getting to the Battle of Charchemish. Josiah was killed by Neco II's men, and the Egyptians continued to Charchemish. After the battle, which resulted in the defeat of the combined Assyrian and Egyptian armies at the hands of Nebuchadnezzar II (605–562 BC) of Babylon, Neco II exacted payback on the kingdom of Judah. The Egyptians deposed Josiah's successor, Joahaz, and made Eliakim (Jehoiakim) king over Judah and Jerusalem (2 Chr 36:4). The king of Egypt also imposed a fine of one hundred talents of silver and one talent of gold (2 Chr 36:3). It is unlikely that the one talent of gold included the ark since the gold of the ark probably easily exceeded one talent (33 kg) of gold.[1]

Furthermore, the prophet Jeremiah tells us that the ark "will not come to mind, nor will they remember it, nor will they miss it, nor will it be made again" (Jer 3:16), which indicates that the ark was either permanently lost or destroyed. If the ark makes a visible return, then it would "come to mind" and be remembered again, contradicting these words of Jeremiah. Josiah died in 610/609 BC. Jeremiah lived between 650 and 570 BC. Nebuchadnezzar II invaded and destroyed Jerusalem in 587/586 BC.

This means that the ark was most likely taken back to Babylon by Nebuchadnezzar II where it was destroyed. The Bible states that Nebuchadnezzar II burned the temple and destroyed "all its valuable articles" (2 Chr 36:19). This means that the most valuable items were destroyed first. Unlike the Egyptian army, the Babylonians paid their soldiers in gold. And funding an army the size of Babylon's created a situation where the royal house was continuously cash strapped and gold poor. The Bablyonians stole whatever gold they could and melted it down.

When the Babylonians destroyed the Solomonic temple, they broke apart and destroyed the bronze pillars, stands, and bronze sea (2 Kgs 25:13). When King Cyrus II (559–530 BC) of Persia returned what remained of the temple vessels, the inventory included both original and duplicated items (Ezra 1:9–10). Essentially, Cyrus II restored some of what had been destroyed to begin temple service again, but not everything was restored as it had been before. Large items like the bronze pillars, bronze sea, and the ark were not replaced.

In the case of large religious furniture like sacred barques and the ark, the Babylonians burned these pieces in large furnaces. The Babylonians routinely melted down royal gifts for their precious metal content.[2] After the furnace cooled, the gold was swept up after all the wood was burned away. This is what became of most Egyptian sacred furniture after the Assyrians ransacked Egypt.

The ark and what remained of the temple furniture was possibly burned in the same kind of furnace that is used in the attempted execution of Shadrach, Meshach, and Abed-nego (Dan 3:20). The destruction of gold-covered furniture for metal recovery gives us a practical reason for a furnace large enough for a man to stand in (Dan 3:25).

Thus, the ark was most likely burned for its gold and the recovered metal was weighed out and distributed to soldiers, who exchanged it for food, drink, and the necessities of life. Over millennia, this metal was remelted and the gold repurposed. Some gold was made into jewelry. Some of that gold has been used in electronics. Where is the ark today? A small piece of it may be on your finger.

# Notes

## Chapter 1

1. Kathryn A. Bard and Rodolfo Fattovich, *Seafaring Expeditions to Punt in the Middle Kingdom: Excavations at Mersa/Wadi Gawasis, Egypt* (Leiden: Brill, 2018), 194.

2. They translated *ἱλαστήριον*, "expiation/propitiation," as the German *Gnadenstuhl*, "mercy seat."

3. *HALOT*, 4:1678.

4. *HALOT*, 1:85.

5. CAD 1.2:231.

6. James E. Hoch, *Semitic Words in Egyptian Texts of the New Kingdom and Third Intermediate Period* (Princeton: Princeton University Press, 1994), 86.

7. Kenneth A. Kitchen and Paul J. N. Lawrence, *Treaty, Law and Covenant in the Ancient Near East*, pt. 3 (Wiesbaden: Harrassowitz, 2012), 262.

8. The term "Asiatic" is a description of region of origin that includes the widest possible region of the Asian portion of the Near East and includes remote areas including Turkey (Asia Minor) and Elam. A narrower term, "Levantine," refers to people from Syria, Israel, Jordan, Lebanon, and broadly includes Turkey, Iraq, and Egypt. The Egyptians referred to the people groups who lived from the Sinai eastward collectively as *áam*, "Asiatics."

9. *P. Chester Beatty III, "The Dream Book."*

10. The use of "seventy sons" is a reference to Jacob's entire clan and includes all males (sons and grandsons) in a direct line of decent.

11. *KRI* 6:257, line 9.

12. David A. Falk, "Brick by Brick: What Did the Israelites Build in Egypt?" *Biblical Archaeology Review* 46 (2020): 54–57.

13. Karin Kopetzky and Manfred Bietak, "A Seal Impression of the Green Jasper Workshop from Tell el-Dabˁa," *Ägypten und Levante* 26 (2016): 357–75.

14. "Great House" is the literal translation of *pharaoh.*

15. This kind of didactic exchange between a teacher and student frequently appears in Egyptian literature (e.g., *The Book of Thoth*). Thus, we could expect exchanges like the one demonstrated here to be quite common. Discussions like this are part of the Egyptian cultural heritage, and the author has even participated in a few of these during his travels in Egypt.

16. The Egyptian month was thirty days. Each month had three weeks of ten days. The typical worker labored nine and a half days and received a half day off. The seven-day week was not invented until after the Israelites left Egypt.

17. Trading worthless promissory notes was a common practice in workmens' villages like Deir el-Medina. People in these villages knowingly traded in worthless promissory notes as a fiction that maintained community continuity and as a way to keep track of who owed what to whom.

18. For example, in the 1970s J. J. Bimson painted William F. Albright as having invented the late exodus view while advocating strongly for an early dating tradition (J. J. Bimson, *Redating the Exodus and*

*Conquest*, 2nd ed. [Sheffield: Almond Press, 1981], 15, 74). Bryant Wood also said, "With new discoveries and additional analysis, the arguments for a 13th-century exodus-conquest have steadily eroded since the death of its founder and main proponent William F. Albright in 1971" (Bryant G. Wood, "The Rise and Fall of the 13th-Century Exodus-Conquest Theory," *JETS* 48 [2005]: 489). Yet, James Orr in 1906 calls the late view the "Rameses-Merneptah Theory" (James Orr, *The Problem of the Old Testament: considered with reference to recent history* [New York:Scribner's Sons, 1906], 422).

19. Jewish Chronicle, "The Date of the Exodus," *Littell's Living Age* 195:2518 (1892), 64; L. Ideler, *Handbuch der mathematischen und technischen Chronologie*, vol. 1 (Berlin, 1825), 569–80.

20. C. R. Lepsius, *Letters from Egypt, Ethiopia, and the Peninsula of Sinai: with extracts from the chronology of the Egyptians, with reference to the Exodus of the Israelites*, trans. L. Horner and J. B. Horner (London, 1853), 449–51, 456.

21. "Piramesses" comes from the Egyptian *per-ramessu,* "House of Ramesses." This is the same as the "Rameses" mentioned in the Bible. Hebrew has the tendency to drop the *pi/per,* "house of" at the beginning of place names since the prefix was common and often understood. This is why the biblical text also refers to Pithom as "Etham." Etham (Exod 13:20; Num 33:6–8) is *per-tem*, "Pithom," with the prefix dropped, leaving *tem*, "Etham."

22. Rob Iliffe, "Biblical Chronology," in *Encyclopedia of the Scientific Revolution from Copernicus to Newton*, ed. W. Applebaum (New York: Garland, 2000), 134.

23. A. O'Connor, *Finding Time for the Old Stone Age: A History of Palaeolithic Archaeology and Quaternary Geology in Britain, 1860–1960* (Oxford: Oxford University Press, 2007), 1–2.

24. P. Bahn, "The Antiquity of Man," in *Archaeology: The Key Concepts*, ed. C. Renfrew and P. Bahn (New York: Routledge, 2005), 7–8. Year 1 of the Julian calendar is 4713 BC. So, year 710 of the Julian calendar is 4713–710 which equals 4004 BC.

25. Orr, *Problem of the Old Testament*, 422.

26. Ibid., 424. Orr knew that he was breaking from tradition when he said that his view of the exodus date was a "new hypothesis." J. W. Jack in 1925 also recognized the late date as the "traditional school" and his own theory as the nontraditional position (L. E. Binns, review of *The Date of the Exodus,* by J. W. Jack, *Theology* 13 [1926]: 175).

27. Orr, *Problem of the Old Testament*, 422–23.

28. E.g., Charles F. Aling, "The Biblical City of Ramses," *JETS* 25 (1982): 129–37.

29. EA 6; EA 7–8,10–11,14; EA 9; EA 1–3 and 5; and EA 15.

30. EA 148, 227, 228, 364.

31. Israel Finkelstein and Neil Asher Silberman, *The Bible Unearthed: Archaeology's New Vision of Ancient Israel and the Origin of Its Sacred Texts* (New York: Free Press, 2001), 90.

32. Manfred Bietak, Nicola Math, and Vera Müller, "Report on the excavations of a Hyksos Palace of Tell el Dabᶜa/Avaris," *Ägypten und Levante* 22/23 (2013): 45.

33. Manfred Bietak, "Harbours and Coastal Military Bases in Egypt in the Second Millennium B.C.: Avaris, Peru-nefer, Pi-Ramesse," in *The Nile: Natural and Cultural Landscape in Egypt*, ed. Harco Willems and Jan-Michael Dahms (Bielfeld: Transcript Verlag, 2017), 63.

34. D. A. Carson, *Exegetical Fallacies* (Grand Rapids: Baker Books, 1984), 45–47.

35. Grant R. Osborne, *The Hermeneutical Spiral: A Comprehensive Introduction to Biblical Interpretation* (Downers Grove, IL: InterVarsity Press, 1991), 72–73.

36. Wood, "Rise and Fall," 486.

37. Umberto Cassuto, *The Documentary Hypothesis and the Composition of the Pentateuch* (Jerusalem: Magnes, 1961), 52. "When the Bible gives us technical or statistical data and the like, it *frequently prefers* the ascending order, since the tendency to exactness in these instances causes the smaller numbers to be given precedence and prominence." [emphasis mine] When Cassuto is quoted, the words "frequently prefers" are often omitted because these words completely change the nature of his argument. "Frequently prefers" means that something has a preference, but a preference is not the same as "always." If I "frequently prefer" to eat vanilla ice cream, this does not mean that I never eat any other kind of ice cream.

Although Cassuto's words are sometimes construed as meaning that numbers in ascending order are "always" meant to be read literally, his argument actually is: if the Bible gives technical data, then the number is sometimes represented in ascending order; the Bible gives technical data; therefore, some numbers in ascending order are technical data.

Some rephrase the argument as: "He [Cassuto] discovered that when a number is written in ascending order . . . the number is intended to be a technically precise figure . . ." (Wood, "Rise and Fall," 486). This changes Cassuto's argument by affirming the consequent, which compounds a logical fallacy upon a "one-meaning" exegetical fallacy. It is the equivalent of the fallacious argument: If X is a dog, then X is an animal; X is an animal; therefore, X is a dog—but what if X were a cat?

38. Umberto Cassuto, *Biblical and Oriental Studies* (Jerusalem: Magnes; Hebrew University, 1973), 1:36.

39. Julian Reade, "Assyrian King-Lists, the Royal Tombs of Ur, and Indus Origins," *JNES* 60 (2001): 3–4.

40. Nebti would have been a Hyksos king because (a) archaeological context (that is, this temple and stela were located at Avaris), (b) Nebti was not in the line of late Dynasty 13 Theban kings, and (c) Nebti's name contained the hieroglyph for the god Seth. The Ramessides venerated Seth because their seat of power was at Avaris. But prior to Dynasty 19, Seth worship was not a practice of the Theban kings. During the late Middle Kingdom and Second Intermediate Period, Seth worship was associated with the Canaanite god Baal and was restricted to areas under Levantine influence.

41. *COS* 2:137.

42. Edwin R. Thiele, *The Mysterious Numbers of the Hebrew Kings*, 2nd ed. (Exeter: Paternoster, 1965), 24–25; see also Kenneth A. Kitchen, *On the Reliability of the Old Testament* (Grand Rapids: Eerdmans, 2003), 181–83. Even though the Bible ascribes twelve years to Omri's reign, the text also states that Omri became king during the 31st year of Asa, king of Judah (1 Kgs 16:23) and died in Asa's 38th year (1 Kgs 16:29). So the twelve years attributed to Omri may have included years when he had not secured dominion over his kingdom or perhaps was an application of the sacred figure "12," similar to how the Moabites used "40" in this context.

43. Thiele, *Mysterious Numbers*, 198–99.

44. Irene Forstner-Müller, Tomasz Herbich, Christian Schweitzer, and Michael Weissl, "Preliminary Report on the Geophysical Survey at Tell el-Dabᶜa/Qantir in Spring 2008," *Ägypten und Levante* 18 (2008): 97–99.

45. Slawomir Rzepka, Mustafa Nour el-Din, Anna Wodzińska, and Łukasz Jarmużek, "Egyptian Mission Rescue Excavations in Tell el-Retabah. Part I: New Kingdom Remains," *Ägypten und Levante* 22/23 (2013): 273. PM IV, 53; W. M. Flinders Petrie, *Hyksos and Israelite Cities* (London: Bernard Quaritch, 1906), 28.

46. *Papyrus Anastasi V*, 20, lines 2–3 (Ricardo A. Caminos, *Late-Egyptian Miscellanies* [London: Oxford University Press, 1954], 255, 258).

47. *Treaty of Ramesses II with Hattusil III* (*KRI* 2:227, line 9).

48. KBo 1.10 + KUB 3.72 (*COS* 3.31:52).

49. Kristina Josephson Hesse, *Contacts and Trade at Late Bronze Age Hazor*, Archaeology and Environment 24 (Umeå, Sweden: Umeå University, 2008), 229–31.

50. Kathleen M. Kenyon, *Excavations at Jericho* (London: British School of Archaeology in Jerusalem, 1981), 3:17.

51. Aidan Dodson and Dyan Hilton, *The Complete Royal Families of Ancient Egypt* (London: Thames & Hudson, 2004), 170, 173. Amenhirkopshef is last attested in Ramesses II's twentieth regnal year, and Ramesses II's second son, Ramesses, ruled as crown prince from around the twenty-fifth to the fiftieth regnal years. This places the death of Amenhirkopshef between ca. 1269 and 1262 BC.

52. Christopher Partridge, *Re-Enchantment of the West: Alternative Spiritualities, Sacralization, Popular Culture and Occulture* (London: T&T Clark International, 2005), 1:84–85.

# Chapter 2

1. "What do National Lottery winners spend their money on?" *The Guardian Datablog*, www.theguardian.com/news/datablog/2012/oct/22/national-lottery-winners-spend-money.

2. Jac. J. Janssen, *Commodity Prices from the Ramessid Period: An Economic Study of the Village of the Necropolis Workmen at Thebes* (Leiden: Brill, 1975), 101.

3. Ibid., 178.

4. Ibid., 109.

5. Ibid., 107.

6. *O. Varille 25* (Janssen, *Commodity Prices*, 106, 337).

7. J. Lowell Lewis, *The Anthropology of Cultural Performance* (New York: Palgrave Macmillan, 2013), 60; William W. McCorkle, *Ritualizing the Disposal of the Deceased: From Corpse to Concept* (New York: Lang, 2010), 7.

8. Sherif El-Sabban, *Temple Festival Calendars of Ancient Egypt* (Liverpool: Liverpool University Press, 2000), 57–58.

9. Robert Kriech Ritner, *The Mechanics of Ancient Egyptian Magical Practice,* 4th ed. (Chicago: University of Chicago Press, 1993), 35, 38.

10. David A. Falk, "The Significance of the Horns (קֶרֶן) of Exodus 27:2: the Egyptian (*ṯst*) and Levantine Four-Horned Altars," in *Did I Not Bring Israel Out of Egypt? Biblical, Archaeological, and Egyptological Perspectives on the Exodus Narratives*, ed. James Karl Hoffmeier, Alan Millard, and Gary Rendsburg (Winona Lake, IN: Eisenbrauns, 2016), 75.

11. Even though the Bible never claims that it is unreasonable to worship the sun, it does make the case that the sun is nothing compared to the glory and power of the God who created the sun (Gen 1:16) and is therefore a detestable thing (Ezek 8:16).

12. A. Egberts, *In Quest of Meaning: A Study of the Ancient Egyptian Rites of Consecrating the Meret-Chests and Driving the Calves* (Leiden: Nederlands Instituut voor het Nabije Oosten, 1995), 1:53.

13. A. S. Hornby, ed., *Oxford Advanced Learner's Dictionary of Current English*, 7th ed. (Oxford: Oxford University Press, 2005), 632.

14. Richard H. Wilkinson, "The Coronational Circuit of the Walls, the Circuit of the *hnw* Barque and the Heb-sed 'Race' in Egyptian Kingship Ideology," *JSSEA* 15 (1985): 45–51.

15. For example, the workshop scene of goldsmiths creating chests and grave goods from the Mastaba of Mereruka, Saqqara (Chamber A3, east wall, scene 2). Prentice Duell, *The Mastaba of Mereruka*, pt. 1 (Chicago: University of Chicago Press, 1938), pl. 30.

16. Herbert E. Winlock, *The Treasure of El Lāhūn* (New York: Metropolitan Museum of Art, 1934), pl. I and pp. 12–22.

17. George Andrew Reisner, *A History of the Giza Necropolis* (Cambridge: Harvard University Press, 1955), 2:16, 23–27, and figs. 28–29.

18. Reisner, *History of the Giza Necropolis*, 2:17–18, 21, 36–40, 43–44 and figs. 38–40, 44.

19. Richard E. Averbeck, "Myth, Ritual, and Order in 'Enki and the World Order,'" *Journal of the American Oriental Society* 123 (2003): 758.

20. Ibid., 767.

21. Saqarrah tomb S.2405 [A3]. J. E. Quibell, *Excavations at Saqqara (1911–12)* (Cairo: L'Institut Français D'Archeologie Orientale, 1913), pl. XVI.

22. Mastaba of Nufer (LG 99), Giza Necropolis (Selim Hassan, *Excavations at Giza*, vol. 3 [Cairo: Government Press, 1941], fig. 175).

23. Commission des sciences et arts d'Egypte, *Description de L'Égypte ou recueil des observations et des recherches qui ont ete faites en Égypte pendant l'expédition de l'armée française*, 2nd ed., vol. 1 (Paris, 1820), pl. 19 [2].

24. N. de Garis Davies, *The Mastaba of Ptahhetep and Akhethetep at Saqqarah*, pt. 2 (London: Egypt Exploration Fund, 1901), pl. viii.

25. Reinhard Grieshammer, "Reinheit, kultische," in *Lexikon der Ägyptologie*, vol. 5, ed. Wolfgang Helck and Eberhard Otto (Weisbaden: Harrassowitz, 1984), 213.

26. Reisner, *History of the Giza Necropolis*, 2:20. Five large chests holding linens were placed against the south wall of the Tomb of Hetepheres (G 7000 X), Giza Necropolis. Markings left by these boxes on the floor of the tomb as the wood decayed indicate their dimensions. A large box 90 x 59 cm supported a second box 58 x 43 cm. A third box measured 50 x 70 cm, a fourth 60 x 90 cm, and a fifth 40 x 120 cm. Pottery was found among the decayed linen inside the boxes.

27. Hermann Junker, *Bericht über die von der Akademie der Wissenschaften in Wien auf gemainsame Kosten mit Dr. Wilhelm Pelizaeus unternommenen Grabungen auf dem Friedhof des Alten Reiches bei den Pyramiden von Gîza*, vol. 5 (Leipzig: Hölder-Pichler-Tempsky, 1941), pl. VIII [b-c].

28. A. T. Sandison and Edmund Tapp, "Disease in ancient Egypt," in *Mummies, Disease and Ancient Cultures*, ed. Thomas Aidan Cockburn, Eve Cockburn, and Theodore A. Reyman (Cambridge: Cambridge University Press, 1998), 39.

29. Mircea Eliade suggested that the manifestation of the sacred transforms an object or space into something fit to participate in the cosmic drama transmuting the mundane into a "supernatural reality" (*The Sacred and the Profane: The Nature of Religion*, trans. Willard R. Trask [New York: Harcourt, Brace & World, 1959], 12). Susan Guettel Cole maintained that sacred space is created through the induction of a new community or ritual but "had to be formally allocated for sacred precincts, altars, and temples" and involved the replication of sacred objects (*Landscapes, Gender, and Ritual Space: The Ancient Greek Experience* [London: University of California Press, 2004], 39). Ronald L. Grimes recognized the dichotomy between ascribed emic meaning and the scholarly inclination to not see beyond materialism ("Ritual, performance, and the sequestering of sacred space," in *Discourse in Ritual Studies*, ed. Hans Schilderman [Leiden: Brill, 2007], 152–53). Conversely, David Weir thought that sacred space is a "human universal" that necessitates a "sacred" and a "profane" dichotomy ("Liminality, Sacred Space and the Diwan," in *Sacred Space: Interdisciplinary Perspectives within Contemporary Contexts*, ed. Steven Brie, Jenny Daggers, and David Torevell [Newcastle upon Tyne: Cambridge Scholars Publishing, 2009], 39).

30. John Baines, "Temple Symbolism," *Royal Anthropological Institute Newsletter* 15 (1976): 10.

31. Jan Assmann, "The Ramesside tomb and the construction of sacred space," in *The Theban Necropolis: Past, Present and Future*, ed. Nigel Strudwick and John H. Taylor (London: British Museum Press, 2003), 47–48.

32. Miriam Lichtheim, *Ancient Egyptian Literature* (Berkeley: University of California Press, 1973), 1:16. From the Fifth Dynasty tomb of Hetep-Her-Akhet, "I made this tomb on the west side in a pure place, in which there was no tomb of anyone, in order to protect the possession of one who has gone to his *ka*. As for any people who would enter this tomb unclean and do something evil to it, there will be judgment against them by the great god."

33. Émile Chassinat, *Edfou*, vol. 5 (Cairo: Institut Français d'Archéologie Orientale, 1930), 334, lines 1–6. "He who leads initiates wrongfully, [he who enters] when unclean, he who speaks falsehood in your house, he who knows right from wrong, he who is pure . . . I write down good for the one who acts justly in your city. I reject the character of the evildoer."

34. Kasia Szpakowska, "Demons of Ancient Egypt," *Religion Compass* 3 (2009): 801–2.

35. Roland De Buck, "On the meaning of the name *ḥꜥpj*," in *Orientalia Neerlandica: A Volume of Oriental Studies* (Leiden: A. W. Sijthoff's Uitgeversmaatschappij N. V., 1948), 13.

36. Denise M. Doxey, *Egyptian Non-Royal Epithets in the Middle Kingdom: A Social and Historical Analysis* (Leiden: Brill, 1998), 27.

37. Marek Marciniak, "Un successeur contemporain de la frise de *khekerou*?" *Mélanges Gamal Eddin Mokhtar* (Cairo: L'Institut Français D'Archéologie Orientale, 1985), 2:110.

38. Ritner, *Mechanics of Ancient Egyptian Magical Practice*, 224.

39. Sally Johnson, "Uraeus statuettes," in *Mummies & Magic: The Funerary Arts of Ancient Egypt*, ed. Sue D'Auria, Peter Lacovara, and Catharine H. Roehrig (Dallas: Dallas Museum of Art, 1992), 144.

40. Norman de Garis Davies and Alan H. Gardiner, eds., *Tombs of Menkheperrasonb, Amenmosě, and Another* (London: Egypt Exploration Society, 1933), pl. 41.

41. Alix Wilkinson, "Symbolism and Design in Ancient Egyptian Gardens," *Garden History* 22 (1994): 2.

42. Anna Stevens, "The Material Evidence for Domestic Religion at Amarna and Preliminary Remarks on Its Interpretation," *JEA* 83 (2003): 163.

43. D'Auria, Lacovara, and Roehrig, *Mummies & Magic*, pl. VII.

44. Egyptian Museum, Temp. 21.11.16.12.

45. John H. Taylor, "Patterns of colouring on ancient Egyptian coffins from the New Kingdom to the Twenty-sixth Dynasty: an overview," in *Colour and Painting in Ancient Egypt,* ed. W. V. Davies (London: British Museum Press, 2001), 164. Note here that the term "resurrecting" is the concept that the dead follow a daily cycle of inhabiting and departing a tomb and is not intended to convey the Judeo-Christian concept of the resurrection of the body.

46. Catharine H. Roehrig, "Tomb group of Henettawy," in D'Auria, Lacovara, and Roehrig, *Mummies & Magic*, 163.

47. J. Vandier, *Manuel d'archéologie égyptienne*, vol. 5 (Paris: A. et J. Picard, 1969), fig. 299.

48. PT 534 (Sethe 1267–1273).

49. Byron E. Shafer, "Temples, Priests, and Rituals: An Overview," in *Temples of Ancient Egypt*, ed. Byron E. Shafer (London: Taurus Publishers, 1997), 24.

50. PT 256 (Sethe 302).

# Chapter 3

1. *O. Petrie 15* (*Hier. Ostr.* pl. 26, ill. 5, line 1).

2. Alan Millard, "The Babylonian Flood Story—A new tablet and an old one misinterpreted," *Faith & Thought* 60 (2016): 28.

3. *Urk*. II, 5, line 16.

4. *CD*, 397.

5. *O. Turin N. 57366* (*=suppl. 9592*) rt 3 (Jesús López, *Ostraca ieratici, n. 57320–57449* [Milan: Istituto Cisalpino la Goliardica, 1982], pl. 113).

6. Jac. J. Janssen, *Furniture at Deir el-Medîna including Wooden Containers of the New Kingdom and Ostracon Varille 19* (London: Golden House Publications, 2009), 49.

7. Carter no. 001k. Jaroslav Černý, *Hieratic Inscriptions from the Tomb of Tutʿankhamūn* (Oxford: Griffith Institute, 1965), 8.

8. *O. Gardiner 119* (*Hier. Ostr.* pl. 33, ill. 3, line 2).

9. *O. Berlin P 12343* vs 2–3 (*KRI* 6:165, line 2).

10. Margaret A. Murray, *Saqqara Mastabas*, pt. 1 (London: Bernard Quartich, 1905), pl. II.

11. *CG 01391* (Ludwig Borchardt, *Denkmäler des Alten Reiches*, pt. 1 [Berlin: Reichsdruckerei, 1937], 52).

12. *P. Ramasseum E*, 9 (Roberto A. Díaz Hernández, "Der Ramesseumpapyrus E, Ein Ritualbuch für Bestattungen aus dem Mittleren Reich," *GM* Beihefte Nr. 15 [2014]: 22). Alan H. Gardiner, "A Unique Funerary Liturgy," *JEA* 41 (1955): 9, 11, and pl. II, col. 9.

13. *P. Geneva D191* vs 3 (Jaroslav Černý, *Late Ramesside Letters* [Brussels: Fondation Égyptologique Reine Élisabeth, 1939], 58, lines 12–13).

14. Janssen, *Furniture at Deir el-Medîna*, 34.

15. *O. BM 5631* (*Hier. Ostr.* pl. 88, line 3).

16. *O. Gardiner 33* (*Hier. Ostr.* pl. 18, ill. 3, line 5).

17. *Hier. Ostr.* pl. 18, ill. 3, line 4.

18. *Urk*. IV, 705, lines 10–15.

19. *P. Anastasi IIIA*, 7–8 (*LEM* 33, lines 10–12).

20. *P. Anastasi IV*, 16, lines 6–7 (*LEM* 53, lines 1–3).

21. *WÄS* V, 153, line 9, "box (with a lid)."
22. Janssen, *Commodity Prices*, 198.
23. *P. Mayer B* (*KRI* 6:516, lines 11–12).
24. *O. Gardiner 44* (*Hier. Ostr.* pl. 24, ill. 1, line 3).
25. *O. Gardiner 44,* lines 2–4.
26. *O. Gardiner 44,* line 5.
27. *O. Petrie 48* (*Hier. Ostr.* pl. 31, line 4).
28. *O. Petrie 48*, lines 9–10.
29. *Naunakhte III* rt 12 and vs 11 (Jaroslav Černý, "The Will of Naunakhte and the Related Documents," *JEA* 31 [1945]: pl. XIa rt 12 and vs 11).
30. *Naunakhte II* rt 11(Černý, "Will of Naunakhte," pl. X rt 11); *Naunakhte III* vs 11 (Černý, "The Will of Naunakhte," pl. XIa vs 11).
31. Junker, *Grabungen auf dem Friedhof des Alten Reiches bei den Pyramiden von Gîza*, vol. 5, 121–22 and pl. VIII [b-c].
32. *P. Harris I,* 13b, line 10 (W. Erichsen, *Papyrus Harris I: Hieroglyphische Transkription* [Brussels: Édition de le Fondation Égyptologique, 1933], 17, lines 12–13).
33. *P. Harris I,* 71a, line 4 (Erichsen, *Papyrus Harris I*, 85, line 10).
34. George R. Hughes, ed., *Medinet Habu*, vol. 5 (Chicago: University of Chicago Press, 1957), pl. 333.
35. Carter no. 14b. Burton photo no. 0074.
36. Quibell, *Excavations at Saqqara (1911–12)*, pl. XVIII.
37. Carter no. 403. Burton photo no. 1307.
38. Raymond O. Faulkner, *A Concise Dictionary of Middle Egyptian* (Oxford: Griffith Institute, 1962), 324.
39. Janssen, *Commodity Prices*, 197.
40. Murray, *Saqqara Mastabas*, pt. 1, pl. II.
41. *KRI* 6:165, line 2; *Hier. Ostr.* pl. 31, ill. 5, line 7; *Hier. Ostr.* pl. 36, ill. 1 recto, line 8.
42. *P. Turin 1887* rt 1, line 8 (*RAD*, 75, line 1).
43. *KRI* 7:382, line 9; *P. Harris I,* 13b, line 11 (Erichsen, *Papyrus Harris I*, 17, line 14).
44. *Hier. Ostr.* pl. 80, ill. recto, lines 1–2.
45. *KRI* 5:577, line 4.
46. *Hier. Ostr.* pl. 80, ill. recto, lines 2–3.
47. Edward Brovarski, "Inventory Offering Lists and the Nomenclature for Boxes and Chests in the Old Kingdom," in *Gold of Praise: Studies on Ancient Egypt in Honor of Edward F. Wente*, ed. Emily Teeter and John A. Larson (Chicago: University of Chicago Press, 1999), 32.
48. Gardiner, "Unique Funerary Liturgy," 13.
49. *WÄS* III, 350–51.
50. *P. Westcar*, 12, lines 4–5 (Aylward M. Blackman, *The Story of King Kheops and the Magicians: Transcribed from Papyrus Westcar (Berlin Papyrus 3033)* [Reading: J. V. Books, 1988], 16, lines 2–4).
51. Ritner, *Mechanics of Ancient Egyptian Magical Practice*, 143n637.
52. *UC 32179 (VI.10)* vs (Mark Collier and Stephen Quirke, *The UCL Lahun Papyri: Accounts* (Oxford: Archaeopress, 2006), 28, col. 2, line 6).
53. *UC 32179 (VI.10)* vs (Collier and Quirke, *The UCL Lahun Papyri*, 28, col. 2, lines 8–10).
54. Percy E. Newberry, *Beni Hasan*, pt. 1 (London, 1893), pl. XIII.
55. *P. Berlin 3027* vs 5, line 2 (Adolf Erman, *Zaubersprüche für Mutter und Kind aus dem Papyrus 3027 des Berliner Museums* [Berlin: Königlichen Akademie der Wissenschaften, 1901], 46, lines 5–6).
56. Ahmed M. Moussa and Hartwig Altenmüller, *Das Grab des Nianchchnum und Chnumhotep* (Mainz: von Zabern, 1977), pl. 16.
57. Heinrich Schäfer, *Principles of Egyptian Art*, trans. John Baines (Oxford: Griffith Institute, 1986), pl. 18.
58. N. de Garis Davies, *Mastaba of Ptahhetep and Akhethetep*, pt. 2, pl xxii. Two groups of men drag *setjet* chests. The caption reads *sekhepet setjet in ḥem-ka(u)*, "bringing of *setjet* chests by the ka-priests."

59. Egberts, *In Quest of Meaning*, 1:425.

60. W. M. Flinders Petrie, *Koptos* (London, 1896), pl. VI.2; Paul Barguet, "Tôd: Rapport de fouilles de la saison février-avril 1950," *BIFAO* 51 (1952): 90; PM II, 351 (35).

61. Cf. Harold Hayden Nelson, *The Wall Reliefs* (Chicago: University of Chicago Press, 1981), pl. 73; with Moussa and Altenmüller, pl. 16.

62. *O. Černý 20* (*KRI* 7:343–44).

63. Siegfried Schott, *Wall Scenes from the Mortuary Chapel of the Mayer Paser at Medinet Habu* (Chicago: University of Chicago Press, 1957), pl. 2.

64. E.g., Nelson, *Wall Reliefs*, pl. 73.

65. *P. Westcar*, 12, lines 4–5 (Blackman, *King Kheops and the Magicians*, 16, lines 2–4).

66. *P. Westcar*, 2, line 1 (Blackman, *King Kheops and the Magicians*, 1, line 11).

67. *WÄS* I, 566, line 15.

68. *P. Anastasi I*, 16, line 3 (Alan H. Gardiner, *Egyptian Hieratic Texts: Series I; Literary Texts of the New Kingdom*, pt. 1 [Leipzig: Hinrichs, 1911], 56, lines 2–3).

69. *P. Anastasi I*, 12, line 2 (Gardiner, *Egyptian Hieratic Texts*, 42, lines 6–7).

70. *P. Leyden 344*, 8, line 5 (Roland Enmarch, *The Dialogue of Ipuwer and the Lord of All* [Oxford: Griffith Institute, 2005], 41).

71. *Legend of Astarte*, 1x+12 (*LESt* 77, lines 9–10).

72. *CG 48862*, 33 (*Urk*. III, 18, lines 5–6).

73. *Urk*. IV, 630.

74. Murray, *Saqqara Mastabas*, pt. 1, pl. II.

75. *UC 16448* (Alan H. Gardiner, *Ancient Egyptian Onomastica* [London: Oxford University Press, 1947], pl. XXIII vs 4).

76. Hughes, *Medinet Habu,* vol. 5, pl. 325.

77. Reisner, *History of the Giza Necropolis*, 2:17–18, 43–44, pl. 37a, and Figs. 38 and 44.

78. Ibid., 2:17.

79. Hughes, *Medinet Habu*, vol. 5, pl. 333.

80. Carter no. 101. Burton photo no. 0137.

81. Howard Carter, excavation card 101–5 for Carter No. 101 (Oxford: Griffith Institute).

82. Hughes, *Medinet Habu*, vol. 5, pl. 325.

83. *Urk*. IV, 388, line 1.

84. *HALOT*, 2:369.

85. David A. Falk, "The products of Hatshepsut's trade mission to Punt: An alternative translation of the Punt reliefs at Deir el-Bahari," *GM* 238 (2013): 52.

86. *Urk*. I, 106, lines 14–17.

87. *Berlin 7306* (Günther Roeder, *Aegyptische Inschriften aus den Staatlichen Museen zu Berlin* [Leipzig: Hinrichs, 1924], 2:131 [C]).

88. Friedrich Wilhelm von Bissing, *Mastaba des Gem-Ni-Kai*, vol. 1 (Berlin: Duncker, 1905), 19, line 5 and pl. V.

89. F. L. Griffith and Percy E. Newberry, *El Bersheh*, pt. 2 (London, 1896), 44.

90. CT 21 (*ECT*, 1:62,c-d); Ritner, *Mechanics of Ancient Egyptian Magical Practice*, 83; Sue D'Auria, "Mummification in Ancient Egypt," in D'Auria, Lacovara, and Roehrig, *Mummies & Magic*, 15.

91. Jean Capart, *Une rue de tombeaux à Saqqarah* (Brussels: Vromant, 1907), pl. LXV.

92. Reisner, *History of the Giza Necropolis*, 2:48.

93. Hughes, *Medinet Habu*, vol. 5, pl. 325.

94. Schott photo 3906.

95. Tomb of Huya (Amarna Tomb 1), first room (N. de Garis Davies, *The Rock Tombs of El Amarna*, [London: Egypt Exploration Fund, 1905], pt. 3, pl. XIII).

96. Johannes Dümichen, *Geographische Inschriften altägyptischer Denkmäler*, pt. 4 (Leipzig, 1885), pl. CXXIV.

97. *WÄS* IV, 551, line 3.

98. Schott photo 3906.

99. Auguste Mariette, *Dendérah: description générale du grand temple de cette ville*, vol. 4 (Paris, 1873), pl. 37, line 66.

100. Amice M. Calverley, *The Temple of King Sethos I at Abydos*, vol. 3 (Chicago: University of Chicago Press, 1938), pl. 16.

101. Victor M. Loret, "La tombe de Khâ-m-hâ," *Mémoires publiés par les membres de la Mission archéologique française au Caire* (Paris, 1889), 1:123.

102. Ibid., 116.

103. Ibid., 124.

104. Ibid., 121. Loret records this determinative as the road sign (Gardiner Sign N31). The *Belegstellen* corrects this rendering as a variant of a chest determinative (*WÄS die Belegstellen*, vol. II, 746).

105. N. de Garis Davies, *Two Ramesside Tombs at Thebes* (New York: Metropolitan Museum of Art, 1927), pl. xviii.

106. Bernard Bruyère, *Rapport sur les fouilles de Deir el Médineh, 1924–1925* (Cairo: Imprimerie de L'Institut Français D'Archéologie Orientale, 1925), fig. 62.

107. Ibid., 93.

108. E.g., Reisner, *History of the Giza Necropolis*, 2:21–22, fig. 44[a]; and Jacques De Morgan, *Fouilles A Dahchour: Mars-Juin 1894*, vol. 1 (Vienna, 1895), fig. 54; Ambrose Lansing and William C. Hayes, "The Museum's Excavations at Thebes," *The Metropolitan Museum of Art Bulletin* 32 (1937): fig. 36.

109. Alexandre Barsanti and Gaston Maspero, "Saqqâra, Around Pyramid complex of Unis," *ASAE* 2 (1901): fig. 6–7.

110. PM I, 662. Egyptian Museum, Temp. 20.12.25.11.

111. Schott photo XIV, 55 a.

112. CT 24 (*ECT*, 1:74,h–i).

# Chapter 4

1. Shafer, "Temples, Priests, and Rituals," 4.

2. Kerry M. Muhlestein, "New Pyramid Structures and Conservation Techniques: The 2018 and 2019 Fag el-Gamous and Seila Pyramid seasons" (paper presented at the 70th Annual Meeting of the American Research Center in Egypt, Washington, DC, 12–14 April 2019). This information is expected to be publishing in Kerry Muhlestein, "Excavations at the Seila Pyramid and Ritual Ramifications" in *Excavations at Fag el-Gamous and the Seila Pyramid*, ed. Kerry Muhlestein, Bethany Jensen, and Krystal Pierce (Leiden: Brill, forthcoming). Special thanks to Dr. Muhlestein for providing me with this information in advance.

3. Mastaba of Seshemnefer III (G 5170), Giza Necropolis (ca. Djedkara) (Junker, *Grabungen auf dem Friedhof des Alten Reiches bei den Pyramiden von Gîza*, vol. 3, pl. IV).

4. W. M. Flinders Petrie, *Denderah* (London, 1898), pl. III.

5. Tomb of Khnumhotep III (Beni Hassan Tomb 3) (Newberry, *Beni Hasan*, pt. 1, pl. XXIX).

6. Sacrophagus of Kemsh, Deir el Bahari (ca. Mentuhotep II, Dynasty 11) (Edouard Naville, *The XI[th] Dynasty Temple at Deir el Bahari*, pt. 1 [London: Egypt Exploration Fund, 1907], pl. XXII).

7. Charles F. Nims, *Tomb of Kheruef: Theban Tomb 192* (Chicago: University of Chicago Press, 1980), pl. 34.

8. Carter no. 37. Burton photo no. 0302.

9. Carter no. 487. Burton photo no. 1706.

10. E.g., the canopic chest pictured on the *Stela of Merymery* (ca. Amenhotep III) (Marcelle Werbrouck, *Les pleureuses dans l'Égypte ancienne* [Brussels: Fondation Égyptologique Reine Élisabeth, 1938], pl. XXXVI).

11. Davies, *Rock Tombs of El Amarna*, pt. 3, pl. xxiv.

12. Auguste Mariette, *Abydos: description des fouilles*, vol. 2 (Paris, 1880), pl. 19[c].

13. Lansing and Hayes, "The Museum's Excavations at Thebes," fig. 36.

14. Dilwyn Jones, *Ancient Egyptian Boats* (London: Trustees of the British Museum Press, 1995), fig. 22 and pl. VII.

15. Aylard M. Blackman, "Notes on Certain Passages in Various Middle Egyptian Texts," *JEA* 16 (1930): 71.

16. PT 260 (Sethe 321b).

17. Faulkner, *Concise Dictionary*, 237; James Karl Hoffmeier, "Tents in Egypt and the Ancient Near East," *Society for the Study of Egyptian Antiquities Newsletter* 7 (1977): 17–19.

18. Thomas George Allen, *The Egyptian Book of the Dead: Documents in the Oriental Institute Museum at the University of Chicago* (Chicago: University of Chicago Press, 1960), 254.

19. Hoffmeier, "Tents in Egypt and the Ancient Near East," 19.

20. PT 184 (Sethe 219a–b).

21. PT 535 (Sethe 1287b–c).

22. CT 45 (*ECT*, 1:195g–196a).

23. *LESt* 41, lines 3–6.

24. *Urk*. IV, 664, line 7.

25. *Urk*. IV, 705, lines 13–14.

26. *P. Anastasi IV*, 11, line 11 (*LEM* 47, lines 9–10).

27. *CG 28086*, *CG 28092*; Pierre Lacau, "Textes religieux," *RecTrav* 27 (1905): 229, lines 41–44.

28. PT 627 (Sethe 1773c).

29. PT 255 (Sethe 300a).

30. PT 255 (Sethe 295).

31. PT 254 (Sethe 276).

32. *P. Leiden T 6* and *P. Louvre N 3092* (Edouard Naville, *Das aegyptische Todtenbuch der XVIII. bis XX. Dynastie*, vol. 2 [Berlin, 1886], ch. 130, line 6).

33. *P. Leiden T 6* and *P. Berlin 3002* (Naville, *Das aegyptische Todtenbuch*, ch. 130, line 7).

34. M. Eaton-Krauss and E. Graefe, *The Small Golden Shrine from the Tomb of Tutankhamun* (Oxford: Griffith Institute, 1985), 2n7.

35. *KRI* 1:42, line 5.

36. *Speos Artimidos Great Inscription*, 7 (*KRI* 1:42, lines 4–5).

37. Faulkner, *Concise Dictionary*, 48.

38. *P. Chester Beatty I* rt (= *P. BM 10681*), 3, line 10 (*LESt* 40, lines 14–15).

39. *P. Harris I,* 4, lines 10–11 (Erichsen, *Papyrus Harris I*, 5, lines 8–9).

40. *P. Harris I,* 6, line 4 (Erichsen, *Papyrus Harris I*, 7, line 4).

41. *P. Harris I,* 45, lines 7–8 (Erichsen, *Papyrus Harris I*, 50, lines 16–17).

42. Mariette, *Dendérah*, vol. 4, pl. 10.

43. This is equal to Staircase Y' of Mariette. PM VI, 26.

44. Mariette, *Abydos*, vol. 1, pl. 50b, line 23. Because of the poor preservation of the staircase texts (Katherine Eaton, "The Ritual Functions of Processional Equipment in the Temple of Seti I at Abydos." [PhD diss., New York University, 2004], 66), Mariette's text has not been superseded by a later edition.

45. *P. Harris I*, 58, line 2 (Erichsen, *Papyrus Harris I*, 67, line 4).

46. *Urk*. IV, 168, line 15.

47. Alan H. Gardiner, "Texts Relating to the Taxation and Transport of Corn," *JEA* 27 (1941): 29.

48. Ibid., 23.

49. *P. Turin 1895+2006*, rt 3, lines 4 and 7 (*RAD*, 38, lines 9 and 14).

50. *P. Turin 1895+2006*, rt 3, line 7 (*RAD*, 38, line 14).

51. Serge Sauneron, "L'hymne au soleil levant des papyrus de Berlin 3050, 3056 at 3048 [avec 1 planche]," *BIFAO* 53 (1953): 84 line II.2–3.

52. Calverley, *Temple of King Sethos I*, vol. 3, pl. 14.

53. Janssen, *Furniture at Deir el-Medîna*, 42.

54. *CG 25517* (Pierre Grandet, "Travaux, grèves et personnages célèbres aux XIXe et XXe dynasties, dans quelques ostraca documentaires de l'IFAO," in *Deir el-Médineh et la Vallée des Rois: La vie en Égypte au temps des pharaons du Nouvel Empire*, ed. Guillemette Andreu [Paris: Musée du Louvre, 2003], 214).

55. *CG 25584* (*KRI* 5:470, lines 4, 7, and 9).

56. *P. Nash 11* (= *O. BM. 65933*) (*Hier. Ostr.* pl. 72, line 2).

57. *O. Liverpool 13626* vs (*Hier. Ostr.* pl. 62, ill. 3 verso, line 3).

58. *P. BM 10054* rt (Thomas Eric Peet, *The Great Tomb-Robberies of the Twentieth Dynasty* [Oxford: Clarendon, 1930], 59).

59. Peet, *Great Tomb-Robberies*, pl. VII, ill. 3 ro, line 12.

60. *WÄS* III, 300, line 5; Jean Capart, "Une liste d'amulettes," *ZÄS* 45 (1908): 19, line 56.

61. *Urk.* IV, 248, line 1.

62. Faulkner, *Concise Dictionary*, 193; Gardiner, "Unique Funerary Liturgy," 13.

63. *Urk.* IV, 237, lines 8–9.

64. *Urk.* IV, 386, line 15.

65. *Urk.* IV, 617, line 15.

66. Eaton-Krauss and Graefe, *Small Golden Shrine*, 2n6.

# Chapter 5

1. Raymond O. Faulkner, *The Ancient Egyptian Coffin Texts* (Oxford: Aris & Phillips, 1977), 2:194.

2. Hierakonpolis may also have had a permanent temple architecture, a temple to Horus of Nekhen, that is earlier than Djoser's funerary temple. However, the excavation was so poorly done that little can be definitively said about the site.

3. E.g., Khnum and Kheper traveling upon mythological barques in the tomb of Ireahor (Lepsius Grave 23) in Saqqara (*LD*, 3:280c).

4. *WÄS* I, 271, line 15–272, line 2; *Urk.* IV, 2030, line 1.

5. *Urk.* IV, 304, line 17 and 307, line 15; Edouard Naville, *The Temple of Deir el Bahari*, vol. 4 (London: Egypt Exploration Fund, 1901), pl. LXXXIX and XCI.

6. See p. 33 for a discussion on the use of the terms *idealized* and *mythological* as used in this thesis.

7. *P. Chester Beatty I* rt (*LESt* 42, line 11).

8. *KRI* 1:48, line 14.

9. *KRI* 1:47, line 5.

10. *KRI* 2:636, lines 4–5.

11. Gardiner, *Ancient Egyptian Onomastica*, pl. XXIII vs 1–3.

12. *CG 20712*, 8.

13. *WÄS* I, 382, line 16–383, line 5.

14. PM III, 464.

15. *Urk.* I, 53, lines 6–7.

16. *Urk.* IV, 97, lines 12–13.

17. *Urk.* IV, 98, lines 1–2.

18. M. Georges Daressy, "Notes et remarques," *RecTrav* 16 (1894): 47, line 9.

19. *Berlin 1204*, 21–22 (Kurt Sethe, *Ägyptische Lesestücke zum Gebrauch im akademischen Unterricht: Texts des Mittleren Reiches* [Hildesheim: Olms, 1959], 71, lines 18–19).

20. Penelope Wilson, *A Ptolemaic Lexikon: A Lexicographical Study of the Texts in the Temple of Edfu* (Leuven: Peeters, 1997), 273.

21. For example, *WÄS* VI, 291, lines 11–13; and Kenneth A. Kitchen, *Ramesside Inscriptions: Translated & Annotated* (Malden, MA: Blackwell, 1993), 1:97.

22. Georges Legrain, "Le logement et transport des barques sacrées et des statues des dieux dans quelques temples égyptiens," *BIFAO* 13 (1917): 4–5.

23. *WÄS* IV, 285, line 7; *WÄS* III, 244, line 10; James Karl Hoffmeier, *Sacred in the Vocabulary of Ancient Egypt: The Term ḎSR, with special Reference to Dynasties I–XX* (Göttingen: Universitätsverlag Freiberg Schweiz; Göttingen: Vandenhoeck & Ruprecht, 1985), 204.

24. *P. Harris I*, 11, line 1. Perhaps, the symbol of the fan as it often held by priests in ritual procession became a symbol synonymous with holiness.

25. *KRI* 1:116, line 4.

26. *CG 00779* (*Urk.* IV, 1909, lines 6–7).

27. *KRI* 1:115, line 16.

28. *KRI* 1:207, line 16–208, line 2.

29. *KRI* 2:546, line 12.

30. *KRI* 2:628, line 6.

31. Auguste Mariette, *Karnak: étude topographique et archéologique* (Leipzig, 1875), pl. 42, line 14.

32. Ibid., pl. 42, line 19.

33. W. M. Flinders Petrie, *Naukratis*, vol. 1 (London, 1886), pl. XII.

34. G. A. Gaballa and Kenneth A. Kitchen, "The Festival of Sokar," *Orientalia* 38 (1969): 14–15.

35. Ibid., 11.

36. Harold Hayden Nelson, *Festival Scenes of Ramses III* (Chicago: University of Chicago Press, 1940), pl. 223.

37. Ibid., pl. 222.

38. Gaballa and Kitchen, "Festival of Sokar," fig. 3.

39. Nelson, *Festival Scenes*, pl. 226.

40. CT 21 (*ECT*, 1:63,b). This text mentions the masculine counterpart of the beer-goddess Tjenmyt.

41. Katherine Eaton, *Ancient Egyptian Temple Ritual: Performance, Pattern, and Practice* (Routledge: London, 2013), 105; Maria Costanza Centrone, "Corn-mummies: a case of «figuring it out»," *Proceedings of the Ninth International Congress of Egyptologists, Grenoble, 6–12 September 2004*, ed. Jean-Claude Goyon and Christine Cardin (Leuven: Peeters, 2007), 1:297.

42. Sue D'Auria, "Corn-Mummy," in D'Auria, Lacovara, and Roehrig, *Mummies & Magic*, 245.

43. Laurence Cotelle-Michel, "Présentation préliminaire des blocs de la Chapelle de Sésostris Ier découverte dan le IXe pylône de Karnak," *Cahiers de Karnak* 11 (2003): fig. 11.

44. A special thank you to Joseph Greene and the Harvard Semitic Museum, who allowed me several hours to examine HSM 1935.4.7 and to conduct my photographic analysis.

45. Gordon J. Hamilton, *The Origins of the West Semitic Alphabet in Egyptian Scripts* (Washington, DC: Catholic Biblical Association of America, 2006), 374.

46. Cf. the Middle Kingdom tomb of Senbi at Meir (Mark Collier and Bill Manley, *How to Read Egyptian Hieroglyphs* [Berkeley: University of California Press, 1998], 13).

47. Jaroslav Černý, *Egyptian Stelae in the Bankes Collection* (Oxford: Griffith Institute, 1958), pl. 8.

48. The ox-head on Sinai 351 has an extended neck that is carved into the next line of text. Sinai 365 has a single line for a neck. The ox-heads on the top-right portion of Sinai 375 also have a neck.

49. CT 934 (*ECT*, 7:136, i).

50. Leonard H. Lesko, *Ancient Egyptian Book of Two Ways* (Berkeley: University of California Press, 1972), 100.

51. Henri Frankfort, *Kingship and the Gods: A Study of Ancient Near Eastern Religion as the Integration of Society and Nature* (Chicago: University of Chicago Press, 1948), 107.

52. Ibid., 96 and 46.

53. PT 256 (Sethe, 302a-b); trans. Raymond O. Faulkner, *The Ancient Egyptian Pyramid Texts* (Oxford: Clarendon, 1969), 66.

54. Elizabeth Blyth, *Karnak: Evolution of a Temple* (New York: Routledge, 2006), 105.

55. B. J. J. Haring, *Divine Households: Administrative and Economic Aspects of the New Kingdom Royal Memorial Temples in Western Thebes* (Leiden: Nederlands Instituut voor het Nabje Oosten, 1997), 45.

56. Christina Karlshausen, "L'évolution de la barque processionnelle d'Amon à la 18e dynastie," *REg* 46 (1995): 121.

57. *P. Harris I*, 45, line 7 (Erichsen, *Papyrus Harris I*, 50, lines 15–16).

58. E.g., the barques found at the Le Chapelle Rouge at Karnak (Legrain, "Le logement et transport des barques sacrées, pl. VII [4]), the Great Hypostyle Hall at Karnak (Nelson, *Wall Reliefs*, pl. 53), and Mortuary Temple of Ramesses III at Medinet Habu (Nelson, *Festival Scenes*, pl. 193).

59. Nelson, *Wall Reliefs*, pls. 180, 197, and 226.

60. Peter J. Brand, "Veils, Votives, and Marginalia: The Use of Sacred Space at Karnak and Luxor," in *Sacred Space and Sacred Function in Ancient Thebes*, ed. Peter F. Dorman and Betsy M. Bryan (Chicago: University of Chicago Press, 2007), 61.

61. M. Maurice Pillet, "Rapport sur les travaux de Karnak (1923–1924)," *ASAE* 24 (1924): pl. III (upper).

62. Georges Legrain, "Le temple et les chapelles d'Osiris a Karnak," *RecTrav* 22 (1900): 129.

63. René Preys, "Nekhbet, l'oeil droit du dieu solaire," *REg* 61 (2010): 169.

64. W. Benson Harer, "Pharmacological and Biological Properties of the Egyptian Lotus," *JARCE* 22 (1985): 54.

65. Nelson, *Wall Reliefs*, pl. 226.

66. PM II, 439.

67. Gaston Maspero, ed., *Rapports relatifs à la consolidation des temples* (Cairo: Institut Français D'Archéologie Orientale, 1911), 1:154–55 and fig. 12.

# Chapter 6

1. Gerard Dowling, "The Liminal Boundary: An Analysis of the Sacral Potency of the Ditch as Ráith na Ríg, Tara, Co. Meath," *The Journal of Irish Archaeology* 15 (2006): 16–17.

2. Dieter Kessler, "Bemerkungen zur Tempel- und Gottesgerichtsbarkett im Neuen Reich," in *Scribe of Justice: Egyptological Studies in honour of Shafik Allam*, ed. Zahi Hawass, Khaled A. Daoud, and Ramadan B. Hussein (Cairo: Ministry of State for Antiquities, 2011), 249–63; Haring, *Divine Households*, 114, 260.

3. N. L. Cantor, *After We Die: The Life and Times of the Human Cadaver* (Washington, DC: Georgetown University Press, 2010), 76.

4. Bert Hayslop Jr., Kenneth W. Sewell, and Russell B. Riddle, "The American Funeral," in *Handbook of Death & Dying*, ed. Clifton D. Bryant and Dennis L. Peck (Thousand Oaks, CA: SAGE Publications, 2003), 590.

5. N. de Garis Davies, *The Tomb of Two Sculptors at Thebes* (New York: Metropolitan Museum of Art, 1925), pl. XXXI and XXIV.

6. Kathlyn M. Cooney, "Coffin Reuse in the Twenty-First Dynasty: The Demands of Ritual Transformation," *Backdirt* (2012): 32.

7. N. de Garis Davies, *The Rock Tombs of Deir el Gebrâwi*, pt. 1 (London: Egypt Exploration Fund, 1902), pl. XIV.

8. Christian T. de Vartavan, "*Pistacia* species in relation to their use as varnish and 'incense' (*sn<u>t</u>r*) in Pharaonic Egypt," *Bulletin of Parthian and Mixed Oriental Studies* 2 (2007): 63.

9. PT 274 (Sethe 404d).

10. *Urk*. IV, 329, line 8. PT 200 (Sethe 116).

11. William Kelly Simpson, *The Mastabas of Kawab, Khafkhufu I and II: G7110–20, 7130–40, and 7150 and subsidiary mastabas of Street G 7100* (Boston: Museum of Fine Arts, 1978), fig. 30.

12. Junker, *Grabungen auf dem Friedhof des Alten Reiches bei den Pyramiden von Gîza*, vol. 5, fig. 5 [b]; Hassan, *Excavations at Giza*, vol. 7, pl. L[B].

13. Hassan, *Excavations at Giza*, vol. 7, pl. L[A].

14. N. de Garis Davies, *Rock Tombs of Deir el Gebrâwi*, pt. 2, pl. VII.

15. Aylward M. Blackman, *Middle-Egyptian Stories* (Brussels: Fondation Égyptologique Reine Élisabeth, 1972), 32, line 9 (=*Sinuhe*, B193–194).

16. *P. Leyden 344*, 7, line 2 (Enmarch, *Dialogue of Ipuwer and the Lord of All*, 39).

17. N. de Garis Davies, *Tomb of Antefoker, Vizier of Sesostris I, and his wife, Senet (No. 60)* (London: Egypt Exploration Society, 1920), pl. XXI–XXII.

18. Werbrouck, *Les pleureuses dans l'Égypte ancienne*, pl. XXVI (upper).

19. Harco Willems, *Chests of Life: A Study of the Typology and Conceptual Development of Middle Kingdom, Standard Class Coffins* (Leiden: Ex Orient Lux, 1958), 46.

20. *P. Berlin 1204*, 22 (Sethe, Ägyptische Lesestücke, 71, line 18).

21. CT 55 (*ECT*, 1:245,b-c).

22. E.g., N. de Garis Davies, *The Tomb of Puyemrê at Thebes*, vol. 2 (New York: Metropolitan Museum of Art, 1923), pl. XLVII; Davies, *Rock Tombs of Deir el Gebrâwi*, pt. 1, pl. x.

23. Werbrouck, *Les pleureuses dans l'Égypte ancienne*, pl. XXXVI.

24. Davies, *Two Ramesside Tombs*, pl. XIII.

25. David A. Falk, "'My Putrefaction Is Myrrh:' The Lexicography of Decay, Gilded Coffins, and the Green Skin of Osiris," *Journal of Ancient Civilizations* 33 (2018): 33.

26. Alan H. Gardiner, "The term , ***pr-n-sṯꜣ*** in Pap. Mayer A.," *ZÄS* 59 (1924): 72.

27. *P. Anastasi II*, 3, line 1 (*LEM*, 13, lines 9–10).

28. Caminos, *Late-Egyptian Miscellanies,* 42.

29. *P. Harris I*, 28, line 2 (Erichsen, *Papyrus Harris I*, 32, line 14).

30. *P. Harris I*, 27, line 8 (Erichsen, *Papyrus Harris I*, 31, line 18).

31. *P. BM 10403*, 1, lines 2–8 (Peet, *Great Tomb-Robberies*, pl. XXXVI).

32. *P. BM 10403*, 1, line 13 and 1, line 8 (Peet, *Great Tomb-Robberies*, pl. XXXVI).

33. *P. BM 10403*, 1, line 2 (Peet, *Great Tomb-Robberies*, pl. XXXVI).

34. *P. BM 10403*, 2, line 3 (Peet, *Great Tomb-Robberies*, pl. XXXVI).

35. *P. Westcar* 7, lines 12–13 (Blackman, *King Kheops and the Magicians*, 9, lines 2–3).

36. Richard S. Hess, *Israelite Religion: An Archaeological and Biblical Survey* (Grand Rapids: Baker Books, 2007), 239, 299–302.

37. *P. BM 10403*, 1, lines 23–25 (Peet, *Great Tomb-Robberies*, pl. XXXVI). *P. Mayer A,* 2, line 7 (*KRI* 6:806, lines 15–16) uses "rings of copper," *shaqu ḥemet,* in reference to the *per-en-setja.*

38. *O. Černý 20* (*KRI* 3:555, line 9).

39. *Paheri* 3, 1 (J. J. Tylor and F. Ll. Griffith, *The Tomb of Paheri at El Kab* [London, 1894], pl. III).

40. *Urk.* IV, 2028, line 13.

41. *P. Harris I*, 46, lines 9–47, line 1 (Erichsen, *Papyrus Harris I*, 51). Pierre Grandet, *Le Papyrus Harris I* (Cairo: Institut Français D'Archéologie Orientale du Caire, 1994), 2:169–70.

42. Mariette, *Karnak*, pl. 42, lines 17–21.

43. Peet, *Great Tomb-Robberies*, 171.

44. *UC 32179*, col. 2, line 9 (Collier and Quirke, *The UCL Lahun Papyri*, 28). *UC 32183*, rt, bottom left, line 6 (Collier and Quirke, *The UCL Lahun Papyri*, 32). J. R. Harris, *Lexicographical Studies in Ancient Egyptian Minerals* (Berlin: Akademie, 1961), 122. Kei Yamamoto, "The materials of Iykhernofret's portable shrine: An alternative translation of *Berlin 1204*, lines 11–12," *GM* 191 (2002): 103.

45. *P. Mayer A,* 2, line 7 (*KRI* 6:806, lines 15–16).

46. Gardiner, *Ancient Egyptian Onomastica*, 64–68, pl. XXIII vs 2.

47. Geoffrey Killen, *Ancient Egyptian Furniture: Boxes, Chests and Footstools* (Oxford: Aris & Phillips, 1994), 53.

48. Legrain, "Le logement et transport des barques sacrées," pl. I.

49. Harold Hayden Nelson, ed., *Ramses III's Temple within the Great Inclosure of Amon* (Chicago: University of Chicago Press, 1936), pt. 1, pl. 21.

50. Ranaan Eichler, "The Poles of the Ark: On the Ins and Outs of a Textual Contradiction," *JBL* 135 (2016): 733–41.

51. Ibid., 740–41.

52. Ludwig Borchardt, *Das Grabenkmal des Königs Śa3ḥ-Re*ʕ, vol. 2 (Leipzig: Hinrichs, 1913), pl. 60.

53. W. M. Flinders Petrie, *Medum* (London, 1892), pl. XXI.

54. Ann Macy Roth, "The Practical Economics of Tomb-Building in the Old Kingdom: A Visit to the Necropolis in a Carrying Chair," in *For His Ka: Essays Offered in Memory of Klaus Baer*, ed. David P. Silverman (Chicago: University of Chicago Press, 1994), 238.

55. *P. Westcar* 7, lines 12–13 (Blackman, *King Kheops and the Magicians*, 9, lines 2–3).

56. Hilda Flinders Petrie and Margaret A. Murray, *Seven Memphite Tomb Chapels* (London: British School of Egyptian Archaeology, 1952), pl. XVII [3(1)].

57. Hassan, *Excavations at Giza*, vol. 2, fig. 240.

58. Ibid., vol. 5, fig. 122.

59. *LD* 2:78b.

60. N. Kanawati and M. Abder-Raziq, *Mereruka and his family*, vol. 2 (Oxford: Aris & Phillips, 2008), pl. 69.

61. PT 571 (Sethe 1470a).

62. PT 570 (Sethe 1452c).

63. PT 81 (Sethe 56c).

64. Junker, *Grabungen auf dem Friedhof des Alten Reiches bei den Pyramiden von Gîza*, vol. 5, fig. 20.

65. PT 438 (Sethe 811a).

66. PT 467 (Sethe 892c).

67. *CG 01570*; Hans Goedicke, "A Fragment of a Biographical Inscription of the Old Kingdom," *JEA* 45 (1959): pl. II.

68. Davies, *Rock Tombs of Deir el Gebrâwi*, pt. 2, pl. X.

69. *WÄS* V, 50, lines 13–16.

70. Janssen, *Commodity Prices,* 187–89.

71. *KRI* 5:470, lines 6, 8, and 10.

72. Gardiner, *Ancient Egyptian Onomastica*, pl. XXIII vs, line 3.

73. *Hier. Ostr.* pl. 24, ill. 1, lines 3–4.

74. Janssen, *Commodity Prices*, 189.

75. *O. Cairo 23800*, II, 4–5.

76. Janssen, *Commodity Prices*, 181.

77. *KRI* 6:257, line 9.

78. *KRI* 6:257, lines 11–12.

79. *Urk.* IV, 666, lines 16–17.

80. *Urk.* IV, 705, lines 10–14.

81. Naville, *Temple of Deir el Bahari*, vol. 5, pl. CXXV.

82. Albert Gayet, *Le temple de Louxor: constructions d'Aménophis III* (Paris, 1894), pl. XVIII.

83. Davies, *Rock Tombs of El Amarna*, pt. 2, pl. XXXVII.

84. *LD* 3:149b.

85. Davies, *Rock Tombs of El Amarna,* pt. 3, pl. XIII.

86. *LD* 3:121a-b.

87. Schott photo 4958.

88. Jaroslav Černý, "Le culte d'Amenophis I chez les ouvriers de la Nécropole thébaine [avec 9 planches]," *BIFAO* 27 (1927): fig. 13.

89. Ibid., fig. 14.

90. Nelson, *Ramses III's Temple*, pt. 2, pl. 101.

91. Nelson, *Festival Scenes*, pl. 197.

92. Shlomo Bunimovitz, "Problems in the 'ethnic' identification of the Philistine material culture," *Tel-Aviv* 17 (1990): 211.

93. James M. Weinstein, "The Egyptian Empire in Palestine: A Reassessment," *BASOR* 241 (1981): 23.

94. Schott photo 4140.

95. Edward F. Wente, *Scenes of King Herihor in the Court: with translations and texts* (Chicago: University of Chicago Press, 1979), pl. 21.

96. Henri Chevrier, "Rapport sur les travaux de Karnak (1933–1934) (avec 4 planches)," *ASAE* 34 (1934): fig. 1.

## Chapter 7

1. David A. Falk, "Ritual Processional Furniture: A Material and Religious Phenomenon in Egypt" (PhD diss., University of Liverpool, 2015). A special thank you to Mark Lanier, whose generous funding made possible my dissertation that served as the foundational research for this book.

## Epilogue

1. Josiah Derby, "The Gold of the Ark," *Jewish Bible Quarterly* 33 (2005): 254.
2. EA 3, lines 13–22; 7, lines 63–72; 10, lines 8–24.

# Bibliography


Aling, Charles F. "The Biblical City of Ramses." *JETS* 25 (1982): 129–37.

Allen, Thomas George. *The Egyptian Book of the Dead: Documents in the Oriental Institute Museum at the University of Chicago*. Chicago: University of Chicago Press, 1960.

Assmann, Jan. "The Ramesside tomb and the construction of sacred space." Pages 46–52 in *The Theban Necropolis: Past, Present and Future*. Edited by Nigel Strudwick and John H. Taylor. London: British Museum Press, 2003.

Averbeck, Richard E. "Myth, Ritual, and Order in 'Enki and the World Order.'" *Journal of the American Oriental Society* 123 (2003): 757–71.

Bahn, P. "The Antiquity of Man." Pages 7–11 in *Archaeology: The Key Concepts*. Edited by C. Renfrew and P. Bahn. New York: Routledge, 2005.

Baines, John. "Temple Symbolism." *Royal Anthropological Institute Newsletter* 15 (1976): 10–15.

Bard, Kathryn A., and Rodolfo Fattovich. *Seafaring Expeditions to Punt in the Middle Kingdom: Excavations at Mersa/Wadi Gawasis, Egypt*. Leiden: Brill, 2018.

Barguet, Paul. "Tôd: Rapport de fouilles de la saison février-avril 1950." *BIFAO* 51 (1952): 80–110.

Barsanti, Alexandre, and Gaston Maspero. "Saqqâra, Around Pyramid complex of Unis." *ASAE* 2 (1901): 97–111.

Bietak, Manfred. "Harbours and Coastal Military Bases in Egypt in the Second Millennium B.C.: Avaris, Peru-nefer, Pi-Ramesse." Pages 53–70 in *The Nile: Natural and Cultural Landscape in Egypt*. Edited by Harco Willems and Jan-Michael Dahms. Bielfeld: Transcript Verlag, 2017.

Bietak, Manfred, Nicola Math, and Vera Müller. "Report on the excavations of a Hyksos Palace of Tell el Dab<sup>c</sup>a/Avaris." Ägypten und Levante 22/23 (2013): 17–53.

Bimson, J. J. *Redating the Exodus and Conquest*. 2nd ed. Sheffield: Almond Press, 1981.

Binns, L. E. Review of *The Date of the Exodus*, by J. W. Jack. *Theology* 13 (1926): 175.

Bissing, Friedrich Wilhelm von. *Mastaba des Gem-Ni-Kai*. vol. 1. Berlin: Duncker, 1905.

Blackman, Aylward M. *Middle-Egyptian Stories*. Brussels: Fondation Égyptologique Reine Élisabeth, 1972.

———. "Notes on Certain Passages in Various Middle Egyptian Texts." *JEA* 16 (1930): 63–72.

———. *The Story of King Kheops and the Magicians: Transcribed from Papyrus Westcar (Berlin Papyrus 3033)*. Reading: J. V. Books, 1988.

Blyth, Elizabeth. *Karnak: Evolution of a Temple.* New York: Routledge, 2006.

Borchardt, Ludwig. *Das Grabenkmal des Königs Śa3ḥ-Reʕ.* vol.2. Leipzig: Hinrichs, 1913.

———. *Denkmäler des Alten Reiches.* Part 1. Berlin: Reichsdruckerei, 1937.

Brand, Peter J. "Veils, Votives, and Marginalia: The Use of Sacred Space at Karnak and Luxor." Pages 51–83 in *Sacred Space and Sacred Function in Ancient Thebes.* Edited by Peter F. Dorman and Betsy M. Bryan. Chicago: University of Chicago Press, 2007.

Brovarski, Edward. "Inventory Offering Lists and the Nomenclature for Boxes and Chests in the Old Kingdom." Pages 27–54 in *Gold of Praise: Studies on Ancient Egypt in Honor of Edward F. Wente.* Edited by Emily Teeter and John A. Larson. Chicago: University of Chicago Press, 1999.

Bruyère, Bernard. *Rapport sur les fouilles de Deir el Médineh, 1924–1925.* Cairo: Imprimerie de L'Institut Français D'Archéologie Orientale, 1925.

Bunimovitz, Shlomo. "Problems in the 'ethnic' identification of the Philistine material culture." *Tel-Aviv* 17 (1990): 210–22.

Calverley, Amice M. *The Temple of King Sethos I at Abydos.* 4 vols. Chicago: University of Chicago Press, 1933–1938.

Caminos, Ricardo A. *Late-Egyptian Miscellanies.* London: Oxford University Press, 1954.

Cantor, N. L. *After We Die: The Life and Times of the Human Cadaver.* Washington, DC: Georgetown University Press, 2010.

Capart, Jean. "Une liste d'amulettes." *ZÄS* 45 (1908): 14–21.

———. *Une rue de tombeaux à Saqqarah.* Brussels: Vromant, 1907.

Carson, D. A. *Exegetical Fallacies.* Grand Rapids: Baker Books, 1984.

Cassuto, Umberto. *Biblical and Oriental Studies.* Vol. 1. Jerusalem: Magnes; Hebrew University, 1973.

———. *The Documentary Hypothesis and the Composition of the Pentateuch.* Jerusalem: Magnes, 1961.

Centrone, Maria Costanza. "Corn-mummies: a case of «figuring it out»." Pages 293–301 in vol. 1 of *Proceedings of the Ninth International Congress of Egyptologists, Grenoble, 6–12 September 2004.* Edited by Jean-Claude Goyon and Christine Cardin. Leuven: Peeters, 2007.

Černý, Jaroslav. *Egyptian Stelae in the Bankes Collection.* Oxford: Griffith Institute, 1958.

———. *Hieratic Inscriptions from the Tomb of Tutʕankhamūn.* Oxford: Griffith Institute, 1965.

———. *Late Ramesside Letters.* Brussels: Fondation Égyptologique Reine Élisabeth, 1939.

———. "Le culte d'Amenophis I chez les ouvriers de la Nécropole thébaine [avec 9 planches]." *BIFAO* 27 (1927): 159–203.

———. "The Will of Naunakhte and the Related Documents." *JEA* 31 (1945): 29–53.

Černý, Jaroslav, and Alan H. Gardiner. *Hieratic Ostraca.* 2 vols. Oxford: Griffith Institute, 1957.

Chassinat, Émile. *Edfou.* Vol. 5. Cairo: Institut Français d'Archéologie Orientale, 1930.

Chevrier, Henri. "Rapport sur les travaux de Karnak (1933–1934) (avec 4 planches)." *ASAE* 34 (1934): 159–75.

Cole, Susan Guettel. *Landscapes, Gender, and Ritual Space: The Ancient Greek Experience.* London: University of California Press, 2004.

Collier, Mark, and Bill Manley. *How to Read Egyptian Hieroglyphs.* London: University of California Press, 1998.

Collier, Mark, and Stephen Quirke. *The UCL Lahun Papyri: Accounts.* Oxford: Archaeopress, 2006.

Commission des sciences et arts d'Egypte. *Description de l'Égypte ou recueil des observations et des recherches qui ont ete faites en Égypte pendant l'expédition de l'armée française.* 2nd ed. Vol. 1. Paris, 1820.

Cooney, Kathlyn M. "Coffin Reuse in the Twenty-First Dynasty: The Demands of Ritual Transformation." *Backdirt* (2012): 22–33.

Cotelle-Michel, Laurence. "Présentation préliminaire des blocs de la Chapelle de Sésostris Ier découverte dan le IXe pylône de Karnak." *Cahiers de Karnak* 11 (2003): 339–53.

Crum, Walter Ewing. *A Coptic Dictionary compiled with the help of many scholars.* Oxford: Clarenden, 1939.

Daressy, M. Georges. "Notes et remarques." *RecTrav* 16 (1894): 42–60.

D'Auria, Sue. "Corn-Mummy." Page 245 in *Mummies & Magic: The Funerary Arts of Ancient Egypt.* Edited by Sue D'Auria, Peter Lacovara, and Catharine H. Roehrig. Boston: Dallas Museum of Art, 1992.

———. "Mummification in Ancient Egypt." Pages 14–19 in *Mummies & Magic: The Funerary Arts of Ancient Egypt.* Edited by Sue D'Auria, Peter Lacovara, and Catharine H. Roehrig. Boston: Dallas Museum of Art, 1992.

Davies, N. de Garis. *The Mastaba of Ptahhetep and Akhethetep at Saqqarah.* 2 pts. London: Egypt Exploration Fund, 1900–1901.

———. *The Rock Tombs of El Amarna.* 6 pts. London: Egypt Exploration Fund, 1905–1908.

———. *The Rock Tombs of Deir el Gebrâwi.* 2 pts. London: Egypt Exploration Fund, 1902.

———. *Tomb of Antefoker, Vizier of Sesostris I, and his wife, Senet (No. 60).* London: Egypt Exploration Society, 1920.

———. *The Tomb of Puymerê at Thebes.* 2 vols. New York: Metropolitan Museum of Art, 1922–1923.

———. *The Tomb of Two Sculptors at Thebes.* New York: Metropolitan Museum of Art, 1925.

———. *Two Ramesside Tombs at Thebes.* New York: Metropolitan Museum of Art, 1927.

Davies, Norman de Garis, and Alan H. Gardiner, eds. *Tombs of Menkheperrasonb, Amenmosě, and Another.* London: Egypt Exploration Society, 1933.

De Buck, Adriaan, and Alan H. Gardiner, eds. *The Egyptian Coffin Texts.* 7 vols. Chicago: University of Chicago Press, 1935–1961.

De Buck, Roland. "On the meaning of the name ***ḥʿpj.***" Pages 1–22 in *Orientalia Neerlandica: A Volume of Oriental Studies.* Leiden: A. W. Sijthoff's Uitgeversmaatschappij N. V, 1948.

De Morgan, Jacques. *Fouilles A Dahchour: Mars-Juin 1894.* Vol. 1. Vienna, 1895.

Derby, Josiah. "The Gold of the Ark." *Jewish Bible Quarterly* 33 (2005): 253–56.

Dodson, Aidan, and Dyan Hilton. *The Complete Royal Families of Ancient Egypt.* London: Thames & Hudson, 2004.

Dowling, Gerard. "The Liminal Boundary: An Analysis of the Sacral Potency of the Ditch as Ráith na Ríg, Tara, Co. Meath." *The Journal of Irish Archaeology* 15 (2006): 15–37.

Doxey, Denise M. *Egyptian Non-Royal Epithets in the Middle Kingdom: A Social and Historical Analysis.* Leiden: Brill, 1998.

Duell, Prentice. *The Mastaba of Mereruka.* 2 pts. Chicago: University of Chicago Press, 1938.

Dümichen, Johannes. *Geographische Inschriften altägyptischer Denkmäler.* Pt. 4. Leipzig, 1885.

Eaton, Katherine. *Ancient Egyptian Temple Ritual: Performance, Pattern, and Practice.* London: Routledge, 2013.

———. "The Ritual Functions of Processional Equipment in the Temple of Seti I at Abydos." PhD diss., New York University, 2004.

Eaton-Krauss, M., and E. Graefe. *The Small Golden Shrine from the Tomb of Tutankhamun.* Oxford: Griffith Institute, 1985.

Egberts, A. *In Quest of Meaning: A Study of the Ancient Egyptian Rites of Consecrating the Meret-Chests and Driving the Calves.* Vol. 1. Leiden: Nederlands Instituut voor het Nabije Oosten, 1995.

Eichler, Ranaan. "The Poles of the Ark: On the Ins and Outs of a Textual Contradiction." *JBL* 135 (2016): 733–41.

Eliade, Mircea. *The Sacred and the Profane: The Nature of Religion.* Translated by Willard R. Trask. New York: Harcourt, Brace & World, 1959.

El-Sabban, Sherif. *Temple Festival Calendars of Ancient Egypt.* Liverpool: Liverpool University Press, 2000.

Enmarch, Roland. *The Dialogue of Ipuwer and the Lord of All.* Oxford: Griffith Institute, 2005.

Erichsen, W. *Papyrus Harris I: Hieroglyphische Transkription.* Brussels: Édition de le Fondation Égyptologique, 1933.

Erman, Adolf. *Zaubersprüche für Mutter und Kind aus dem Papyrus 3027 des Berliner Museums.* Berlin: Königlichen Akademie der Wissenschaften, 1901.

Erman, Adolf, and Hermann Grapow. *Wörterbuch der aegyptischen Sprache.* 5 vols. Leipzig: Hinrichs; Berlin: Akademie, 1926–1931. Repr., 1971.

Falk, David A. "Brick by Brick: What Did the Israelites Build in Egypt?" *Biblical Archaeology Review* 46 (2020): 54–57.

———. "'My Putrefaction is Myrrh:' The Lexicography of Decay, Gilded Coffins, and the Green Skin of Osiris." *Journal of Ancient Civilizations* 33 (2018): 27–39.

———. "The products of Hatshepsut's trade mission to Punt: An alternative translation of the Punt refliefs at Deir el-Bahari." *GM* 238 (2013): 51–61.

———. "Ritual Processional Furniture: A Material and Religious Phenomenon in Egypt." PhD diss., University of Liverpool, 2015.

———. "The Significance of the Horns (קֶרֶן) of Exodus 27:2: the Egyptian (*ṯst*) and Levantine Four-Horned Altars." Pages 69–75 in *Did I Not Bring Israel Out of Egypt? Biblical, Archaeological, and Egyptological Perspectives on the Exodus Narratives*. Edited by James Karl Hoffmeier, Alan Millard, and Gary Rendsburg. Winona Lake, IN: Eisenbrauns, 2016.

Faulkner, Raymond O. *The Ancient Egyptian Coffin Texts*. 3 vols. Oxford: Aris & Phillips, 1973–1978.

———. *The Ancient Egyptian Pyramid Texts*. Oxford: Clarendon, 1969.

———. *A Concise Dictionary of Middle Egyptian*. Oxford: Griffith Institute, 1962.

Finkelstein, Israel, and Neil Asher Silberman. *The Bible Unearthed: Archaeology's New Vision of Ancient Israel and the Origin of Its Sacred Texts*. New York: Free Press, 2001.

Forstner-Müller, Irene, Tomasz Herbich, Christian Schweitzer, and Michael Weissl. "Preliminary Report on the Geophysical Survey at Tell el-Dab$^{c}$a/Qantir in Spring 2008." *Ägypten und Levante* 18 (2008): 87–106.

Frankfort, Henri. *Kingship and the Gods: A Study of Ancient Near Eastern Religion as the Integration of Society and Nature*. Chicago: University of Chicago Press, 1948.

Gaballa, G. A., and Kenneth A. Kitchen. "The Festival of Sokar." *Orientalia* 38 (1969): 1–76.

Gardiner, Alan H. *Ancient Egyptian Onomastica*. London: Oxford University Press, 1947.

———. *Egyptian Hieratic Texts: Series I; Literary Texts of the New Kingdom*. Pt. 1. Leipzig: Hinrichs, 1911.

———. *Late-Egyptian Miscellanies*. Brussels: Fondation Egyptologique Reine Elisabeth, 1937.

———. *Late-Egyptian Stories*. Brussels: Fondation Egyptologique Reine Elisabeth, 1932.

———. *Ramesside Administrative Documents*. Oxford: Griffith Institute, 1948.

———. "The term 𓉐𓈖𓋴, *pr-n-sṯ3* in Pap. Mayer A." *ZÄS* 59 (1924): 72.

———. "Texts Relating to the Taxation and Transport of Corn." *JEA* 27 (1941): 19–73.

———. "A Unique Funerary Liturgy." *JEA* 41 (1955): 9–17.

Gayet, Albert. *Le temple de Louxor: constructions d'Aménophis III*. Paris, 1894.

Gelb, Ignace J., et al. *The Assyrian Dictionary of the Oriental Institute of the University of Chicago*. 21 vols. Chicago: The Oriental Institute of the University of Chicago, 1956–2010.

Goedicke, Hans. "A Fragment of a Biographical Inscription of the Old Kingdom." *JEA* 45 (1959): 8–11.

Grandet, Pierre. *Le Papyrus Harris I*. Vol. 2. Cairo: Institut Français D'Archéologie Orientale du Caire, 1994.

———. "Travaux, grèves et personnages célèbres aux XIX$^{e}$ et XX$^{e}$ dynasties, dans quelques ostraca documentaires de l'IFAO." Pages 209–34 in *Deir el-Médineh et la Vallée des Rois: La vie en Égypte au temps des pharaons du Nouvel Empire*. Edited by Guillemette Andreu. Paris: Musée du Louvre, 2003.

Grieshammer, Reinhard. "Reinheit, kultische." Pages 213–14 in *Lexikon der Ägyptologie*. Vol. 5. Edited by Wolfgang Helck and Eberhard Otto. Weisbaden: Harrassowitz, 1984.

Griffith, F. L., and Percy E. Newberry. *El Bersheh*. Pt. 2. London, 1896.

Grimes, Ronald L. "Ritual, performance, and the sequestering of sacred space." Pages 149–68 in *Discourse in Ritual Studies*. Edited by Hans Schilderman. Leiden: Brill, 2007.

Hallo, William W., and K. Lawson Younger. *The Context of Scripture: Canonical Compositions from the Biblical World*. 3 vols. Leiden: Brill, 2003.

Hamilton, Gordon J. *The Origins of the West Semitic Alphabet in Egyptian Scripts*. Washington, DC: Catholic Biblical Association of America, 2006.

Harer, W. Benson. "Pharmacological and Biological Properties of the Egyptian Lotus." *JARCE* 22 (1985): 49–54.

Haring, B. J. J. *Divine Households: Administrative and Economic Aspects of the New Kingdom Royal Memorial Temples in Western Thebes*. Leiden: Nederlands Instituut voor het Nabje Oosten, 1997.

Harris, J. R. *Lexicographical Studies in Ancient Egyptian Minerals*. Berlin: Akademie, 1961.

Hassan, Selim. *Excavations at Gîza*. 10 vols. Cairo: Government Press, 1930–1960.

Hayslop, Bert Jr., Kenneth W. Sewell, and Russell B. Riddle. "The American Funeral." Pages 587–97 in *Handbook of Death & Dying*. Edited by Clifton D. Bryant and Dennis L. Peck. Thousand Oaks, CA: SAGE Publications, 2003.

Hernández, Roberto A. Díaz. "Der Ramesseumpapyrus E, Ein Ritualbuch für Bestattungen aus dem Mittleren Reich." *GM* Beihefte Nr. 15, 2014.

Hess, Richard S. *Israelite Religion: An Archaeological and Biblical Survey*. Grand Rapids: Baker Books, 2007.

Hesse, Kristina Josephson. *Contacts and Trade at Late Bronze Age Hazor*. Archaeology and Environment 24. Umeå, Sweden: Umeå University, 2008.

Hoch, James E. *Semitic Words in Egyptian Texts of the New Kingdom and Third Intermediate Period*. Princeton: Princeton University Press, 1994.

Hoffmeier, James Karl. *Sacred in the Vocabulary of Ancient Egypt: The Term D̲SR, with special Reference to Dynasties I–XX*. Göttingen: Universitätsverlag Freiberg Schweiz; Göttingen: Vandenhoeck & Ruprecht, 1985.

———. "Tents in Egypt and the Ancient Near East." *Society for the Study of Egyptian Antiquities Newsletter* 7 (1977): 13–28.

Hornby, A. S., ed. *Oxford Advanced Learner's Dictionary of Current English*. 7th ed. Oxford: Oxford University Press, 2005.

Hughes, George R., ed. *Medinet Habu*. Vol. 5. Chicago: University of Chicago Press, 1957.

Ideler, L. *Handbuch der mathematischen und technischen Chronologie*. Vol. 1. Berlin, 1825.

Iliffe, Rob. "Biblical Chronology." Pages 133–35 in *Encyclopedia of the Scientific Revolution from Copernicus to Newton*. Edited by W. Applebaum. New York: Garland, 2000.

Janssen, Jac. J. *Commodity Prices from the Ramessid Period: An Economic Study of the Village of the Necropolis Workmen at Thebes*. Leiden: Brill, 1975.

———. *Furniture at Deir el-Medîna including Wooden Containers of the New Kingdom and Ostracon Varille 19.* London: Golden House Publications, 2009.

Jewish Chronicle. "The Date of the Exodus." *Littell's Living Age* 195:2518 (1892): 64.

Johnson, Sally. "Uraeus statuettes." Pages 143–44 in *Mummies & Magic: The Funerary Arts of Ancient Egypt.* Edited by Sue D'Auria, Peter Lacovara, and Catharine H. Roehrig. Boston: Dallas Museum of Art, 1992.

Jones, Dilwyn. *Ancient Egyptian Boats.* London: Trustees of the British Museum Press, 1995.

Junker, Hermann. *Bericht über die von der Akademie der Wissenschaften in Wien auf gemeinsame Kosten mit Dr. Wilhelm Pelizaeus unternommenen Grabungen auf dem Friedhof des Alten Reiches bei den Pyramiden von Gîza.* 12 vols. Leipzig: Hölder-Pichler-Tempsky, 1921–1955.

Kanawati, N., and M. Abder-Raziq. *Mereruka and his family.* 3 vols. Oxford: Aris & Phillips, 2004–2010.

Karlshausen, Christina. "L'évolution de la barque processionnelle d'Amon à la 18ᵉ dynastie." *REg* 46 (1995): 119–37.

Kenyon, Kathleen M. *Excavations at Jericho.* Vol. 3. London: British School of Archaeology in Jerusalem, 1981.

Kessler, Dieter. "Bemerkungen zur Tempel- und Gottesgerichtsbarkett im Neuen Reich." Pages 249–63 in *Scribe of Justice: Egyptological Studies in honour of Shafik Allam.* Edited by Zahi Hawass, Khaled A. Daoud, and Ramadan B. Hussein. Cairo: Ministry of State for Antiquities, 2011.

Killen, Geoffrey. *Ancient Egyptian Furniture: Boxes, Chests and Footstools.* Oxford: Aris & Phillips, 1994.

Kitchen, Kenneth A. *On the Reliability of the Old Testament.* Grand Rapids: Eerdmans, 2003.

———. *Ramesside Inscriptions: Historical and Biographical.* 8 vols. Malden, MA: Blackwell, 1975–1990.

———. *Ramesside Inscriptions: Translated & Annotated.* 5 vols. Malden, MA: Blackwell, 1993–2008.

Kitchen, Kenneth A., and Paul J. N. Lawrence. *Treaty, Law and Covenant in the Ancient Near East.* Pt. 3. Wiesbaden: Harrassowitz, 2012.

Koehler, Ludwig, Walter Baumgartner, and Johann J. Stamm. Translated and edited under the supervision of Mervyn E. J. Richardson. *The Hebrew and Aramaic Lexicon of the Old Testament.* 4 vols. Leiden: Brill, 1994–1999.

Kopetzky, Karin, and Manfred Bietak. "A Seal Impression of the Green Jasper Workshop from Tell el-Dabʿa." Ägypten und Levante 26 (2016): 357–75.

Lacau, Pierre. "Textes religieux." *RecTrav* 27 (1905): 217–33.

Lansing, Ambrose, and William C. Hayes. "The Museum's Excavations at Thebes." *The Metropolitan Museum of Art Bulletin* 32 (1937): 4–39.

Legrain, Georges. "Le logement et transport des barques sacrées et des statues des dieux dans quelques temples égyptiens." *BIFAO* 13 (1917): 1–76.

———. "Le temple et les chapelles d'Osiris a Karnak." *RecTrav* 22 (1900): 125–36.

Lepsius, C. R. *Denkmäler aus Aegypten und Aethiopien*. 5 vols. Leipzig, 1897.

———. *Letters from Egypt, Ethiopia, and the Peninsula of Sinai: with extracts from the chronology of the Egyptians, with reference to the Exodus of the Israelites*. Translated by L. Horner and J. B. Horner. London, 1853.

Lesko, Leonard H. *Ancient Egyptian Book of Two Ways*. Berkeley: University of California Press, 1972.

Lewis, J. Lowell. *The Anthropology of Cultural Performance*. New York: Palgrave Macmillan, 2013.

Lichtheim, Miriam. *Ancient Egyptian Literature*. Vol. 1. Berkeley: University of California Press, 1973.

López, Jesús. *Ostraca ieratici, n. 57320–57449*. Milan: Istituto Cisalpino la Goliardica, 1982.

Loret, M. Victor. "La tombe de Khâ-m-hâ." Pages 113–32 in vol. 1 of *Mémoires publiés par les membres de la Mission archéologique française au Caire*. Paris, 1889.

Marciniak, Marek. "Un successeur contemporain de la frise de *khekerou*?" Pages 109–10 in vol. 2 of *Mélanges Gamal Eddin Mokhtar*. Cairo: L'Institut Français D'Archéologie Orientale, 1985.

Mariette, Auguste. *Abydos: description des fouilles*. 2 vols. Paris, 1869–1880.

———. *Dendérah: description générale du grand temple de cette ville*. 6 vols. Paris, 1870–1875.

———. *Karnak: étude topographique et archéologique*. Leipzig, 1875.

Maspero, Gaston, ed. *Rapports relatifs à la consolidation des temples*. 2 vols. Cairo: Institut Français D'Archéologie Orientale, 1911.

McCorkle, William W. *Ritualizing the Disposal of the Deceased: From Corpse to Concept*. New York: Lang, 2010.

Millard, Alan. "The Babylonian Flood Story—A new tablet and an old one misinterpreted." *Faith & Thought* 60 (2016): 25–30.

Moussa, Ahmed M., and Hartwig Altenmüller. *Das Grab des Nianchchnum und Chnumhotep*. Mainz: von Zabern, 1977.

Muhlestein, Kerry M. "New Pyramid Structures and Conservation Techniques: The 2018 and 2019 Fag el-Gamous and Seila Pyramid seasons." Paper presented at the 70th Annual Meeting of the American Research Center in Egypt, Washington, DC, 12–14 April 2019.

Murray, Margaret A. *Saqqara Mastabas*. 2 pts. London: Bernard Quartich, 1905.

Naville, Edouard. *Das aegyptische Todtenbuch der XVIII. bis XX. Dynastie*. Vol. 2. Berlin, 1886.

———. *The Temple of Deir el Bahari*. 6 pts. London: Egypt Exploration Fund, 1895–1908.

———. *The XI$^{th}$ Dynasty Temple at Deir el Bahari*. 3 pts. London: Egypt Exploration Fund, 1907–1913.

Nelson, Harold Hayden. *Festival Scenes of Ramses III*. Chicago: University of Chicago Press, 1940.

———. *Ramses III's Temple within the Great Inclosure of Amon*. 2 pts. Chicago: University of Chicago Press, 1936.

———. *The Wall Reliefs*. Chicago: University of Chicago Press, 1981.

Newberry, Percy E. *Beni Hasan*. 4 pts. London, 1893–1900.

Nims, Charles F. *Tomb of Kheruef: Theban Tomb 192*. Chicago: University of Chicago Press, 1980.

O'Connor, A. *Finding Time for the Old Stone Age: A History of Palaeolithic Archaeology and Quaternary Geology in Britain, 1860–1960*. Oxford: Oxford University Press, 2007.

Orr, James. *The Problem of the Old Testament: considered with reference to recent history*. New York: Scribner's Sons, 1906.

Osborne, Grant R. *The Hermeneutical Spiral: A Comprehensive Introduction to Biblical Interpretation*. Downers Grove, IL: InterVarsity Press, 1991.

Partridge, Christopher. *Re-Enchantment of the West: Alternative Spiritualities, Sacralization, Popular Culture and Occulture*. Vol. 1. London: T&T Clark International, 2005.

Peet, Thomas Eric. *The Great Tomb-Robberies of the Twentieth Dynasty*. Oxford: Clarendon, 1930.

Petrie, Hilda Flinders, and Margaret A. Murray. *Seven Memphite Tomb Chapels*. London: British School of Egyptian Archaeology, 1952.

Petrie, W. M. Flinders. *Dendereh*. London, 1898.

———. *Hyksos and Israelite Cities*. London: Bernard Quaritch, 1906.

———. *Koptos*. London, 1896.

———. *Medum*. London, 1892.

———. *Naukratis*. London, 1886.

Pillet, M. Maurice. "Rapport sur les travaux de Karnak (1923–1924)." *ASAE* 24 (1924): 53–88.

Porter, Bertha, and Rosalind L. B. Moss. *Topographical Bibliography of Ancient Egyptian Hieroglyphic Texts, Reliefs, and Paintings*. 2nd ed. 7 pts. Oxford: Clarendon, 1960–1995.

Preys, René. "Nekhbet, l'oeil droit du dieu solaire." *REg* 61 (2010): 159–77.

Quibell, J. E. *Excavations at Saqqara (1911–12)*. Cairo: L'Institut Français D'Archeologie Orientale, 1913.

Reade, Julian. "Assyrian King-Lists, the Royal Tombs of Ur, and Indus Origins." *JNES* 60 (2001): 1–29.

Reisner, George Andrew. *A History of the Giza Necropolis*. 2 vols. Cambridge: Harvard University Press, 1942–1955.

Ritner, Robert Kriech. *The Mechanics of Ancient Egyptian Magical Practice*. 4th ed. Chicago: University of Chicago Press, 1993.

Roeder, Günther. *Aegyptische Inschriften aus den Staatlichen Museen zu Berlin*. 2 vols. Leipzig: Hinrichs, 1913–1924.

Roehrig, Catharine H. "Tomb group of Henettawy." Pages 162–63 in *Mummies & Magic: The Funerary Arts of Ancient Egypt*. Edited by Sue D'Auria, Peter Lacovara, and Catharine H. Roehrig. Boston: Dallas Museum of Art, 1992.

Roth, Ann Macy. "The Practical Economics of Tomb-Building in the Old Kingdom: A Visit to the Necropolis in a Carrying Chair." Pages 225–40 in *For His Ka: Essays Offered in*

*Memory of Klaus Baer*. Edited by David P. Silverman. Chicago: University of Chicago Press, 1994.

Rzepka, Slawomir, Mustafa Nour el-Din, Anna Wodzińska, and Łukasz Jarmużek. "Egyptian Mission Rescue Excavations in Tell el-Retabah. Part I: New Kingdom Remains." Ägypten und Levante 22/23 (2013): 253–87.

Sandison, A. T., and Edmund Tapp. "Disease in ancient Egypt." Pages 38–58 in *Mummies, Disease and Ancient Cultures*. Edited by Thomas Aidan Cockburn, Eve Cockburn, and Theodore A. Reyman. 2nd ed. Cambridge: Cambridge University Press, 1998.

Sauneron, Serge. "L'hymne au soleil levant des papyrus de Berlin 3050, 3056 at 3048 [avec 1 planche]." *BIFAO* 53 (1953): 65–90.

Schäfer, Heinrich. *Principles of Egyptian Art*. Translated by John Baines. Oxford: Griffith Institute, 1986.

Schott, Siegfried. *Wall Scenes from the Mortuary Chapel of the Mayer Paser at Medinet Habu*. Chicago: University of Chicago Press, 1957.

Sethe, Kurt. Ägyptische Lesestücke zum Gebrauch im akademischen Unterricht: Texts des Mittleren Reiches. Hildesheim: Olms, 1959.

———. *Die altaegyptischen Pyramidentexte*. 2 vols. Leipzig: Hinrichs, 1908.

Sethe, Kurt, Heinrich Schäfer, Siegfried Schott, and Herman Grapow, eds. *Urkunden des ägyptischen Altertums*. 7 vols. Leipzig: Hinrichs, 1904–1958.

Shafer, Byron E. "Temples, Priests, and Rituals: An Overview." Pages 1–30 in *Temples of Ancient Egypt*. Edited by Byron E. Shafer. London: Taurus Publishers, 1997.

Simpson, William Kelly. *The Mastabas of Kawab, Khafkhufu I and II: G7110–20, 7130–40, and 7150 and subsidiary mastabas of Street G 7100*. Boston: Museum of Fine Arts, 1978.

Stevens, Anna. "The Material Evidence for Domestic Religion at Amarna and Preliminary Remarks on Its Interpretation." *JEA* 83 (2003): 143–68.

Szpakowska, Kasia. "Demons of Ancient Egypt." *Religion Compass* 3 (2009): 799–805.

Taylor, John H. "Patterns of colouring on ancient Egyptian coffins from the New Kingdom to the Twenty-sixth Dynasty: an overview." Pages 164–81 in *Colour and Painting in Ancient Egypt*. Edited by W. V. Davies. London: British Museum Press, 2001.

Thiele, Edwin R. *The Mysterious Numbers of the Hebrew Kings*. 2nd ed. Exeter: Paternoster, 1965.

Tylor, J. J., and F. Ll. Griffith. *The Tomb of Paheri at El Kab*. London, 1894.

Vandier, J. *Manuel d'archéologie égyptienne*. Vol. 5. Paris: A. et J. Picard, 1969.

Vartavan, Christian T. de. "*Pistacia* species in relation to their use as varnish and 'incense' (*snṯr*) in Pharaonic Egypt." *Bulletin of Parthian and Mixed Oriental Studies* 2 (2007): 63–92.

Weigall, Authur E. P. *Travels in the Upper Egyptian Deserts*. London: William Blackwood and Sons, 1913.

Weinstein, James M. "The Egyptian Empire in Palestine: A Reassessment." *BASOR* 241 (1981): 1–28.

Weir, David. "Liminality, Sacred Space and the Diwan." Pages 39–54 in *Sacred Space: Interdisciplinary Perspectives within Contemporary Contexts.* Edited by Steven Brie, Jenny Daggers, and David Torevell. Newcastle upon Tyne: Cambridge Scholars Publishing, 2009.

Wente, Edward F. *Scenes of King Herihor in the Court: with translations and texts.* Chicago: University of Chicago Press, 1979.

Werbrouck, Marcelle. *Les pleureuses dans l'*Égypte ancienne. Brussels: Fondation Égyptologique Reine Élisabeth, 1938.

"What do National Lottery winners spend their money on?" *The Guardian Datablog.* www.theguardian.com/news/datablog/2012/oct/22/national-lottery-winners-spend-money.

Wilkinson, Alix. "Symbolism and Design in Ancient Egyptian Gardens." *Garden History* 22 (1994): 1–17.

Wilkinson, Richard H. "The Coronational Circuit of the Walls, the Circuit of the *hnw* Barque and the Heb-sed 'Race' in Egyptian Kingship Ideology." *JSSEA* 15 (1985): 45–51.

Willems, Harco. *Chests of Life: A Study of the Typology and Conceptual Development of Middle Kingdom, Standard Class Coffins.* Leiden: Ex Orient Lux, 1958.

Wilson, Penelope. *A Ptolemaic Lexikon: A Lexicographical Study of the Texts in the Temple of Edfu.* Leuven: Peeters, 1997.

Winlock, Herbert E. *The Treasure of El Lāhūn.* New York: Metropolitan Museum of Art, 1934.

Wood, Bryant G. "The Rise and Fall of the 13th-Century Exodus-Conquest Theory." *JETS* 48 (2005): 475–89.

Yamamoto, Kei. "The materials of Iykhernofret's portable shrine: An alternative translation of Berlin 1204, lines 11–12." *GM* 191 (2002): 101–6.

# Index of Subjects

# Index of Personal Names

# Index of Place Names

# Index of Scripture References

# Index of Foreign Words